REINCARNATION
—A REASONABLE
INQUIRY

REINCARNATION —A REASONABLE INQUIRY

Erich Z. Petrovsky

Quadrakoff Publications Group, LLC
Wilmington, Delaware
USA

Copyright © 2020, 2019 Quadrakoff Publications Group, LLC All rights reserved.

Except as noted, All Scripture passages taken from The Holy Bible, King James Version.
All NASB scriptures taken from The New American Standard Bible® Copyright © 1960, 1962, 1963, 1968, 1971, 1972, 1973, 1975, 1977, 1995 by the Lockman Foundation, LaHabra, CA.

Special thanks to the Lockman Foundation for the finest Bible version available; as well as for their permission to use the same. All Scripture passages taken from The Holy Bible, King James Version, are as noted.

ISBN: 978-1-948219-74-7

All rights reserved. No part of this publication may be reproduced, stored in a retrieval system or transmitted, in any form, or by any means, electronic, mechanical, recorded, photocopied, or otherwise, without the prior written permission of both the copyright owner and the above publisher of this book, except by a reviewer who may quote brief passages in a review.

The scanning, uploading, and distribution of this book via the Internet or via any other means without the permission of the publisher is illegal and punishable by law. Please purchase only authorized electronic editions and do not participate in or encourage electronic piracy of copyrightable materials. Your support of the author's rights is appreciated.

Any and all characters appearing that are not in any of the versions of the Bible are fictional. Any resemblance to any living person is strictly coincidental.

Printed in the United States of America.

"He that answereth a matter before he heareth it, it is folly and shame unto him."
—Proverbs 18:13 (KJV)

CONTENTS

Foreword ———————————————————— xv

Introduction ——————————————————— xxi

Chapter 1
Controversy ——————————————————— 1

Chapter 2
It Happens to Everyone ——————————————— 9

Chapter 3
Divination ———————————————————— 31

Chapter 4
That One Called Elijah —————————————— 63

Chapter 5
Religious Commentary on Elijah et al. ———————— 91

Chapter 6
Why the Fuss? —————————————————— 117

Chapter 7
On the Nature of the Matter ———————————— 143

Chapter 8
"The Force" ———————————————— 159

Chapter 9
Internals—Externals ————————————— 187

About the MeekRaker Series Title ————————— 225

Glossary ——————————————————— 231

Bibliography —————————————————— 247

FOREWORD

It seems a bit odd to be writing this, given my functions as a part of QPG. But it also seems appropriate to explain the genesis of this work, as well as the types of projects that each of us at QPG are actually involved.

Some time ago, Erich came to me seeking my assistance with a project in which *he* was involved: "I want you should help me with this book about the reincarnation."

I explained to "Zee," that I knew very little about "the reincarnation," so it was not clear how I could be of any assistance. But nevertheless, that I would most certainly be willing to help him in any way I was able.

"Zee" indicated that he was not in need of any help in *writing* it, as the rough draft had already been completed. What he needed, was some help with the vernacular. "Zee" was raised in a different culture, and often communicates in a manner difficult for many to easily comprehend. He often describes this as: "The catch of the twenty-two."

"Zee's" work was a true masterpiece—albeit a bit difficult to understand in its original form. Many hours were spent in rephrasing, and changing the style, (without changing any of the content); in order to better reflect that which is in "normal" common usage today. I would like to take this opportunity to thank all of those who also assisted in this; as I did not provide, and could never have provided this assistance alone.

The final product represents what I consider to be the finest work on reincarnation in existence. Generally, works on this subject are quite short on facts, and quite long on opinion. Most, if not all, are purely emotionally driven "advocacy" works attempting to sway the reader one way or the other regarding the existence of this phenomenon known as reincarnation. And many are merely purported "case studies" of dubious value. This is precisely why personally at that time: I knew "very little about 'the reincarnation.'" The key is "to know," as opposed "to have heard."

But "Zee" did not take this approach. He had no desire to advocate: "either the one way or the way of the other." Instead, he thoroughly researched the matter, including and most particularly Biblically. This research even included what others over the centuries had to say about this matter, and some of these same known Biblical references.

Thus the purpose of this work is not advocacy. The purpose is to provide "known" *reliable* evidence, so that the reader can make up his or her own mind, based strictly upon *reliable* evidence.

While involved in this project, it was amazing to see firsthand the efforts undertaken by many of these "advocates." It is intellectually dishonest to intentionally derive a meaning or meanings for evidence that is or are "way down on the probability list," simply because the most obvious meaning or meanings cause some degree of emotional discord.

Emotions are fine as the *driving* force for the undertaking of a project. But emotions should never be utilized in determining "what is the truth." US President James Garfield once stated: "The truth will set you free, but first it will make you miserable." Thus choosing unlikely meanings in order to avoid this "misery," causes one to likewise avoid obtaining the "truth," as well as any associated "freedom." After all: "A thing that *is*, *is*; and cannot *not* be"—no matter what the emotional result.

It was also amazing to see what *Biblical* evidence actually exists regarding the condition of the "soul" after leaving the body, as well the *Biblical* evidence regarding reincarnation. Surely intellectual

Foreword

honesty requires the presentation of *all* of this available evidence, and not simply one piece of "evidence" in furtherance of a particular position. Neither does intellectual honesty permit the presentation of "evidence" out of context with this very same intention. These types of behaviors are best left to the "advocates," as they have no place in true analysis.

This work "tells it like it is." It is thorough, well referenced, and honest. If it is truth that is sought, this work is where it can be found.

I remain thankful for the opportunity to have had some small part in the genesis of this work. And I learned much about this subject in the process.

Well done "Zee."

—Malcom F. Sutton
Editor in Chief
QPG, LLC
Wilmington, DE

INTRODUCTION

"You're wrong!"
"I am *not* wrong. It is *you* who are wrong!"
"I'm telling you, it is *you* who are wrong!"
"I am not wrong!"
"Who says?!"
"God."
"How do you know God says so?"
"The preacher told me."
"Will you please stop believing what some man tells you God said. And by the way, His *written* Word says differently."

Sound familiar? Just look on "social media"—it seems to go on and on—*ad infinitum* and *ad nauseam*.
But how can this be? God's word says what it says—right?
Well, not exactly, because if one were to consider God's word as a long story, then it is a story with *many many* "versions." It must be noted that these various versions of His Word are openly called *versions*; and are not referred to as *translations*. One might ask why a difference of opinion about the best English synonyms for Hebrew or Greek words would not simply be considered as different *translations*?

The answer; is that generally it is not a difference of opinion about the best English synonyms. Rather it is a difference of opinion about the *meanings* of these various words. Thus the various "versions" represent the best English words for that which those who are or were in charge of these "versions," believe or believed the "facts" are. These versions are written with preconceived notions about the meanings; and words are chosen to best reflect these preconceptions—whether synonymic to the original Hebrew and Greek terminology or not. These versions are not then proffered as commentary or analyses, but rather staunchly defended as the *true* "Word of God." And as long as the desire for a particular meaning is the motivating factor, truth and subsequent wisdom will never be attained.

The Supreme Court of the United States; well known for lexiconic frippery; has routinely engaged in a somewhat similar practice. They often make decisions based upon not what the Constitution actually *states*; but rather they make decisions based upon what others have claimed the Constitution *means*. This permits some justification of extra-constitutional rulings to their liking. They simply "shop for," and then cite the opinions of others as "evidence;" rather than utilizing "best evidence;" i.e.; what the actual words of the Constitution actually state, and what they reasonably mean.

In Isaac Asimov's *"Foundation"* series, there is a character claiming to be an expert archaeologist. When he is asked about all of the various sites he had visited, he is appalled at the idea that someone would think that would be necessary. He simply reads what others wrote about these various sites, and this makes him an "expert."

Three examples of serious problems caused by the various "versions" of the Bible written by various "experts" easily come to mind:

The *first* is the controversy between OSAS (Once Saved Always Saved) believers, and OSAS deniers. The OSAS deniers believe in an analog and arcane system of "works based" salvation. Unlike what the Bible clearly states (OSAS), they put a "price tag" of

Introduction

various unknown amounts on salvation. The problem here is that not only is this Biblically false, but it causes many to not accept salvation. This is because these same "many," believe the various prices are too high; tend to be quite different depending upon the denomination; and often make little or no sense. This also tends to discredit the Bible in its entirety, since all claim the Bible as their source.

The *second* example, is the conflation of the *creation* (H. bârâ), of the original human beings from *nothing* in Genesis 1:26-27; with the *formation* (H. yâtsar) of Adam from *something* (H. âphâr) in Genesis 2:7. Already being so certain that Adam was the first human being, Genesis 2:7 is automatically and quite erroneously assumed to be merely a detailed recapitulation of that which was described earlier in Genesis 1:26-27.

If the original Hebrew terminology were of any serious concern, it can easily be seen that *bârâ* and *yâtsar* are mutually exclusive processes, and thus cannot possibly represent the same event. Bârâ (created) requires that matter *not be* utilized; and yâtsar (formed) requires that matter *be* utilized (here âphâr), in order for that matter to be "formed."

Since Adam can genealogically be traced, it is certain that Adam was formed less than ten thousand years ago. This conflation error is the main reason why science and the Bible conflict with respect to the amount of time man has been on the earth; and thus consequently denies sufficient time for evolution.

In addition, the insistence that the Hebrew word *yom* must mean a literal "day," and staunchly refusing to consider the equally acceptable definition of a "period of activity;" results in the earth being Biblically less than ten thousand years old. This is because the original *created* hosts came to be on the sixth *yom*.

These errors force people to choose between science and the Bible. And many; based upon what they were *told* the Bible states; will disregard the Bible entirely; instead choosing science, as science appears to makes the most sense.

And the *third*, is the very subject of the pages that follow—

CHAPTER 1

Controversy

To some, even the *word* reincarnation is a literal profanity—meaning; that reincarnation is, [and can only be]; a subject that could be taken seriously only by others—specifically *only* by those who are "profane." *Profane* here generally being considered as derived from: *pro* (before), and *fanum* (a temple).

Profane and its offspring *profanity*, are often misused words. Obscene is not synonymous with profane. Obscene in the general sense refers to *offensive*, although in recent history obscene is usually associated with some type of sexual matter. Many consider the religious beliefs of others as offensive, and simply because of their beliefs; even those *persons*; could and often are considered as *obscene* by many.

However; it must be asked if the *lack* of knowledge by an individual or individuals; as opposed to believing *differently*, should reasonably be considered either *obscene* or *profane*; or should this better be considered as a teaching opportunity. It seems that Jesus believed the latter.

It must also be remembered that it was those who were believed to have the greatest level of "fanum" knowledge that petitioned the Romans for assistance in His *attempted* murder. [It must be noted that it was actually Jesus Himself who commanded his "spirit" to leave his body.] To be fair; the assistance of these particular "fanumites" was necessary in order to facilitate God's will. But clearly "God's will" was not any type of motivational factor for those active participants in said attempted murder at that time.

Thus it remains unclear as to precisely what this "pro" or *before* in "profane" refers:

This "pro" may refer to those who have *as of yet* either know nothing; or know not enough of the "civilized goings on;" to not only not be in any need of any type of temple; but to not even *know* they are in need of any type of temple. The old saying: "When you don't know that is bad. When you don't know you don't know, that is worse."

Here these simply "do not know what they do not know." In this sense, these "profane" persons are either *judged* as obscene or offensive by others and shunned, (by the "true fanumites"); or (although rarely today), their "agnosticism" is considered by the "true fanumites" as an opportunity for these "profane" people to be "taught."

This use of "profane" may also refer to those who "know" (actually *believe*) things; but these "believed things" disagree with "other things" believed by "other persons" in "other temples."

Or as believed by many, the "pro" could also refer to those who must remain physically *outside* of the temple, (standing before the temple); as they have not yet been deemed suitable for admission *into* this "true and correct" temple. This of course represents the antithesis of the actual purported purpose of any "house of worship."

It must be asked why this is done, instead of welcoming these "profane" persons into said temple? One answer could be that because what is purported to be a *fanum* or temple, has in fact become much more of a country club—rather than any type of house of worship.

And a second reason would be the direct result of the first. The literally profane petitioner standing outside (before) the temple lacks the *earthly* requirements for admission, and this cannot be helped. The only other possible reason for the "profane's" admission would be to teach them these "truths"—*but too often there is no one left in there who is capable of this—if reason and logic are truly prerequisites.*

Distinctions must be made, and care must be exercised with respect to the use of the term "knowledge." Knowledge; or that which is *truly known*; as opposed to that which is *known to be true*, can be a tricky entity. One can truly know all of the attributes of a character in a fictional work, but the actual existence, (actuality), of any fictional character is known by all to *not* be true.

Thus if it is stipulated that this character has no actuality, then although all of this character's attributes can in fact be truly known; *all* of this knowledge is about a thing whose existence is in fact known by all involved to not be true. This represents true knowledge about an entity having a *reality*, but in fact having no *actuality*; i.e.; it does not exist, except as a *reality* or *perception*.

Solipsists state that one's "I am" is all that is or can be *truly* known; and a fair argument can be made for this position. This is not to say that solipsism requires an *admission* that nothing else exists. (That likewise is not possible for a true solipsist, for obvious reasons.)

The issue is not actually whether anything exists beyond ones "I am;" but whether or not the existence of anything beyond one's "I am" can be truly known. But of course this causes serious problems, in that one solipsist can never be certain that one is actually communicating with another "I am." Neither can one be certain that whatever the subject of the communication may actually be; actually exists; unless the subject is one's (and only one's) "I am." Given the level of narcissism existing in the US today, a fair argument exists that major portions of the population currently are "schizoid solipsists." They do not *think* like solipsists, but *behave* as though they were.

Thus in order for life to have any meaning, assumptions must be made. The first being that something *other than* one's "I am" exists;

e.g.; "I am hungry. When I eat this, I am no longer hungry." An individual's hunger pangs comport with solipsism, but what about the existence of the food? Since the consumption of the food removes the hunger pangs, it is reasonable to assume that the food exists beyond one's "I am;" else why not merely "I am" the pangs away?

"In normal every day life, levels of evidence for the existence of actualities are generally presumed to be based upon "common sense"—even if the term "common sense" is considered as oxymoronic by some. Unless some assumptions about the existence of actualities are made based upon commonly accepted levels of evidence, nothing would ever be able to happen. Sometimes; as in the case of a mirage; these levels fall short.

"This is seen with the legal levels of proof, ranging from: "probable cause," through "preponderance of evidence," through "clear and convincing evidence," and "proof beyond a reasonable doubt." And generally; the more severe that the legal penalty is; the higher the level of proof that is required. And sometimes a "mirage" occurs, where the incorrect decision is made. This is one reason why the severity of a penalty is proportional to the "certainty" of the evidence required; i.e.; requires more "certain" evidence. "Probable cause" may allow limited interference with one's rights, but "proof beyond a reasonable doubt" is generally required for the penalties of incarceration or death.

"When levels of proof are such that the evidence for the existence of an actuality falls below that which is "normally" considered as "sufficient;" the term "believe" is often incorporated. When one "knows in his heart of hearts," this may be overwhelming *subjective* evidence; but falls short of the level of *objective* evidence required by others. Hence here; unlike as is the case with counting apples; statements regarding *belief* are appropriate."¹ [Excerpt from: *"Statists Saving One"* Reprinted by Permission]

The Greek word *lŏgŏs* in the general sense, means "the word." However when the word *lŏgŏs* is used alone, particularly when it is capitalized (*Lŏgŏs*); this usually refers to "Divine Word" or "Word of God." When lŏgŏs is used as the "root of a suffix," this forms the basis of many of the various "ologies;" ranging from perhaps "Aardvarkology" through Zoology. [One notable exception is *astronomy*. *Astronomy* roughly meaning "star namer," as in the word *nomenclature*; is utilized to denote the *scientific* study of the stars, likely because the term *astrology* was "already taken."]

This "ology" suffix has various meanings such as: "the study of;" or "the branch of knowledge of;" or the "science of." Here there is a requirement of an accepted level of proof regarding the truth of that which is purported as "known" by said various "ologists."

History shows us that once this accepted level of "proof threshold" is achieved; by *any* of that which is contained in that which is recognized as part of the purpose(s) for the existence of *any* temple or *fanum*; the same is generally moved out of the "fanum department," and into the "ology department." A lot of words here, but this simply means that once what is merely "believed" can be "reasonably proven" to exist, this particular belief is now considered as "knowledge" *outside* of the temple or "fanum."

It is believed that much of what today is now considered as science, was originally a part of one or more of the ancient "mystery schools." Over time, this knowledge branched out from these "temples," and is now considered a part of mainstream science; roughly meaning "to know."

Thus that which is contained solely within any temple or *fanum*, is essentially inevitably doomed to a level of proof less than that which is required by science. If the secret of hyperspace travel were discovered in a temple, and proven to be true; "hyperspaceology" would immediately be born, and the majority of research and discovery would take place in laboratories outside of that same or any other temple from which the same was "dis-covered."

Any "temple related" matters which are otherwise characterized as any type of "ology," should be considered a correct usage; if and only if the same is solely concerned with describing what it is that those in the temple *believe*; and never correct if concerned with the truth or falsity of what it is that is in fact *believed* by them.

It is *truly known* that Catholics believe that the wafer is *transubstantiated*. But it is not known whether or not this *transubstantiation* process itself is in fact truth—with most non-Catholics believing it is not. Stated another way, it is an *actuality* that Catholics believe this. But whether this *believed* to be "transubstantiation process" itself is an *actuality*, or merely a *reality*, is not known. To be clear, a distinction must be made between this transubstantiation *always* occurring, and *ever* occurring. If this transubstantiation process were proven to be in fact true, or an *actuality*; this would be then be moved outside of Catholicism to the *scientific*, (now to be known as the *"transubstantiantionology"*), departments.

And it does not require a particularly high level of skepticism to predict that laws would then be passed prohibiting "transubstantiation without a license." The Church would then have to substitute this "true" transubstantiation process, with some ersatz "non-transubstantiation" mummery.

Any organization necessarily utilizing levels of proof less than those required by science, is likely to be under the influence of factors other than what is actually "known." Often times it is *emotion(s)* and not facts that determine what it is that is believed to be "in fact so." And this happens even with science. Max Planck; (1918 Nobel Prize winner for "energy quanta"); is attributed with having stated: *"Science advances one funeral at a time."*

So as previously stated, there are those who believe that "even the *word* reincarnation is a literal profanity—meaning; that reincarnation is, [and can only be]; a subject that could be taken seriously only by others—specifically *only* by those who are 'profane.'" But to others, reincarnation is an integral part of the very belief system that represents the "civilized goings on" in their particular temple.

With regard to those to whom reincarnation represents an integral part of *their* belief system; those who *shun* reincarnation are considered as the literally "profane" ones. Here these "non-believers" in reincarnation are considered as profane, because they either have yet to discover any temple; or to have yet discovered the "true and correct" temple.

Judeo-Christian beliefs seem to be a bit split in this matter. Reincarnation is generally not considered to be a part of either Modern Judaism or Modern Christianity. Yet even today many Jewish families name their children after deceased family members, in the hope that these same deceased family members will return as their children. The matter of Passover and Elijah will be addressed later.

But there is one inescapable fact: It is a certainty that reincarnation cannot simultaneously be both fact and fiction—either it is true, or it is not.

Irrespective of one's position on the matter, it is important to filter out that which is emotional, and to *understand* the background information regarding the two positions; in order to reasonably try to determine that which is: "fact."

In furtherance of this, prudence requires that some terms be defined, as used in this endeavor:

- "actuality" is "what a thing is or is not" irrespective of any reality of the same
- "alive" in the *general* sense, refers to a *connection*, or connected
- "body" or "soma" refers to that *material* or *physical* part of man; i.e.; the physical structure which is designed to contain the immaterial part of man
- "dead" in the *general* sense refers to a *disconnection*, or disconnected
- "death" is roughly synonymous with "dead," but refers to the *event* of disconnection, rather than that *general state* where

there is no connection—"death" is when this disconnection occurs; and "dead" is the state after this occurrence
- "life" or "living" is reasonably synonymous with "alive," and thus also refers to that *general* state where there is some type of connection
- "physical death" refers to that state where the immaterial part of man (soul), is no longer connected to the material part of man (body)
- "physical life" is that condition where the immaterial part of man (soul) is connected to the material part (body)
- "reality" is that belief or "understanding" of "what a thing is or is not," and is based upon some level of *perception*
- "soul" refers to that *immaterial* part of man, often inadequately described as "will, intellect and emotions"
- "spiritual" can refer to a myriad of immaterial or "breath like" entities
- "spiritual death" refers to that state where the immaterial part of man (soul) is disconnected from its original source
- "spiritual life" refers to that state where the immaterial part of man (soul) is connected to its original source

CHAPTER 2

It Happens to Everyone

". . . "Waking up," and having no idea what happened, how I got "here," or what to do—with the only things known are that "I am," and that I need something. What is needed (what I need), changes from time to time, but that "I am" persists. I can't remember when "I wasn't," only knowing that "I am."

"Having no reliable way to communicate, at least for now; the best I can do is a binary. I can show when I am content, and show when I am not. I must leave it to others to guess what the current issue is, by my offering of either the resolution or the continuance of one state or the other. When I get what I need, I just flip from not content, to content—until the next need arises. I have no idea that this will "never ever" change."

"As time goes on; whatever that means; I begin to learn how to communicate. I also find new needs arising—needs that I never had before. I have no idea that this also will "never ever" change."

"One of the *new* needs that I find, is the (my) need for those around me to also be in the content state. This has nothing to do with the feelings of others, but only my own. I do not like the way I feel when those around me behave the way that I do when I need something—even though I am unaware of this similarity. When I do certain things, those around me change from either being not content to content, or content to not content. I have no idea why this change, but I learn to do or not do things based upon the way that I feel about the reactions of those around me. It is unimportant to me what anyone else may be "feeling,"—in fact I have never even thought about it. I just don't like the way that *I* "feel" when others are not content, so I learn to behave in order to keep them content—at least until I need something, and then I temporarily don't care."

"It's not a bad "life" really. Things are getting better and it works out well. As long as I watch the reactions around me, I can get away with a lot. If I keep the little rules, I can break the big ones. I learn that there are little sins and there are big ones, and I try to stay away from those that I cannot get away with. All seems well, but I wonder where this is all going..."

18,746 words omitted...

"She always dragged me out to places and made me try on all kinds of things she calls clothes. But this time, she practically bought out the store. And she keeps talking about this thing called "school." I have no idea what this really means, but both of them seem pretty excited about it."

"And then it happened. Oh my God, what a mess! I had always thought there were only a few of us, but now there is an entire building full of those who are similar to me. They are nowhere near as good as me of course—just ask mom; but they are still there. The rules here are different, and I don't like them at all."

"Except for some basic needs, no one seems to care about what I want. I can't do whatever I want; and now find that I must do things I am told to do, or else—and a lot of them are pretty stupid too. I understand others here have it even worse because of their bad decision to come here. If *I* had to look at those stupid blots of ink all day long, and then talk about if I can see who is "running," I'd be screaming."

"I am glad that it is finally over. I told mom that I tried it with an open mind; but that it was horrible, and was not for me. I also told her how much I now appreciate my "other life," and look forward to its resumption."

"I can't describe the look she gave me. She kept opening *her* mouth, but no sound came out. Dad overheard us and opened *his* mouth, but no sound came out. She finally explained to me that "school" was not an option. Then I kept opening *my* mouth, but nothing would come out."

"So it went on and on, year after year. Then all of a sudden it was over. And believe it or not, things got even worse. At least while I was in "school," almost all of my needs were taken care of by mom and pop. But now I have to actually work to get the stuff I need (and want). When I first went to school, I longed for the days when I *didn't have* to go to school. Now that I am out of school and working, I long for the days when I *did* have to go to school."

"Then I met someone, and the next thing I knew the entire cycle seemed to be repeating itself. Now I had the role that my folks had from my first memory, and there was another doing exactly what I was doing when I first knew that "I am." So now the perspective has changed a bit, as now there is not only my "I am," but also a "he is." And I have just been informed that soon it will be "they are.""

But did the cycle actually repeat itself?

Material

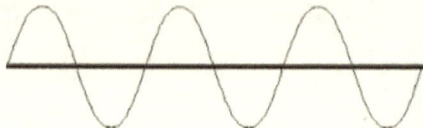

Immaterial

A bove is a rough "graph" of a "sine wave." If one drops a pebble into a small body of water, a similar phenomenon can be seen if viewed from the side. For the present, we are concerned with only the upper half, (alternation), of the very first "wave" or "curve." And as will soon be seen, "wave" and "curve" are not synonymous.

Here the *horizontal* line refers to the division between the material and the immaterial realms, with the material being *above* this line, and the immaterial *below* this line. It is also stipulated that "time" on the material realm runs from left to right; and also that the first upper curve represent among other things, the overall *condition* of the physical vessel, (the body or *soma*); when "physically alive" or *connected*, with respect to this *time*. Many believe that the peak; or maximum physical condition; generally occurs at about thirty-three years of age.

The very first curve is a representation of the "I am," to which was previously referred. This begins or began when this wave begins at/intersects the horizontal (time) line, which is what is seen on the far left. This represents physical *birth*. This type of "I am," represents the time that the "soul" is first contained in the physical body; with total "physical life" or "incarnation" (*literally—in the flesh*), represented by the entire "positive" half of the wave above this horizontal line; i.e.; one *lifetime*.

It must be noted that there are limitations to any graphical representation. When this first upper curve *again intersects* the horizontal time line, but here (on the "way down"), with "negative slope;" this is physical death or disconnection. This represents a "split," in that the soul returns to the immaterial below the line, but the body "remains" in the material.

However; the level of *organization* of the body "remains," does roughly obey this downward curve, in the sense of *catabolism*, but "remains" in the *material* realm. The condition or complexity of the physical body continues to decline as per the curve; until ultimately in a sense some degree of complexity begins to rise or *anabolism*, as the components are utilized by other life forms.

Another type of "I am" can be seen in Genesis 3:14 (KJV):

> *"And God said unto Moses, I AM THAT I AM:*
> *and he said, Thus shalt thou say unto*
> *the children of Israel,*
> *I AM hath sent me unto you"*[2]

Since in this passage it is God that is speaking to Moses, it is clear that this refers to the Father, and not the Son. Thus this is both similar to, but also different than, the "I am" with physical incarnation. One *similarity* is self-awareness. One *difference* here is the existence of this self-awareness (God's) *without* a physical vessel. This will be addressed in greater detail later.

It is obvious that on this "graph," the intersection of this "wave" with the line or axis at the very beginning; requires a "preexisting" vessel capable of containing this "I am." It is also logical that this generally must be done by an "I am" other than the "soon to be I am," (not yet physically alive), "life form" depicted by the "wave."

We are told how this was done *directly* by God in Genesis 2:7 (KJV):

> *"And God formed man of the dust of the ground,*
> *and breathed into his nostrils the breath of life;*
> *and man became a living soul."*[3]

Here in Genesis 2:7, it is God Who Himself alone is *first* forming the material vessel; and it is God Who *then* introduces this "breath of life." Although we are not told how long this process took; it would nevertheless most certainly be fair to ask *why* we are told this.

An extremely important detail, is that here God is *forming* the vessel from *something*. This is an entirely different process than that which resulted in the original *created* hosts. Those original created hosts were not *formed* from any-*thing* [not via yâtsar (H) as here in Genesis 2:7]; but rather, they were *created* from *nothing* [via bârâ' (H)]. It is this confusion that is responsible for the controversy regarding the age of the earth. Once it is understood that the *formation* of that which would be called Adam occurred less than ten thousand years ago; but those original *created* hosts were created likely hundreds of thousands of years ago; much, but not all, of this controversy is resolved.

It would seem to be fair to assume that at the time of Adam's *formation*, the descendants of the original *created* hosts knew full well how (euphemism) it is that; (or the process by which); any new "I am" is or was brought into physical existence. So then why are we told of this process?

The truth is that at that time, many if not most, in fact *did not know* of this—if physical "life" *in-toto*; i.e.; a "living soul;" is the subject.

And it is also true, that it is not only "even," but *most especially* today; that it is more than just that many do not *understand* this process, but in fact many have *no knowledge whatsoever* of this actual "two-fold" process.

To be clear, "this actual process" does not mean the mere creation of the physical vessel. Most know all about that, at least in terms of how that process is begun. But *"that"* process represents only a part of *"this"* process. A corpse is a vessel. An unborn baby represents a vessel. But neither is a "living soul" according to Genesis 2:7. The corpse once *was*, and the unborn *will be* by this definition. [Any serious discussion of abortion is a very complex matter, and thus is purposely avoided here.]

Thus there are at least two reasons we are told this in Genesis 2:7:

Firstly: to make sure that it is understood that the source of that which *animates* the physical body comes directly from God. It is God who chooses that which it is that animates (breathed into) any body or soma. Here in Genesis 2:7 God also "chose to choose" the vessel. [A variant of this is, or "will be" seen later with Mary.]

But normally, it is man who in a sense can *ethically* at least partially choose some of the characteristics the *vessel*, by determining the two parties who are to be involved in the vessel's formation. And today, one can *unethically*; (some would argue also sinfully); increase the desired characteristics of the vessel, by choosing means beyond this "normal" means. But although man can *petition* for the insertion of some particular "I am" to his liking; it seems this nevertheless currently remains God's decision alone.

The *second* reason; is to let man know that "something else is happening" or "happened" here. In light of Adam's original intended domicile, and ultimate purpose; Adam's vessel had to be formed in a manner slightly different than others who were "alive" at that time; and those yet to be. The purpose(s) for which Adam was formed, required that sin could not be a factor either directly or indirectly in the formation of this (Adam's) vessel. [Although an extensive litigation of this is beyond the scope of this work, the same can be found in "*MeekRaker Beginnings...*"]

Adam was to be "the first Adam." Jesus is sometimes referred to as "The Last Adam;" and there are reasons for this. Although there are references to the "first" and the "last" Adam, it seems that there are no "Adams" in between. [Years ago, when the USSR competed with the US in two team sporting events and lost; they would often report that the USSR came in at "second place," and the US came in "next to last."]

These physical vessels of the two "Adams" (first and last) have similar, but not identical, origins.

The "first Adam" was formed from *'âphâr*, or that which is often translated as "dust of the ground" or "dust of the earth." This was done *unilaterally* by God. We are told this, in order to distinguish this *formation* of Adam from the actual *creation* or *bârâ'* of the original created hosts. Depending upon one's definitions of "virgin" and "birth;" this could arguably be considered literally as a "virgin birth." But by this same definition, the same could be said about the bringing into existence of the originally *created* hosts.

The "Last Adam" was brought into existence in a sort of "hybrid" manner. Mary provided one part of the physical requirements for the vessel, and God provided the other part. Whether this is believed to have already happened, (history); or will happen sometime in the future, (prophesy), as prophesied; changes nothing with regard to the nature of the event. Thus this either was, or *also* was a "virgin birth." Whether this was the first and only time this process occurred; or the third time this process occurred, being a matter of one's definitions.

Adam's unique purpose was to begin the bloodline for Messiah. Adam was *formed* by God, and thus with no tinge of sin possible. Adam resided in a sinless environment, without even the *knowledge* of evil. But evil came to him, and he sinned.

Because he, (Adam), sinned, he had to leave this or his original environment. When he left this *gan* (H), or "guarded area," (often translated as *garden*); he encountered other human beings outside the area who were the descendants of the original *created* hosts. In their native language, (likely the true and original Chaldean); they called Adam and Co. "one from the other side" of this *gan*. Their Chaldean word for "one from the other side," is or was the word *Hebrew*. These circumstances explain precisely why so much of Hebrew is considered by experts to be of Chaldean origin.

Had Adam not sinned, it seems likely, if not a certainty; that Adam would have remained in the *gan*. As explained in the monograph: *"It's Not Just a Theory,"* sin, health, and longevity are inextricably related. It is at least arguable that without sin, Adam may have lived in the *gan* forever. But this was not God's purpose. Thus here in the *gan*, the enemy; as would also happen sometime later at Calvary; unknowingly acted in a manner in furtherance of God's will.

Jesus was born with a body or vessel formed partially by that which was of man; and partially by that which was of God. Mary was female, and thus by definition had no "y chromosome." Jesus was male; and thus by definition had said "y chromosome." He resided in a sinful environment, but yet never sinned. And for the same reason as was the case with Adam before Adam sinned, had Jesus not *chosen* to release His immaterial part to the Father, He also may have physically lived in His earthly body forever. No one had been able to kill Jesus up to this point, and likely could not have succeeded then. Thus the entire "Adamic" purpose was completed at Calvary, when it was stated by "The Last Adam"—"It is finished."

Back to the "wave" or "curve."

Material

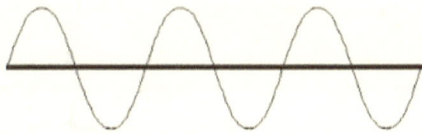

Immaterial

If here the magnitude or height of the wave is considered to represent the condition or "status" of the physical vessel, it can be seen that the "soul" enters the vessel at birth, generally at the point when this vessel is just *minimally* capable of containing it. It can also be seen that the soul at some unspecified time later, exits the vessel as the vessel becomes just *less* than minimally capable of containing it, here where the wave drops *below* the horizontal line.

And since as God stated in Genesis 2:7; the former, or physical *birth*, happens with the first breath, (soul entrance); thus as previously stated, it logically follows that the latter, or so-called physical *death*, (soul exit); occurs with the last breath.

It is usually at some point within the top half of this first "wave," (menarche to menopause); where additional cycles of "I am" (children) are brought into existence. These cycles begin in a similar fashion to the above, with respect to *their* or these *new* waves; but chronologically generally occur slightly before the peak, at the peak, or just after the peak of the "curves" of the parties responsible for bringing them into physical existence.

From most mainstream religion's viewpoint there is no argument that in an absolute sense this "I am" continues to exist beyond the point where the "I am" is no longer contained in the physical vessel—i.e.; the point where the curve with "negative slope" drops below the horizontal (time) line. Thus here this is the graphic representation of the beginning of the *afterlife*. Without belief in an afterlife, it seems that there would not be all that much for most religions to talk about.

Where all the "shouting seems to start;" is in the understanding the *trajectory* or *slope* of this "sine wave," *at* or just *after* it again intersects this horizontal (time) line. This is *after* the slope becomes "negative," and at the point where the curve or wave intersects and drops *below* the horizontal line.

These same mainstream religions generally believe that said trajectory or the *slope* of this wave or curve remains "negative" either for eternity; or until some point in time in the far distant future—depending upon one's interpretation of the *Apocalypse* (literally: "revealed things"), or that which is today known as the "*Book of Revelation.*" "Remains negative;" here meaning that this wave does not and will not ever again take on a "positive slope" and again intersect this horizontal (time) line, except perhaps only once as noted at "end times."

In this "religious" view, there then is not actually a *wave*, but rather merely a *curve* (curve theory), whose slope once becoming negative essentially remains negative, except possibly as noted.

Others believe that this is not so. It is true that both believe that there is in fact something *similar* to a wave (wave theory), with positive, (above the horizontal), portion; as well as some type of a negative, (below the horizontal), portion. The main difference here, is in the additional belief there is also *oscillation*, or repetition of this cycle by the *same* immaterial portion of a given individual; by again being "breathed into the nostrils" of another (different) vessel, at some future point in time (wave theory). Meaning that here; irrespective of any differences of either the magnitude or frequency of this "wave;" the "wave theory" is that the process repeats itself at least once, or perhaps on some "regular" basis.

This is to be distinguished from the reintroduction into the *same* vessel, as is the case in *resurrection*, resuscitation, or "return" from "near death" experiences. In these instances, the height of the wave is diminished because of the condition of the vessel, but either does not actually drop below the horizontal, or does in fact drop below but nevertheless returns.

It must again be noted, that the use of this graphic falls short once this wave or curve falls below the "material/immaterial line." This is simply due to time, space, and matter; which although clearly exist in and in fact *define* the *material* realm (above the horizontal line); likely do not exist in the *immaterial* realm (below the horizontal line)—by definition.

If so, then both the *immateriality* and the *immortality* of this "soul" is necessarily likewise proved. The immateriality is the easy one, as God is generally considered as an immaterial (*spiritual* or *breath-like*) being. Since unlike earlier in Genesis, there are no "let there be(s)" contained in Genesis 2:7; it seems likely that that which is breathed into man's nostrils is likewise immaterial.

It must be noted, that in the early 20th century there was a fellow named Duncan McDougall who claimed that H. Sapiens lost about 21 grams ($\approx$ ¾ oz.) at death. This would of course tend to suggest that the "soul" could be material in nature. He also claimed that this did not happen with dogs, hence dogs had no "soul."[4]

His work is not even taken seriously by mainstream science. And of course, *anything* having the breath of life in fact necessarily has a "soul." "Soul" is often (inadequately) defined as: "will, intellect, and emotions." No living entity can possess that which this even limited definition describes, without possessing that which it is that is being defined.

And with respect to *immortality*; since by definition there is no time in a realm with no time; there seems to be no reasonable or logical way to determine past, present, or future events within this immaterial realm. This of course is unlike what is the case from the material realm or *earthly* perspective. With no time there can be no *duration* or *sequencing*; thus there can be no beginning or end. God had to have no beginning or end, because no such other possibility can exist in a realm without time. [And there is also that matter of the ultimate requirement of a *"primum movens"* or effect with no cause, to initially "get things rolling." (possible tautology duly noted)] Thus at least with respect to immortality, the same can be said regarding that which is emitted from God that animates the human vessel.

Revelation 6:9-11 (KJV) tells us:

> *"And when he had opened the fifth seal,*
> *I saw under the altar the souls of them*
> *that were slain for the word of God,*
> *and for the testimony which they held:*
>
> *And they cried with a loud voice, saying,*
> *How long, O Lord, holy and true, dost thou not judge and*
> *avenge our blood on them that dwell on the earth?*
>
> *And white robes were given unto every one of them;*
> *and it was said unto them, that they should rest*
> *yet for a little season, until their fellowservants*
> *also and their brethren, that should be killed*
> *as they were, should be fulfilled."*[5]

Much is made of what these passages actually mean—as seems to often be the case with much of the "Book of Revelation" in general.

Nevertheless, some inarguable and important points are evident, as well as are some interesting corollaries.

These souls must have once been physically alive, as we are told that they had been "*slain.*" We are also told *why* they were slain: "*for the word of God, and for the testimony which they held.*" We are not told that they were slain because of any actions they had done, but rather for the *word* and *testimony* they *held*. This of course in no way precludes one being slain for *actions*, but only that this is not the case here with these particular souls.

The actual Greek word translated as here "testimony" here is:

> "*3141* marturia from *3144*; *evidence* given (judicially or gen.): - record, report, testimony, witness."[6]

And the original Greek word translated as "word" is:

> "*3056* lŏgŏs; from *3004*; something *said* (including the *thought*); by impl. a *topic* (subject of discourse), also *reasoning* (the mental faculty) or *motive*; by extens. a *computation*; spec. (with the art. in John) the Divine *Expression* (i.e. *Christ*)"[7]

This "lŏgŏs" in *general*, is as in the aforementioned "ologies;" but here in this particular passage specifically refers to the word "*of God.*" Thus they were killed not for *works*; but for *possession* of both *lŏgŏs* (here *Lŏgŏs*) or knowledge; and *marturia* or evidence. They were not slain simply because of knowledge, or simply because of evidence. They were slain because they had *both*.

Again, what is also clear is that these were once living beings, but were not *living* beings at that time; meaning that these "souls" were no longer contained in a physical vessel at that time; as clearly the context is that these were *disembodied* souls. Any entity such as a soul which was either previously "blown into" a vessel, but is now disembodied; or was *designed* to be contained in a physical vessel, but is not; is technically called a *ghost*. The relevance of this will be seen shortly.

These "souls" were capable of *recollection*: "*How long, O Lord, holy and true, dost thou not judge and avenge our blood on them that dwell on the earth.*" They were capable of judging *duration*: "*how long*", and "*rest yet for a little season;*" despite the fact that they were in a realm with no time. They were capable of *communication*. They also were obviously capable of *thought*.

The "*rest yet for a little season*" is even more revealing. Here it is again clear that these "souls" are capable of judging duration.

The Greek word translated as "season" is:

"5550 chrŏnŏs; of uncert. der.; a space of *time* (in gen. and thus prop. distinguished from *2540*, which designates *fixed* or special occasion; and from *165*, which denotes a particular *period*) or *interval* by extens. an individ. *opportunity*; by impl. *delay*"[8]

Chrŏnŏs; in all of its various spellings is also the root of the word *chronometer*.

The meaning of the "*under the altar*" and the provision of the "*white robes*" is unclear. Why were these "*under the altar*," rather than "with God?" The most likely answer is that they were "*slain*" before salvation was *available* to them. If so, then the meaning of the "*white robes*" may in fact be the provision of the now; (but not at that time); available salvation to these souls?" "Under the Altar" may be another way of stating the *kŏlpŏs* or "Abraham's Bosom." [See the Monograph: "*OSTIUM AB INFERNO*" [*The Opening From Hell*]]

We are not told whether or not these souls continued to be "*under the altar*," as the next verse (verse 12) is about another and entirely different "seal."

Although these passages do not actually state that these "souls" are in fact immortal, (*were* immortal seems a bit oxymoronic); it is clear that these souls once were physically alive.

It is also clear that they were slain, and that their immaterial portions, (souls), continued to exist afterward.

It is also clear that these same "souls" would continue to exist in this state at least "*for a little season, until their fellowservants also and their brethren, that should be killed as they were, should be fulfilled."*

And there is no indication given that once the *"season"* to *"judge and avenge our blood on them that dwell on the earth"* had come and gone; that they would then cease to exist. Thus the immortality of the soul remains the most likely conclusion.

Although it may *seem* that said judging and avenging would certainly be completed by the time all of the contemporaries of these disembodied souls were no longer physically alive, this may or may not be so. This may be a reference to the time of "Armageddon," which is often confused with "Apocalypse." The latter simply means "revealed things;" as opposed to its quasi-antonym "Apocrypha" which simply means "hidden things."

To those who believe in and proclaim the "unconsciousness" of the soul after it leaves the physical vessel, these passages clearly disprove this belief. One might try to make an exception, such as purporting that these "souls" were somehow special and thus atypical—perhaps suggesting that these represented Jesus' disciples. The problem with this particular "purportation;" is that it seems reasonable to believe that each of Jesus' disciples, (perhaps even Judas), received salvation while *they* were physically alive.

So it must be asked why then would any of Jesus' disciples be "under the altar," rather than "with God," AKA: "spiritually alive?" And of course this would then require another explanation for the "white robes."

Matthew 23:27 (KJV) tells us:

> *"O Jerusalem, Jerusalem, thou that killest the prophets,and stonest them which are sent unto thee, how often would I have gathered thy children together, even as a hen gathereth her chickens under her wings, and ye would not!"*[9]

If it can be stipulated that a *prophet* is one who has both *"the word of God,"* (*lŏgŏs*); and *"testimony,"* (*marturia "evidence"*); then it seems likely that it was at least some, or perhaps all of these prophets referenced above in Matthew, whose souls were *"under the altar."* Again, this *"under the altar"* may refer to the *kŏlpŏs* or "Abraham's Bosom."

And since it is a physically alive Jesus speaking here in Matthew 23:27, it is a certainty that these earlier *"prophets,"* (who were *"killest"* and *"stonest"*); did not receive salvation while physically alive. This is because as Jesus more than intimated, (*killest*); that they were not physically alive at the time Jesus stated this, but of course Jesus was; and salvation was not available until after Jesus' "death."

There is also another matter in the previous passages from Revelation requiring clarification. This matter being any relationship between: *"Avenge our blood on them that dwell on the earth;"* and *"until their fellowservants also and their brethren, that should be killed as they were, should be fulfilled."*

It must be asked if these two statements; i.e.; descriptions; refer to the same entity; or if they refer to two entirely different entities? More specifically; does *"them that dwell on the earth,"* refer to the same entity as does *"their fellowservants also and their brethren?"*

These souls *"under the altar"* are asking God about how long until there is vengeance against *"them that dwell on the earth."* But these "souls" are told to wait (rest) *"until "their fellowservants also and their brethren, that should be killed as they were, should be fulfilled."* The key to this is the statement: *"as they were."*

Clearly there is commonality between what had been (past) the fate of those "souls" under the altar; and the fate (future) of those *"fellowservants"* and *"brethren;"* with the difference being merely one of timing." It seems reasonable to conclude that the "avenging" for those under the altar will not take place until their *"fellowservants and brethren"* are also *"slain for the word of God, and for the testimony"* which *"as they* (those under the altar) *were."*

Thus it also seems clear that *"them that dwell on the earth"* represent(s) a third and entirely different entity than those; who from that "time" perspective; had either already been *"slain for the word of God, and for the testimony which they held;"* or *would* be *"slain for the word of God, and for the testimony which they held."*

This leaves several possibilities for *"them that dwell on the earth."* Clearly this group would not be part of those slain *"as they* (those under the altar) *were."* Instead it seems that these would be the *targets* or the *"them"* of the *"judge and avenge our blood on them."*

And it seems clear that *"them that dwell on the earth"* would *not* be *"slain for the word of God, and for the testimony which they held;"* but rather; would be judged and avenged for the *slaying* of those who did have this word and testimony: e.g.; perhaps those referred to by Jesus in the above passage as "Jerusalem." But this in itself presents a problem, as they too originally were brought into existence in the image and likeness of God.

The descriptions of these two (or three) entities should not be overlooked. Those slain and those who would later be slain, share characteristics in terms of having both the word of God and having testimony. They are also described as *"fellowservants also and their brethren."*

But *"them that dwell on the earth"* are only described by where they "dwell." It seems unclear as to where else except earth those slain, and even those yet "un-slain" *"fellowservants also and their brethren"* dwelled or could have dwelled when they were *physically* alive—with the same being the source of the confusion. Likewise, it seems unclear where else *"them that dwell on the earth"* could have dwelled when they had engaged in these past and future acts of slaying, for which they would ultimately be judged and avenged. Even today no one actually "dwells" on any other planet, "asteroid base" or on, (actually *in*), the moon.

The truth is that anyone physically alive, or known to have ever been physically alive at any time, had to at some point dwell on the earth. [There *will be* at some point in the future; H. Sapiens born, who will never set foot upon the earth. But this has yet to happen.] Thus utilizing any form of "dwelling" as a definitive description; seems to be an inadequate means of differentiation.

And the truth; is that in Genesis 1:28 (KJV) we are told:

> *"And God blessed them, and God said unto them,*
> *Be fruitful, and multiply, and replenish the earth,*
> *and subdue it: and have dominion over the fish*
> *of the sea, and over the fowl of the air,*
> *and over every living thing that moveth*
> *upon the earth."*[10]

So here it is obvious that man dwelling on earth was not a secret. The corollaries to this passage are enormous, and will be addressed shortly. For now, it is clear that there are several named "parties" in this particular (Genesis 1:28) passage. There is God, the earth, and there are the recipients of His instructions; (man); expressed here as "them." There are also those or that which man is instructed to have "dominion over" (fish, fowl, etc.).

What is necessarily *missing* from that which man is instructed to have dominion over is *man*; as these were the very *them* being blessed and instructed at this time; and thus not included as part of *"every living thing that moveth upon the earth"* at that same time. It is not God's stated will here that any man have *dominion* over any other man. This idea of "dominion" is of course entirely different than the concept of *governing* with the consent of the governed. [See: "Statists Saving One"]

However there is a critical question which yet remains unanswered here. The word translated as "subdue" in this passage is the Hebrew word:

> "3533 kâbash; a prim. root; to *tread* down; hence neg. to *disregard*; pos. to *conquer, subjugate, violate*..."[11]

Kâbash is the source from which the English word *kibosh*, (kiboshing or kyboshing), is derived.

Hence it must be asked which of the following conditions was present at the time these instructions were given to man:

Was it the case that God *chose* to create an earth that was in a sense incomplete? Meaning that the earth was deliberately created in need of being "kiboshed"—*tread down*," conquered, and subjugated by man.

Or alternatively; that although God wanted to create an earth not requiring "kiboshing," (alternate spelling: kyboshing); He simply was incapable of accomplishing this? Meaning that either way, man was required to "finish the job" for God.

If the former; this would seem to make little if any sense. And if the latter; this of course would then necessarily render God less than omnipotent.

Or was it the case that the earth was completed as per God's wishes, but then something had happened? Meaning; that the effect we are told of in Genesis 1:1; (the creation of the heavens and the earth); was completed as stated, but somehow something then happened that altered the earth to a state requiring "kiboshing."

Luke 10:18-20 (KJV) tells us:

> *"And he said unto them, I beheld Satan as*
> *lightning fall from heaven.*
>
> *Behold, I give unto you power to tread*
> *on serpents and scorpions,*
> *and over all the power of the enemy:*
> *and nothing shall*
> *by any means hurt you.*
>
> *Notwithstanding in this rejoice not,*
> *that the spirits are subject unto you;*
> *but rather rejoice, because your*
> *names are written in heaven."*[12]

Here in Luke, Jesus is speaking to His disciples. The "*as lightning fall from heaven,*" is the likely source of the name "Lucifer." So we are told of this fall from heaven, but although this passage tells us the *origin*, it tells us not of the *destination*. But since Jesus is or was speaking here on earth, to those who are or were also on earth, about power available to them while on the earth; it seems likely that the *destination* of Satan was earth.

Revelation 12:7-9 (KJV) tells us:

> *"And there was war in heaven:*
> *Michael and his angels fought against the dragon;*
> *and the dragon fought and his angels,*
> *And prevailed not; neither was their place*
> *found any more in heaven.*
>
> *And the great dragon was cast out,*
> *that old serpent, called the Devil, and Satan,*
> *which deceiveth the whole world:*
>
> *he was cast out into the earth,*
> *and his angels were cast out with him."*[13]

So unless the position is taken that Satan fell down twice or more, confirmation of the *destination* (earth), of the "fall" previously referenced by Jesus in Luke 10:18, is provided here in the text of Revelation 12:7-9.

Thus it seems most likely that it was Satan, who *"deceiveth" the whole world; he was cast out into the earth, and his angels were cast out with him;"* that represents the *"them"* in the: *"How long, O Lord, holy and true, dost thou not judge and avenge our blood on them that dwell on the earth?"* question. It matters little that those referred to by Jesus back in Matthew 23:27 as *"Jerusalem,"* did the actual slaying; because they were not the *source*; but merely pawns now long dead, and much slaying of prophets continued to go on.

But they; (the souls under the altar); were at that time told, and we now know; that this "judging and avenging" would not take place *"until their fellowservants also and their brethren, that should be killed as they were, should be fulfilled."* Thus it seems likely that this refers to the aforementioned "end times."

But the question they had asked had to do with "judging and avenging." The passages do not address if and/or when they would be returned to active duty as hosts or tsâbâ'. Thus the "waiting" required for what was asked by them does not appear to be in any way *directly* related to the subject of reincarnation. But there is clear evidence of the capabilities of what can reasonably be characterized as disembodied souls. It also seems that these souls were "ready to go." It is important to understand the nature of that which *could* be reincarnated.

Nothing in these passages tells us what ultimately happened to these souls under the altar. It seems that they were provided salvation, and thus likely are no longer *"under the altar,"* but we are not actually told this.

Thus there are unanswered questions, such as: Are they currently "with God?" Who were these people/prophets? Were any of these souls ever reincarnated?

And most importantly; was there one soul *"under the altar"* whose name was Elijah? But first, in order to better understand the nature of that immaterial entity that leaves the body, there is another matter to address. . .

Reincarnation—A Reasonable Inquiry

CHAPTER 3

Divination

Any "non-comedic" discussion of the subject of "divination," is likely to cause substantial unrest among those who believe that they are currently "inside the fanum" or temple, (fanumites). And perhaps in some particular instances, with some particular groups; cause perhaps even greater unrest than any discussion of reincarnation ever would or could. Most if not all "fanumites" would agree that divination must be both *sinful* and *dangerous*—because (after all) the Bible "says so."

Often it is Deuteronomy 18:9-13 that is cited as the evidence for this.

Deuteronomy 18:9-13 (KJV) tells us:

> *"When thou art come into the land which*
> *the Lord thy God giveth thee,*
> *thou shalt not learn to do after the*
> *abominations of those nations.*

*There shall not be found among you any one
that maketh his son or his daughter
to pass through the fire, or that useth divination,
or an observer of times, or an enchanter, or a witch.
Or a charmer, or a consulter with familiar spirits,
or a wizard, or a necromancer.*

*For all that do these things are an abomination unto
the Lord: and because of these abominations the Lord thy
God doth drive them out from before thee.
Thou shalt be perfect with the Lord thy God.*"[14]

That seems to be about it. After all, if Moses (presumably) said it, (not... "*useth divination*"), it must be so.

But the *very first* verse of Deuteronomy (Deuteronomy 1:1 KJV) tells us:

*"These be the words which Moses spake
unto all Israel on this side Jordan
in the wilderness,
in the plain over against the Red sea,
between Paran, and Tophel,
and Laban, and Hazeroth, and Dizahab."*[15]

So at least according to the very *beginning* of Deuteronomy, Deuteronomy is in fact not the actual words Moses spoke, but rather merely the words that some person or persons *purport* that Moses spoke; and Moses is therefore presented here in the third person. "These be the words that he (Moses) spoke (at least according to I)," would also be a fair translation.

Many today believe that Deuteronomy was in fact not written by Moses in his lifetime—somewhere around 1400 BC; but rather was written by others somewhere around 800 BC. Thus the inclusion of Deuteronomy in its purported *entirety* as part of the actual "Word of God;" instead of perhaps its inclusion in the *Talmud*, which is *derived* and was written much later; is likely erroneous.

Deuteronomy is generally believed to mean "second law." It is unclear why there is a need for a "second law." If it is stipulated that God's law is the "first law," then it necessarily follows that a "second law" would have been written by someone other than God.

However an equally compelling argument is that the "nomy" suffix is actually derived from the Latin infinitive "*nominare,*" meaning to "name;" e.g.; as in *nominate*, [as in the previous *astronomy* v. *astrology*], rather than from the Greek *nomos* meaning "law."

If so, then rather than meaning "second law," Deuteronomy would then mean "second name." It must then be asked precisely what is it that is signified by the "first name," and why was there a need for a "second name? It would then also have to be asked why Deuteronomy means merely "second name," but the actual name is not stated—this name considered by the author(s) as *ineffable* perhaps? The significance of this will become obvious in the next chapter.

The same is likely so with much of that which follows the appearance of the "Commandments" in Exodus 20, such as all that business about the "Hebrew slaves." There is a simple test: Is what we are being told consistent or inconsistent with what we know is true about God?

And if Moses did in fact write Deuteronomy, it must be asked precisely how and when he wrote the following part of Deuteronomy:

Deuteronomy 34:5-8 (KJV) tells us:

"So Moses the servant of the Lord died there
in the land of Moab, according to the word of the Lord.

And he buried him in a valley in the land of Moab,
over against Bethpeor: but no man knoweth
of his sepulchre unto this day.

> *And Moses was an hundred and twenty years old*
> *when he died: his eye was not dim,*
> *nor his natural force abated.*
>
> *And the children of Israel wept for Moses*
> *in the plains of Moab thirty days:*
> *so the days of weeping and mourning*
> *for Moses were ended."*[16]

Since theses passages describe events *after* the death of Moses, it must be asked precisely how Moses could have been the author—*divination* perhaps?

Whatever may or may not be true about divination, it seems a good idea to find out precisely what divination actually is. After all, if the truth about divination is as presented by those who purport to speak for Moses about what it is he actually said are correct; then knowing what divination actually is, can help one avoid it. And if they are incorrect, then efforts should be undertaken to determine what the *truth* about divination in fact is.

"Chambers Dictionary of Etymology" defines *divine* as:

> *"adj.* about 1380 *devyne* of God or a god; godlike,..."[17]

Chambers further indicates that *divination* is:

> *"n.* before 1384 *dyvynacioun* foretelling, in the Wycliffe Bible; borrowed from Old French *divination*, learned borrowing from Latin *dīvīnātiōnem* (nominative *divinātiō*), from *divināre* foretell, predict; for suffix see -ATION."[18]

Thus a baseline for understanding *divination*, seems to be that it has something to do with either "of God or a god" or being "godlike;" as well as involving *foretelling*, (roughly telling before), or *prediction*, (roughly speaking before).

Thus it follows; that if the *origin* of whatever the foretelling is concerned with is *not* of God, or that which is "godlike;" then by Hobson's choice, the source must be the enemy. Ergo; whatever this type of "foretelling," (not of God), may otherwise be; it is not "divination."

A distinction must be made here between that which is considered *lŏgŏs*, as in the *lŏgŏs* of the aforementioned "ologies;" and the *precursor* to the same. The use of "precursor" here does not refer to the etymological root of the word *lŏgŏs*, but rather an *action*.

Assuming Moses authored early Genesis, it must be asked precisely how he obtained the information provided therein about certain events that had happened long before he or any other human being was born?

When that which is to be foretold or predicted exists nowhere within the material world "reach" of a given individual, this is *subjectively* equivalent to the information not existing. Of course the information exists in the *immaterial* realm (Akashic records?); but here it is either not available at that time in the material world of that individual; or perhaps is not available anywhere in the entire *material* realm. At a minimum, the former was the situation with respect to Moses. It is not known whether this information (lŏgŏs) was available elsewhere outside of Moses' "reach," but either way, it was the same thing to Moses and his culture.

This "precursor" word is the Greek word rhēma, and means:

> "rhēma 4487 from 4483; an *utterance* (individ., collect. or spec); by impl. a *matter* or *topic* (espec. of narration, command or dispute)..."[19]

This word is related to *rhetoric*, and possibly various medical conditions with the "rhea" suffix; all related to "flowing."

Divination can be an individual who is experiencing this rhēma from God, which when *revealed* to others results in foretelling; (i.e.; Daniel, Ezekiel, Book of Revelation/The Apocalypse or "revealed things," etc.); or, prediction, or soothsaying (or *truth saying* in its original meaning). Once a record of this *rhēma* is made; written or otherwise; this same information then becomes *lŏgŏs*. Rhēma is received "live" or "real time;" and lŏgŏs is "recorded."

When Moses was receiving "real time," the information that was ultimately contained in early Genesis, this was *rhēma*. When it is read today, to the extent that it has not been contaminated, this same information is *lŏgŏs*. Thus the *direct* source of *rhēma* is God, if it is *rhēma*; with God then being the *indirect* source of *lŏgŏs*, if it is *lŏgŏs*.

In the previous chapter, those under the altar were "slayed" because of the Word of God (*lŏgŏs*); and evidence (*marturia*).

And it could be argued that at the time Jesus walked the earth, it was the both His *capability* of rhēma, as well as the *meaning* of the revealed rhēma; that were two of the main reasons why the "religious" leaders at that time hated Jesus so.

According to Strong, there are three words translated as *divination* (singular) in the Old Testament.[20]

The most common word for "divination" (singular) found in the *Old Testament*, is the Hebrew word:

> "7081 qeçem; from 7080; a lot; also divination (includ. its fee) oracle; - (reward of) divination, divine sentence, witchcraft." (qeçem appears eight times in the OT)[21]

Qeçem is an interesting word for several reasons:

There is in this definition, the mention of both oracle and fee. At first blush, this may seem to refer to payment *to the oracle*, for the services (divination) provided by the oracle; and this may in fact be so. But then divination *without* this fee being charged or paid would not fit this definition, and thus could not be qeçem—which again according to Strong, is the most common Hebrew word for divination in the Old Testament.

Perhaps this "fee" means something entirely different.

Proverbs 30:1 (KJV) tells us:

> "*The words of Agur the son of Jakeh,*
> *even the prophecy:*

Divination

> *the man spake unto Ithiel, even
> unto Ithiel and Ucal,"*²²

The Hebrew word translated as "prophesy" here in Proverbs is:

> "*4853* massâ' from *5375*; a burden; spec. tribute, or (abstr.) porterage; fig. an utterance, chiefly a doom, espec. singing; mental desire: - burden, carry away, prophesy..."²³

In Hebrew; as can be seen, the word massâ can refer to either prophesy or burden; and thus sometimes is translated as *prophesy*, [note the inclusion of *utterance* in the definition]; and sometimes is translated as *burden*. How can this be so?

In New Testament Greek; particularly in that which is commonly referred to as the "Talent Man Story" in Matthew 25, there are two words worthy of note:

The actual Greek word appearing in Matthew 25 translated as "talent" is:

> "*5007* talantŏn; neut. Of a presumed der. of the orig. form of tiaō (to *bear*; equiv. to *5342*); a *balance* (as *supporting* weights), i.e. (by impl.) a certain *weight* (and thence a *coin* or rather *sum* of money) or "*talent*": - talent."²⁴

And the actual *Greek* word translated in Matthew 25 as "ability" is:

> "*1411* dunamis; from *1410*; *force* (lit. or fig.); spec. miraculous *power* (usually by impl. a *miracle* itself)..."²⁵

This word *dunamis*; which refers to *supernatural* power, must clearly be distinguished from the English word "*dynamic*;" which is derived from the Greek word *dynamikós*, which refers to *natural* power.

These (talent) men were each given different amounts of *talantŏn*, or balancing weight, based upon their level of *dunamis*—their supernatural or miraculous abilities. It must be noted that they were not each given *talantŏn* according to their *accomplishments*, but rather according to their *abilities*—not according to what they had *done*, but rather according to what they were *capable* of doing. [For a strictly non-political analysis of this process with a modern day example, see: "*Wisdom Essentials*: *Donald Trump Candidacy According to Matthew?*"]

In Hebrew it is understood that supernatural power comes along with the burden; hence the use of *massâ*. Thus *massâ* can be translated with either meaning, as it is understood that they occur together.

In Greek, the use of *dunamis* and *talantŏn* may appear to separate the ability and the burden, but the "Talent Man Story," (actually a parable), in Matthew 25; explains why this is not so. A *talantŏn* can be ignored (buried) and there will be little or no *dunamis*. But if there is *dunamis*, there must also be the burden or *talantŏn*.

Thus *dunamis* or supernatural power, cannot exist without the corresponding *talantŏn*, or burden or balancing weight. Divination is one form of *dunamis* or supernatural power. Thus qeçem, if correctly translated as divination, must include this "fee" or burden; or it cannot be supernatural power. If there is no "fee" or *talantŏn*; then there is no *dunamis*; of which divination is one manifestation.

The next word in the *Old Testament* translated as "divination" in the singular is the Hebrew word:

"4738 miqçâm; from 7080; an *augury*: - divination" (*miqçâm* appears twice in OT)[26]

If this word augury seems to sound a bit familiar, it may be because of what is contained in the aforementioned Proverbs 30: *Agur the son of Jakeh*. Augury means omen, foretelling, divination, etc.

And finally the third *Old Testament* Hebrew word translated as "divination" in the singular is:

Divination

"7080 qâçam; a prim. root; prop. to *distribute*, i.e. *determine* by lot or magical scroll; by impl. to *divine* : - divine (-r, -ation), prudent, soothsayer, use [divination]." (*qâçam* appears (only) once in OT)[27]

Here there seems to be an implication of divination or foretelling based upon something other than *rhēma*. By the use of "determine by lot or magical scroll," it seems other methods are employed. It is unclear as to precisely what Strong means by a "magical scroll." But either way, here some *physical* or other device is utilized as a means of foretelling.

Regarding the *New Testament*; according to Strong, the translation as *divination* (singular) occurs only once in the New Testament.[28]

This actual Greek word is:

"*4436* Puthōn; from Puthō (the name of the region where Delphi, the seat of the famous *oracle*, was located); a *python* i.e. (by anal. with the supposed *diviner* there) *inspiration* (*soothsaying*): - divination."[29]

According to Strong, the word "divinations," (here in the plural), appears only once in the *entire* Bible (in Ezekiel 13:23), and that word is not the above 7080 *qâçam*; but somehow the aforementioned singular 7081 *qeçem*.[30]

"7081 qeçem; from 7080; a *lot*; also *divination* (includ. its *fee*), *oracle*: - (reward of) divination, divine sentence, witchcraft."[31]

Jeremiah 14:14 (KJV) tells us:

> "*Then the Lord said unto me,*
> *The prophets prophesy lies*
> *in my name:I sent them not,*
> *neither have I commanded them,*

> *neither spake unto them:*
> *they prophesy unto you a false vision*
> *and divination, and a thing of nought,*
> *and the deceit of their heart.*"[32]

Here in Jeremiah, we have reference to "*a false vision and divination.*" Given the context, it is obvious that the "*false*" likely also applies to the "*divination,*" as well as the "*vision*" The actual word translated here as "divination" is also 7081 qeçem.[33]

And by qualifying this divination with "false," it is clear that *divination* without this "false" qualifier is presumed to be true. The *reductio ad absurdum* alternative of course, being that if true divination is presumed to always be false; then the inclusion of the qualifier of false, then "false divination" would a double negative and thus be true.

Ezekiel 12:24-25 (KJV) tells us:

> "*For there shall be no more any vain vision*
> *nor flattering divination within the house of Israel.*
> *For I am the Lord: I will speak, and the*
> *word that I shall speak shall come to pass;*
> *it shall be no more prolonged: for in your days,*
> *O rebellious house, will I say the word, and*
> *will perform it, saith the Lord God.*"[34]

This reference is to a "*flattering*" divination. The true meaning of that "old one" generally attributed to Charles Colton about "imitation being the sincerest form of flattery" is unclear; as flattery is generally considered as, unwarranted, excessive or undeserved praise; often with insincere intent.

The actual Hebrew word translated as "*flattering*" is:

> "2509 châlâq; from 2505; smooth (espec. of tongue): - flattering"[35]

Divination

The actual word translated as "*divination*" here in Ezekiel 12:24-25, is the aforementioned 4738 miqçâm.[36]

Thus the "flattering" qualifier for this divination also likely represents falsehood, (a false divination); and the same rules apply. Ezekiel 13:6-9 (KJV) tells us:

"*They have seen vanity and lying divination,
saying, The Lord saith: and the Lord
hath not sent them:
and they have made others to
hope that they would confirm the word.*

*Have ye not seen a vain vision,
and have ye not spoken a lying divination,
whereas ye say, The Lord saith it;
albeit I have not spoken?*

*Therefore thus saith the Lord God;
Because ye have spoken vanity,
and seen lies, therefore, behold,
I am against you, saith the Lord God.*

*And mine hand shall be upon the prophets
that see vanity, and that divine lies:*

*they shall not be in the assembly
of my people, neither shall they be
written in the writing of the house
of Israel,*

*neither shall they enter into
the land of Israel; and ye shall
know that I am the Lord God.*"[37]

Here we have two references to "*lying divination.*" The actual words translated as "divination" are: 7081 qeçem, and 4738 miqçâm, respectively.[38]

In these three passages, the adjectives false, flattering, and lying are applied to "divination." There are also references to *"vanity"* and *"seen lies."* As per the established criteria, this makes sense as divination has something to do with either: "of God or a god," or being "godlike;" as well as involving "foretelling." And this is clear in these passages. Again; by the use of these adjectives, (false, flattering, lying); this again tends to distinguish "divination" as true divination; requiring these adjectives only if *false* divination.

The previously referenced appearance of divination as Puthōn; a place or region "with the supposed diviner there" is in Acts 16:16-18.

Acts 16:16-18 (KJV) tells us:

> *"And it came to pass, as we went to prayer, a certain damsel possessed with a spirit of divination met us; which brought her masters much gain by soothsaying:*
>
> *The same followed Paul and us, and cried, saying, These men are the servants of the most high God, which shew unto us the way of salvation.*
>
> *And this did she many days. But Paul, being grieved, turned and said to the spirit, I command thee in the name of Jesus Christ to come out of her. And he came out the same hour."*[39]

We are told here that this woman was possessed with *"a spirit of divination,"* and had *"brought her masters much gain by 'soothsaying'."*

The actual Greek word translated here as "soothsaying," is:

"*3132* mantĕuŏmai; from a der. of *3105* (mean. a *prophet*, as supposed to *rave* through *inspiration*); to *divine*, i.e.

utter spells (under pretense of foretelling): - by soothsaying."⁴⁰

Thus is seems this woman was in fact capable of soothsaying. The likely error of "as supposed to" instead of "as opposed to;" and the inclusion of "pretense" by Strong notwithstanding.

And she did make money for her masters utilizing this power. And she was telling the truth when she: *"followed Paul and us, and cried, saying: "These men are the servants of the most high God, which shew unto us the way of salvation."*

If her divinations were already false, lying, or flattering; i.e.; not having "something to do with either "of God or a god," or being "godlike;" as well as involving "foretelling;" why would Satan then wish this woman to go around proclaiming salvation; particularly when what she was saying was true?

It should be noted that the word "grieved" is actually:

"*1278* diapŏněō; from *1223* and a der. of *4192*; to *toil through*, i.e. (pass.) *be worried*..."⁴¹

It seems that Paul had "toiled through" this for days before becoming "crabby." There should be an "old saying" which is coined here for the very first time: "It seems that you can take the Paul out of Saul, but you cannot take the Saul out of Paul."

So it must be asked precisely what spirit (crabby) Paul cast "*out of her?*" Was it the "spirit" that resulted in her divination ability; or was it another, and perhaps *evil* spirit, resulting in something else unrelated to any divination capabilities?

It is not uncommon for people of faith to confuse the "voice" of God with that of the enemy; and while believing they are dismissing that which is evil and unsolicited, are in fact dismissing that which is good, and perhaps the answer to a prayer. And surely if *anyone*, it was Paul who previously had been a bit confused in this matter.

Nevertheless; if as many of those today "inside the temple" (fanumites) believe—that divination is not of God; then again one must ask precisely what it is that then constitutes a "false" divination, a "flattering" divination, or a "lying" divination. Either God was deliberately being quasi-oxymoronic; or these adjectives present a double negative; and thus these particular "false" divinations were in fact true.

As previously addressed, this would be because calling a falsehood either false, a lie, or flattering (false praise), negates the falsehood. But this simply cannot be so given the Biblical context. And again; if all divinations are false, then "false divinations" would logically then necessarily be true.

And some simply believe that divination; at least communicating with deceased persons; is simply not possible.

One way to "get around" any possibility of reincarnation, would be to try and Biblically establish that the soul is, and remains completely inactive after separation from the physical body at physical death.

On the "official" website of the Seventh Day Adventists, the following can readily and quite easily be found:

> "Seventh-day Adventists accept the Bible as the only source of our beliefs."[42]

Thus it seems quite clear that all of the beliefs of Seventh Day Adventists are strictly Bible based, in that the word "only" is included.

At a beginning of an article titled: *"Dead Men Can't Save You,"* contained in their "beliefs" subsection, the following appears:

> "Once you're dead, you can't interact with anyone who's still alive. It doesn't matter whether the dead person is Superman, Spiderman, your father, your big sister or your spouse. Communication is no longer possible."[43]

There is an interesting Biblical *story*, (not a parable), that begins in 1 Samuel 28:1-3 (KJV):

Divination

> *"And it came to pass in those days,*
> *that the Philistines gathered their armies together*
> *for warfare, to fight with Israel.*
>
> *And Achish said unto David, Know thou assuredly,*
> *that thou shalt go out with me to battle,*
> *thou and thy men.*
>
> *And David said to Achish, Surely thou shalt*
> *know what thy servant can do.*
>
> *And Achish said to David, Therefore will*
> *I make thee keeper of mine head for ever.*
>
> *Now Samuel was dead, and all Israel had*
> *lamented him, and buried him in Ramah,*
> *even in his own city.*
>
> *And Saul had put away those that had familiar*
> *spirits, and the wizards, out of the land."*[44]

Two important things worthy of note are happening here. Samuel had died and was buried. And this particular Saul; (an entirely different Saul, one whose name would never become Paul, and whose tendency; if any; towards crabbiness is unstated); had *"put away those that had familiar spirits and the wizards out of the land."*

One would naturally first ask precisely what are *"those that had familiar spirits"* who were now *"out of the land?"*

Strong offers as the original Hebrew word translated here as *"familiar spirits"*:

> "178 'ôwv; from the same as 1 (appar. through the idea of *prattling* a father's name) prop. a *mumble*, i.e. a water – skin (from its hollow sound); hence a *necromancer* (ventriloquist, as from a jar): - bottle, familiar spirit;"[45]

According to Chambers, necromancy is:

> "*n.* foretelling of the future by communicating with the dead... divination from an exhumed corpse, from Greek *nekromanteiā* (*nekrós* dead body + *manteiā* divination, oracle, from *manteúesthai* to prophesy...*"*[46]

And according to Strong, "put away" is the translation of:

> "5493 çûwr, or sûwr; a prim. root; to *turn off* (lit. or fig.)..."[47]

It is not known at this point whether this *çûwr* amounted to mere banishment *"out of the land,"* or murder.

The story continues in the next verses, 1 Samuel 28:4-7 (KJV):

> *"And the Philistines gathered themselves together,*
> *and came and pitched in Shunem:*
> *and Saul gathered allIsrael together,*
> *and they pitched in Gilboa.*
>
> *And when Saul saw the host of the Philistines,*
> *he was afraid, and his heart greatly trembled.*
>
> *And when Saul enquired of the Lord,*
> *the Lord answered him not, neither by dreams,*
> *nor by Urim, nor by prophets.*
>
> *Then said Saul unto his servants,*
> *Seek me a woman that hath a familiar spirit,*
> *that I may go to her, and enquire of her.*
> *And his servants said to him,*
> *Behold, there is a woman that*
> *hath a familiar spirit at Endor."*[48]

Divination

So here Saul becomes afraid, and inquires *"of the Lord,"* but he receives no answer. Neither does Saul receive a response *"by dreams,"* *"nor by prophets."* Heck; not even Urim gives Saul a response. Who is this Urim guy anyway(s)?

According to Strong, Urim is:

> "224 'Ûwrîym; plur. of 217; *lights*; *Urim*, the oracular brilliancy of the figures in the Hight Priest's breastplate: - Urim."[49]

So it seems that even the "oracular brilliancy" of the High Priest's mummery could not provide an answer to Saul. Similar situations would occur thousands of years later, when sick children would be brought to the "Vicar of Christ" seeking healing, but; unlike as was the case with Jesus; to depart with only a "Holy Kiss" and a "blessing."

So Saul then tells his servants to find a woman that has a *"familiar spirit."* And not only this, but Saul is willing to *go to her*. Saul just got finished either banishing or murdering those with said "familiar spirits," and likely the "word got out;" so now he must travel *to them* in order to meet with one.

But is this even possible; as anyone with a "familiar spirit" would see Saul coming, and likely assume that he was coming to çûwr, or sûwr; or "turn off" them as well? It seems that at first those with *"familiar spirits"* were "neither oblong nor square" to Saul; but now may be the very key Saul is seeking.

The story again continues in 1 Samuel 28:8-10 (KJV):

> "And Saul disguised himself, and put on other raiment, and he went, and two men with him, and they came to the woman by night: and he said, I pray thee, divine unto me by the familiar spirit, and bring me him up, whom I shall name unto thee.
>
> And the woman said unto him, Behold, thou knowest what Saul hath done,

> how he hath cut off those that have familiar spirits,
> and the wizards, out of the land:
> wherefore then layest thou a snare for my life,
> to cause me to die?
>
> And Saul sware to her by the Lord, saying,
> As the Lord liveth, there shall no punishment
> happen to thee for this thing."⁵⁰

Saul had to disguise himself, likely because of what he had done to the others who had *"familiar spirits."* Here we are told which form of çûwr, or sûwr; or "turned off" was done to these people. Since the woman is fearful that Saul will *"cause me* (her) *to die,"* it is now clear what Saul had actually done when he *"had put away those that had familiar spirits, and the wizards, out of the land;"*—he murdered them. And her fear was so great; that she suspected treachery even before she knew who this disguised man was.

The story again continues in 1 Samuel 28:11-14 (KJV):

> "Then said the woman, Whom shall
> I bring up unto thee?
>
> And he said, Bring me up Samuel.
> And when the woman saw Samuel,
> she cried with a loud voice: and
> the woman spake to Saul, saying, Why
> hast thou deceived me? for thou art Saul.
>
> And the king said unto her, Be not afraid:
> for what sawest thou?
>
> And the woman said unto Saul,
> I saw gods ascending out of the earth.
>
> And he said unto her, What form is he of?

And she said, An old man cometh up;
and he is covered with a mantle.
And Saul perceived that it was Samuel,
and he stooped with his face to the ground,
and bowed himself."[51]

It is interesting that this woman knew how to *"bring up"* Samuel, but it is not clear that she knew *who* it was (other than his name) that she "brought up." But once she "brought him up" she did know that the *disguised* man was Saul. Perhaps Samuel somehow had told her this, but this also is not clear.

The woman saw *"gods ascending out of the earth."* According to Strong, the original text was "see a god."[52]

And also according to Strong the original Hebrew word translated as "gods" or "god" is:

> "430 'ĕlôhîym; plur. of 433: *gods* in the ordinary sense but spec. used (in the plur. thus, esp. with the art.) of the supreme *God*; occasionally applied by way of *deference* to *magistrates*; and sometimes as a superlative..."[53]

It is also interesting that Saul asked her: "What form is he of?" The original Hebrew word translated as "form" here is:

> "8389 tô'ar; from 8388; *outline*, i.e. *figure* or *appearance*..."[54]

This Saul; (not the later Saul who would become Paul, and go on to write one third of the New Testament); had murdered those with *"familiar spirits,"* likely because he believed them to be not of God. So he likely was extremely skeptical regarding who or what it would be that this woman would *"bring up;"* quite likely expecting something demonic.

It seems clear that although the woman actually saw some type of apparition of Samuel, Saul at first did not. But when Saul *"perceived"* that it was actually Samuel, he humbled himself.

The story again continues in 1 Samuel 28:15-16 (KJV):

*"And Samuel said to Saul,
Why hast thou disquieted me,
to bring me up?*

*And Saul answered, I am sore distressed;
for the Philistines make war against me,
and God is departed from me, and answereth
me no more, neither by prophets, nor by
dreams: therefore I have
called thee, that thou
mayest make known unto me
what I shall do.*

*Then said Samuel, Wherefore then dost
thou ask of me, seeing the Lord is departed from thee,
and is become thine enemy?"*[55]

Here it seems Samuel is both inquiring and rebuking Saul. "Why are you bothering me?" would be a fair translation today. And Saul tells Samuel that this is because God doesn't answer him anymore.

Saul mentions the prophets and the dreams, but not the Urim. Likely he does not want Samuel to know that even the High Priest could not help him. Saul then tells Samuel that he needs "info" from him, so he knows *"what I shall do."* And Samuel then asks Saul, (paraphrased): "Why ask me since the Lord departed from you and is has become your enemy?"

The next verses (1 Samuel 28:17-19 (KJV)) provide the *key* to the main issue:

"And the Lord hath done to him, as he spake by me:

*for the Lord hath rent the kingdom out of thine hand,
and given it to thy neighbour, even to David:*

*Because thou obeyedst not the voice of the Lord,
nor executedst his fierce wrath upon Amalek,
therefore hath the Lord done this thing unto thee this day.*

*Moreover the Lord will also deliver Israel with thee
into the hand of the Philistines: and to morrow
shalt thou and thy sons be with me:
the Lord also shall deliver the host of Israel
into the hand of the Philistines.*"[56]

These verses consist of two timeframes; with the words "*this day*" and "*moreover*" representing the junction between these two timeframes.

Samuel is first recollecting to Saul what had already happened in the *past*, which ends with "*this day.*"

This was all likely because Saul had previously disobeyed God when he did not "*go and utterly destroy the sinners, the Amalekites;*"[57] resulting in the famous question from Samuel to Saul when Samuel was still *physically* alive: "*What meaneth then this bleating of the sheep in mine ears, and the lowing of the oxen which I hear?*"[58]

But from the appearance of the word "*moreover,*" which today might be phrased as: "and another thing;" this is no longer a recollection of the past, but prophesy, as the word "*will*" appears.

Samuel is also stating here; (while Samuel is no longer physically alive); that: "*to morrow shalt thou and thy sons be with me.*" Samuel is telling Saul that "*to morrow*" Saul (and Saul's sons), will be dead. What Samuel did not tell Saul; but *we* are told later in 1 Samuel 31:4; is that Saul killed (at that time *will* kill) himself, by falling upon his own sword.[59]

These passages in Samuel, Biblically clearly establish the potential condition of consciousness in disembodied souls. Earlier it was shown that souls, ("under the altar"), were capable of communicating with God. But here in Samuel, we are told that a disembodied soul is capable of communicating with "physically alive" man, and even able to *prophesy*.

So it seems that *"true* divination;" as opposed to "false," "flattering," or "lying" divination; in all of its various forms is in fact an actuality—it does in fact exist—at least according to the Bible.

It also seems that it is appropriately named, as "it has something to do with either "of God or a god" or being "godlike;" as well as involving *foretelling* (roughly telling before), or *prediction* (roughly speaking before);" *if* it is in fact (true) divination.

The truth is that there is no need for qualifiers with respect to divination. Only true divination is divination. Whatever else that which is called "false, flattering, or lying divination" may be, it is not divination of any sort, because it has nothing to do with God; and any resultant predictions or foretelling are either derived from other factors, or can only be correct serendipitously.

Where was Samuel when Saul communicated with him via the woman with *"familiar spirits?"*

Was Samuel in heaven? If so, then Samuel must have led a sinless life, because salvation was not available at that time; and this of course is not in any way possible.

Was Samuel in hell? This is unlikely, because it seems that Samuel was much more comfortable before he was disturbed by Saul and the woman, as he had asked Saul: *"Why hast thou disquieted me, to bring me up?"*

So; if Samuel could not have been in heaven; and it does not seem like he was in any type of "hellish" environment; then where was he?

Perhaps Samuel was also "under the altar." But wait; in order for this to be possible, then Samuel would have to have been slain "for the word of God, and for the testimony which they (he) held?" Right? And 1 Samuel 25:1 simply states: *"Now Samuel died."*[60]

But when we are told: *"I saw under the altar the souls of them that were slain for the word of God, and for the testimony which they held;"* this simply tells us what or whom John *saw*. This is generally understood to mean that *"the souls of them that were slain for the word of God, and for the testimony which they held;"* represents all who were present *"under the altar."* Thus it is considered as an

Divination

established fact that only *"them that were slain for the word of God, and for the testimony which they held;"* were or could possibly have been present *"under the altar."* But that is not what this actually states.

John's statements refer only to what he *saw*. Simply because John was permitted to "see" *those* souls only, this in no way precludes other "souls" also being "under the altar," that for whatever reason(s) John was not permitted to see. There is no rational basis for concluding that simply because any person states what they see or saw, that therefore nothing else exists.

If today John were asked what he saw "under the altar," he would likely respond: "Like I already told you, I saw the souls of them that were *'slain for the word of God, and for the testimony which they held.'*" If he were then asked if there were any other souls "under the altar" or anywhere else, he would likely respond: "I don't know—perhaps. I was only speaking of, and *can* only speak of what I saw."

It would be blatantly unfair to condemn the souls of those who never had the opportunity to accept salvation, to the same fate as those who had, or *would have* had this opportunity; but *refused* salvation.

Whether referred to as *kŏlpŏs*, the "Limbo of the Patriarchs," "Bosom of Abraham," or jut plain "Limbo;" this is likely the "where" John saw, and perhaps Samuel was "there," even if John could not see him. [See: *"OSTIUM AB INFERNO—The Opening From Hell"* for a clearer understanding of the *kŏlpŏs*.]

This presents a bit of a paradoxical "time warp."

By the time John saw what he saw *"under the altar,"* Jesus had already come and gone. So those souls he saw did in fact have the ability to be saved. If the "robes" incident is or was the provision of salvation, this likely had already happened a long time before John saw it. If this is so, then what he saw was not "real time," and this was provided for knowledge. In a realm without time or duration, "real time" becomes difficult to define at best. The same is so with distance.

Possibly John did not see Samuel, because Samuel was not *"slain for the word of God, and for the testimony which they* (he) *held."* Or perhaps Samuel had not yet physically died, or was long gone; and thus no longer in the "under the altar" state. "Time paradoxes" can be like this.

But the previous question had nothing to do with where Samuel was when *John* was alive; but rather where Samuel was when *Saul* was alive. Jesus was a long way off at the time Saul was physically alive, and thus salvation, (robes?), was unavailable at that time.

Assuming hell is not a potential destination, what are the alternatives to "rest in peace?" We are told that Samuel was "*disquieted*" because of Saul. Ergo; he was "quiet" or "in peace" prior to this. And "rest" does not mean sleep, but *inactivity*, as seen in musical notation. Thus; unlike those "*under the altar*," at least at the "time" they were witnessed by John; it seems that Samuel was "resting in peace." This would be so whether Samuel was under the altar, or in the kŏlpŏs—assuming of course that they are not the same "place."

As stated, *divination* must be "true," else it is not divination. Divination must have God involved, and there must be some level of foretelling or prediction involved. If either is missing, then it is not divination.

But the *means* or *type* of divination is a separate matter. *Type* as used here does not mean true or false divination, as previously addressed. "False divination" is essentially an oxymoronic term.

Divination requires "real time" *dunamis* or supernatural power.

Two distinctions must be made here:

Firstly: In the *material* realm, there is time and duration. "Real time *dunamis*," (real time supernatural power), has the *material* realm and not the immaterial realm as the reference. Meaning that from our perspective, the requisite dunamis is a *current* thing. This requires God's "real time" involvement. [Comparing and

Divination

contrasting "real time" *dunamis* with *ĕxŏusia*, is beyond the scope of this work.]

Secondly: The requisite foretelling or prediction does not have to be concerned only with future events, or *prophesy*. It can also be concerned with past events or *retrophesy*, (Walker/Quadrakoff terminology); if information about these past events is otherwise unavailable. This is precisely how, (retrophesy), Moses wrote about the events in Genesis that had happened long before his birth. And even if Mosaic authorship is disputed, the *means* remain unchanged.

The aforementioned *rhēma* is one type or means. Again this is as opposed to *lŏgŏs*, which may have been the product of *rhēma* at one time in the past, but is now recorded. *Finding* or *understanding* "pre-existing" lŏgŏs may involve "real time dunamis," but the lŏgŏs itself is a record of past real time dunamis; e.g.; *rhēma*, and thus lŏgŏs represents "non-real time" dunamis. As previously stated, when Moses was writing Genesis, he was receiving *rhēma*. Once it had been written, it became *lŏgŏs*. The same can be said regarding learning the subjects of the various "ologies"—as opposed to new, or yet to be "dis-cover-ies."

And there is the word "mancy." This appeared earlier, as the suffix of necro*mancy*. As previously stated, according to Chambers, mancy is derived from "*manteiā* divination, oracle, from *manteúesthai* to prophesy, from *mántis* prophet; MANTIS..." This is the root of many other types of means of foretelling or prediction.

There are many forms of "mancies." Palm reading is sometimes called *palmistry*, and sometimes called *chiromancy*; ("chiro" means hand). *Cleromancy* is the casting of lots, believing that the outcome will be influenced by God and reveal unknown truths.

Acts 1:24-26 (NAS) recounts the "selection process" for the replacement of Judas Iscariot:

> "And they prayed and said, "You, Lord,
> who know the hearts of all men,
> show which one of these two
> You have chosen to occupy this ministry

*and apostleship from which Judas turned
aside to go to his own place."*

*And they drew lots for them,
and the lot fell to Matthias;
and he was added to the eleven apostles.*"[61]

This can range from "rolling dice" to "casting bones." There is *rhabdomancy* or the use of a wand or rod, such as in searching for underground water; (dowsing using a "divining rod"). There is *bibliomancy*, which uses a book, often "randomly" opening a book, and often it is the Bible. There are many types of "mancies," depending upon what is utilized.

To be truthful, not all attempts at any of these types of divinations are successful; neither are they always unsuccessful. And simply because any given attempt is unsuccessful, this does not mean that the particular type of "mancy" utilized does not work. For any of these to be successful, there must be "real time dunamis" provided by God. In the case of failure, one could argue that the entire process is nonsense. Alternatively; it could be argued that it was simply the absence of said dunamis with regard to that specific event that caused the failure.

Thus far these have all been *deliberate* attempts at some type of mancy. There is also *unintentional* mancy.

In *deliberate* mancy, the active party is in search of something; e.g.; information; and deliberately undertakes some type of action (mancy), in furtherance of, and with the hope of, obtaining the same. This is usually *specific*, in the sense that something specific is desired. Many people will just randomly open a Bible to learn something about a particular problem currently in their lives. This is deliberate, and specific; i.e.; *deliberate specific* mancy. These are utilizing bibliomancy, but likely most do not realize this.

Other people will just randomly open a Bible to learn "something." This is deliberate, but not necessarily specific; i.e.; *deliberate non-specific mancy*. They are merely seeking "wisdom for the day." These are also utilizing bibliomancy, and also likely most do not realize this.

Unintentional specific mancy, can be where one is seeking specific knowledge; but is not willfully engaging, in or even attempting to engage in, any type of mancy in order to obtain it.

Watson and Crick are credited with discovering the structure of DNA in 1953. Most believe that this was strictly the result of painstaking hours of research, until finally this research finally bore the desired fruit—and "this one" may be true.

But there is also another "story." There were painstaking hours of research, and this is beyond dispute. But this other "story" is a bit different.

As this "other story" goes, Watson and Crick had been using children's toys to discover the structure of DNA. They were assembling what basically looked like a long ladder, but it just wasn't right. This "story" does not specify which one it was, but one of them became angry, and threw this "ladder" down—likely utilizing some "colorful metaphors" before suggesting lunch. And when he then looked at this ladder, it had twisted as the result of being "thrown down." This was the double helix structure of DNA.

There was no known attempt at any type of cleromancy, but that is what actually happened; either unintentional or otherwise—and "this story" may also be true.

And there is *unintentional non-specific* mancy.

Frederic Chopin was once watching a little dog chase its tail. As the story goes, he watched it for a while, being quite amused. He then went and wrote *"Petit Chien,"* (meaning little or small dog), more commonly known as the *"Minute Waltz"*—one of his most famous works.

But wait a minute, how is this any kind of mancy? The purpose of any mancy is to obtain something (usually information) not currently available. Surely it is possible that watching a dog chase its tail was a method commonly employed by Chopin to write musical compositions, but there seems to be no evidence to support this.

Chopin was a composer, and he wrote things that never existed before. Moses was a prophet, and wrote things that never existed before (or at least not known to exist). The fact is that is was Chopin's knowledge of what to write in this waltz; rather than the description of the Big Bang" as contained in Genesis 1:1; matters little. Thus there is commonality in what Moses wrote and what Chopin wrote; in that in both instances something was provided that never existed before, and was capable of producing change.

The process of each of the various "xxx-mancy" is both entirely different; and yet at the same time precisely the same.

Each mancy is an expression of Newton's F=MA. Whether throwing dice, randomly opening a book, or speaking with the dead, each is an expression of man's will. This is to be distinguished from merely *wishing*, (desire); or *hoping*, (desire plus expectation), for something; *without* taking said action.

The expression of will creates a force in both the material and immaterial realms. One produces a balanced physical result (the MA) in the *material* realm, (the dice moved, the book was opened, etc.); and the other produces a non-physical imbalance in the *immaterial* realm. And this non-physical (immaterial) imbalance must and will be *balanced* (via another MA). This is also the simple explanation of that which is often called *karma*. [For a detailed description of this *process*, see the monograph: *"Inevitable Balance,"* also contained in the pentalogy: *"Wisdom Essentials."*]

Engaging in any type of mancy, is providing an *immaterial* imbalance in furtherance of obtaining something; and it matters little what specific *physical* action, (*type* of mancy), is undertaken.

If the imbalance is sufficient, then it will be balanced by the provision of that which is the purpose for the mancy. Meaning; that just as in the physical, when the magnitude of the imbalance or the F is sufficient (it moved, or the MA); if the *immaterial* imbalance is sufficient to move that which is in the *immaterial*, then that which is desired will be received. This is also the basis for, and mechanism of, intercessory prayer. [This entire mechanism is explained in much greater detail in *"MeekRaker Beginnings..."*]

But wait—mancies sometimes fail. This is true, and can happen for at least three reasons:

Divination

The *first*; is that the imbalance created is insufficient to "pay for" that which is desired; e.g.; engaging in a mancy solely as a "parlor trick," without any sincere desire for the knowledge.

The *second*; is that that which is requested is in fact provided, but via a means different than that which was expected; and thus ignored and/or unseen. Often there is an exclusive "man centered" expectation as in precisely how and where the desired result will be provided.

There is "that one" about the man in a flooded area, praying while waiting to be rescued. First a jeep comes to rescue him, but the man refuses, because he is certain "God will save me." As the waters rise, the man climbs to the second floor, and a boat comes to rescue him. Again the man refuses, because he is waiting for God to rescue him. As the waters continue to rise, the man climbs on the roof, and a helicopter comes to rescue him. Again the man refuses, because he is waiting for God to rescue him. Finally the waters rise even more, and the man drowns. In heaven, the disappointed man asks God why He did not rescue him. God then asks the man who is it that he thinks sent the jeep, the boat, and the helicopter?

The *third*; is that provision of what was requested; e.g.; the date time and year of Armageddon; will cause even greater imbalances. But even here, there will be some type of balancing.

In the aforementioned story of Saul, it must be asked: "Where was the dunamis (supernatural power)?" In seeking out one with "familiar spirits," Saul created a force both in the material, as he actually moved or changed his physical location in furtherance of this. This action also created an imbalance in the immaterial as there were specific reasons for the action, or why he traveled—to find one with "familiar spirits," as Saul had all those close by him murdered.

Saul either did not have the capability for necromancy; or at a minimum Saul did not believe that he had said capability. Yet according to the story, Saul did have the capability to communicate with Samuel, once the woman was able to *"bring up unto thee."* Was the dunamis in Saul's ability to communicate with Samuel; in the ability of the woman to "bring up" Samuel; or both?

It could be fairly asked what any of this has to do with reincarnation. But although the term reincarnation is concerned with the "return" of the *immaterial* portion, it largely has to do with the physical *perception*. Meaning; that it is a different *physical* body that purportedly now contains an entity that was previously incarnated. It is generally the presence of this living physical entity or physical body that is under consideration, and is the matter of "grave" dispute.

The immaterial portion of a previously "physically alive" being, continues to exist after exiting the physical body. And this immaterial portion can be at "rest;" or can be involved in activities such as those who were "under the altar," or the situation with Samuel—once Samuel was "disquieted." This is clearly Biblically supported, and thus beyond any rational Biblical dispute.

Thus reincarnation has nothing to do with any question of the continued existence of that particular "I am" in the *immaterial*. If the Bible is the reference, this "I am" will continue to exist whether reincarnated or not. The only relevant consideration here; is whether or not there is *once again* the introduction of this soul into a physical body such as described in Genesis 2:7, or by some other means.

But that which is purportedly reincarnated, or once again introduced into another (a different) body or flesh; has an existence of its own at least during, and after the first incarnation. Little is actually known about the "structure" of that which was incarnated, and then separated from the physical body by physical death.

If the information in the Biblical verses cited in this chapter is in fact true, then this provides substantial information about that which left the previously incarnated body. It is Biblically stated, that a soul maintains its identity, memory, ability to communicate; and more than arguably can provide information about the future.

How was it that Samuel was capable of providing information about the future to Saul? For the same reason John could do the same in Revelation, from roughly Chapter 4 onward. The immaterial part of Samuel was in some part of the immaterial realm where time is not a factor. John was permitted to "see" into the immaterial realm where time is not a factor. This is why some of

Divination

the "Book of Revelation" is historical (retrophesy), some is prophesy; and some may be "current events," depending upon "when," (from the material perspective), it is read.

Finally it seems that something which is often stated with little understanding of the actual meaning, now makes a bit more sense. "Rest in Peace" means: that when one is in a state of "rest;" here "rest" meaning an absence of activity rather than literal sleep; one should do so "in peace," or with lack of trouble or "stirring." This explains why Samuel asked Saul: *"Why hast thou disquieted me, to bring me up?"*

Reincarnation—A Reasonable Inquiry

CHAPTER 4

That One Called Elijah

Two questions:
First: "Who is this fellow Elijah, and why should anyone care about him?"
Second: "And what; if anything; does this fellow Elijah have to do with reincarnation?"
These are fair questions.
2 Kings 2: 8-9 (KJV) tells us:

> *"Elijah took his mantle and folded it together and struck the waters, and they were divided here and there, so that the two of them crossed over on dry ground.*
>
> *When they had crossed over, Elijah said to Elisha, "Ask what I shall do for you before I am taken from you."*

> *And Elisha said, "Please, let a double portion*
> *of your spirit be upon me.""*[62]

So here Elijah and Elisha are walking along, until they reach an impassable body of water. Elijah then simply strikes the water with his folded mantle; the waters "*divided*;" and both of them cross the area previously covered by water like it was never there, and they then just walk on like nothing happened.

This event sounds a bit *Mosaic*, and after all, who would not want to be able to part a body of water, simply by striking it with a folded mantle? *Elisha* was not only included in the group who would want this type of capability; but we are told that Elisha wanted even more, as he requested a "*double portion.*"

The story continues, as 2 Kings 2: 10-11 (KJV) then tells us:

> *"He said, "You have asked a hard thing.*
> *Nevertheless, if you see me when I am taken from you,*
> *it shall be so for you; but if not, it shall not be so."*
>
> *As they were going along and talking, behold,*
> *there appeared a chariot of fire and horses of fire*
> *which separated the two of them.*
>
> *And Elijah went up by a whirlwind to heaven."*[63]

So here Elijah is taken into heaven *in corpus*, with Elisha watching the entire time. This is a rather rare event, with the Ascension of Jesus immediately coming to mind; and perhaps Enoch. But of course the Ascension of Jesus was not to be for nearly a millennium after this.

2 Kings 2: 12-14 (KJV) chronologically then tells us:

> *"Elisha saw it and cried out, "My father,*

my father, the chariots of Israel and its horsemen!"
And he saw Elijah no more.

Then he took hold of his own clothes
and tore them in two pieces.
He also took up the mantle of Elijah
that fell from him and returned and stood
by the bank of the Jordan.

He took the mantle of Elijah that fell
from him and struck the waters and said,
"Where is the LORD, the God of Elijah?"
And when he also had struck the waters,
they were divided here and there;
and Elisha crossed over."[64]

It seems Elisha may have gotten what he asked for.

Who was this Elijah, and why is this relevant?
Elijah was a "fellow" who had "packed" some serious power. In addition to parting the waters, so that he and Elisha (his protégé) could walk over dry ground, as previously stated in verse eight; he also, among many other things: resurrected a child, (1 Kings 17:22);[65] multiplied food, (1 Kings 17:14);[66] and killed two groups of 51 men with fire from heaven, (2 Kings 1:10).[67]
Elijah first appears in the Bible in 1 Kings 17:1 (KJV):

"Now Elijah the Tishbite, who was
of the settlers of Gilead..."[68]

There is nothing actually Scripturally known about his birth, early life or very much else; until he just "shows up" as an adult in this passage. He is referred to as a *Tishbite*, which sounds a bit like something requiring immediate medical attention, but is not.

There are many different opinions about the meaning of "tishbite," but the actual Hebrew word from which Tishbite is derived is:

> "8664 Tishbîy; patrial from an unused name mean. *recourse*; a *Tishbite* or inhab. of Tishbeh (in Gilead); - Tishbite."[69]

Thus, it would seem to be fair to say that this term "Tishbite," refers to someone from an area of Gilead, (Tishbeh); from which we are told Elijah *"was of."*

The problem is that we do not actually know this, because we know not of the chronology. Meaning; that this area may have *later* been referred to as Tishbeh, *because* of Elijah; the same area formerly being known as just Gilead, until after Elijah became famous.

If this were not so, then 1 Kings 17:1 *"Now Elijah the Tishbite, who was of the settlers of Gilead..."* seems a bit redundant. Substituting the words, it would literally read: "Now Elijah, who was from the Tisbeh section of Gilead, who was of the settlers of Gilead...;" which or course seems a bit silly. However if the use of the term Tishbite is because of the *purpose* of what he actually did, or performed, or because of his calling, (Tishbîy); then the verse begins to make a bit more sense.

So there are "patrial," "unused name," and "recourse" from which to understand precisely what a "Tishbite" is.

It is important to precisely understand the meaning of the word "recourse." This word is generally considered to be synonymous with "ability or means of some type of action," but this is incorrect.

The key to this meaning, is that it describes a *turning* of one's course, specifically and exclusively, in order to obtain assistance from another source—a source other than one's self.

Thus, if it is assumed that Tishbite refers to what Elijah *did*; as opposed to where he was *from*; then in a broad sense, he as well as anyone else who is or was involved in a similar type of *recourse* (Tishbîy), is a Tishbite. But what does this mean?

Does it matter one whit that Elijah himself may have at some point been involved in recourse, because of something he could not have accomplished himself? The answer is that this question is irrelevant. It is not because Elijah may have at some point in time *sought* recourse that is significant; but rather that he was the *object* of another "living" entity's need for assistance—and that living entity was God.

The meaning of Tishbîy is first described as "patrial from an unused name mean(ing) *recourse.*"

The word "patrial" is an archaic term today, and if used at all today, is generally understood to refer to the right to live in England. But the root of the word is *"pater,"* which of course is Latin for father. Thus, it could be argued that this "patrial" is merely consistent with the idea of Gilead as being his "fatherland; if we define "patrial" as father-like or fatherly, which is a fair definition. But this "theory" does little to explain the "unused name" part.

Granted that at this juncture, this may at first in fact *appear* to be a bit of a "stretch;" it nevertheless remains the fact that the actual Hebrew word usually translated in Genesis as "hosts" is:

> "6635 tsâbâ' or ts^{e}bâ'âh from 6633; a *mass* of persons (or fig. things), espec. reg. organized for war (an *army*); by impl. a *campaign*, lit. or fig. (spec. *hardship, worship*): - appointed time, (+) army, (+) battle, company, host, service, soldiers, waiting upon..."[70]

Thus there seems to be a striking similarity between the words *Tishbîy*, meaning recourse; and *"tsâbâ'* or *ts^{e}bâ'âh"* as defined above. If the president cannot convince an enemy to "straighten up and fly right;" then using "a *mass* of persons (or fig. things), espec. reg. organized for war (an *army*);" is recourse; and perhaps the only means of recourse capable of succeeding.

It also might be asked as to why a word meaning "recourse," (8664 Tishbîy), is capitalized. The question is not why the word Tishbite is capitalized, but rather why the actual root of Tishbite "Tishbîy; patrial from an unused name mean. *recourse;*" is capitalized? After all, if one is from Bakersville, Carpentersville, or Idiotsville; the corresponding *root* of the name of the town; baker, carpenter or idiot; is generally not capitalized.

It is true that if one is *from* any of those towns, capitalization in: Bakersvillian, Carpentersvillian, or Idiotite is the norm. But that is because this usage then represents a proper noun. Here however, Tishbîy is capitalized, likely because of the normal capitalization of the name, (proper noun), from which; although largely unused; is always capitalized.

What does an "unused name" mean? This seems a bit oxymoronic in that generally, the purpose of any name is to identify a person, place, or thing. A name is designed to be *used*, else what need is there for it? To have a name that is not used; is not substantially more helpful than not having any name at all. So it would be fair to ask, where in the Bible is there any record of anything that has to do with a name that is not used?

> "Rabbinical Judaism teaches the four-letter name of God, YHVH, is forbidden to be uttered except by the High Priest in the Holy Temple on Yom Kippur."[71]

Sometimes the name of God is considered to be *ineffable*; with "ineffable" roughly meaning: "unable to be put into words." YHVH in all of its various spellings is referred to as the *tetragrammaton*. This ineffability of the name of God can be considered simply as a matter of respect, (minority view); or because no word exist which can adequately describe the nature of a limitless God. There is much disagreement regarding which four letters are appropriate, and whether or not the vowels were deliberately removed in order to make pronunciation impossible—except of course by the "Arcanum" of the time.

Thus, often the names that refer to God in the Bible are actually a description or a title; e.g.; Creator, Lord, etc., rather than His actual "name." Nevertheless, whatever is the actual truth; it seems that here we have an excellent example of an unused name.

Unfortunately, no matter how one attempts to pronounce YHVH, it cannot reasonably be made to sound anything like Tishbîy.

However, according to Jewishencyclopedia.com:

"The names Yhwh and Elohim frequently occur with the word Ẓeba'ot ("hosts"), as Yhwh Elohe Ẓeba'ot ("Yhwh God of Hosts") or "God of Hosts"; or, most frequently, "Yhwh of Hosts.""[72]

This same source then cites 1 Samuel 17:45 as to the source of the original meaning of Ẓeba'ot.[73]

1 Samuel 17:45 (KJV) tells us:

"Then David said to the Philistine, "You come to me with a sword, a spear, and a javelin, but I come to you in the name of the LORD of hosts, the God of the armies of Israel, whom you have taunted..."[74]

The original Hebrew word translated as "hosts" in this cited verse from 1 Samuel is in fact the aforementioned: "6635 tsâbâ' or tsᵉbâ'âh...."[75]

Thus, the name YHVH Ẓeba'ot is the same as YHVH tsâbâ' or YHVH tsᵉbâ'âh, albeit spelled a bit differently. Thus YHVH tsâbâ' or YHVH tsᵉbâ'âh; with the ineffable name of God left unspoken, leaves tsâbâ' or tsᵉbâ'âh, meaning remarkably: "hosts." And again; with Tishbîy meaning *recourse*, this is in fact remarkably quite similar.

In fact, the similarities between these two words; tsâbâ' or tsᵉbâ'âh and Tishbîy; is much greater than the similarity between the word Ẓeba'ot and the word tsâbâ' or tsᵉbâ'âh from which

Ẓeba'ot seems to be derived. The capitalization of Tishbîy, as opposed to Tishbite, is likely because it refers to a proper noun, as part of a name for God.

Thus, Elijah as a "Tishbite," likely actually means one who is a tsâbâ' or ts^{e}bâ'âh, or host or vehicle for recourse; in this case on the behalf of YHVH, with the YHVH unspoken or "unused name" for all or the aforementioned reasons.

Thus it should read: "Now Elijah the Ts^{e}bâ'âh(ite) or host for God (hence the capitalization, as well as the *patrial* or father reference), who was, (either genealogical or geographical), of the settlers of Gilead..." And it is inarguable that Elijah was armed with substantial *dunamis*, or supernatural power; in furtherance of his role; at least at the time he first enters the Scriptural scene, and "turns off the rain."

In fact, Elijah's name, if broken down; is actually some permissible combination of this ineffable name of God or YHVH; and the word El, (from *'ĕlôhîym*), commonly used to describe "God." It can be translated as YHVH is God, or YHVH is my God, or arguably God is YHVH, or perhaps in other manners.

For those unfamiliar with the analyses provided in the first Chapter of *"MeekRaker Beginnings...;"* Genesis 1:1 provides the complete statement of what God did or accomplished in the (very) "Beginning."

This event (Genesis 1:1) happened a time long before, (how long is unstated), the description of conditions "on the ground" as contained in the first half of Genesis 1:2. Thus that which is described in Genesis 1:2, is *not* merely a "more detailed" recapitulation of Genesis 1:1; but rather occurred chronologically long after "The Beginning" referenced in Genesis 1:1.

Contained in the second half of Genesis 1:2, is the description of how God Himself and acting alone; (long after the "end" of "The Beginning"); began to restore the conditions "on the ground;" thereby beginning the process in which we are involved to this very day—*whether mankind is aware of this fact or not.*

The very first known Divine Act of God seeking "recourse," occurs in Genesis 1:26-28, where God creates the "hosts;" and gives them dominion over the earth.

Genesis 1:26-28 (KJV) tells us:

> *"And God said, Let us make man
> in our image, after our
> likeness: and let them have
> dominion over the fish of the sea,
> and over the fowl of the air, and over the cattle,
> and over all the earth, and over every creeping
> thing that creepeth upon the earth.*
>
> *So God created man in his own image,
> in the image of God created he him;
> male and female created he them.*
>
> *And God blessed them, and God
> said unto them, Be fruitful, and multiply,
> and replenish the earth, and subdue it:
> and have dominion over the fish of the sea,
> and over the fowl of the air, and over every
> living thing that moveth upon the earth."*[76]

This terminology of "hosts" first appears in Genesis 2:1, and again this actual terminology is: "tsâbâ' or ts^{e}bâ'âh."[77]

The issue of why God chose "recourse," rather than just continuing the process himself is not stated. Clearly the establishment of "a mass of persons, (or fig. things), espec. reg. organized for war (an army);" represents recourse, and surely had some rational basis.

Again it must be asked why any leader would incorporate the services of, (and also here the actual *creation* of), an army; if said leader was both *capable of*, and *permitted to*, accomplish the same ends himself? Since this cannot be because of God's *inability* to continue the fight himself, as he is omnipotent; and omnipotence necessarily includes no act of which one who is omnipotent is *incapable*; there then must be another reason or reasons why God chose to engage in recourse by the establishment of the hosts, as "tsâbâ' or tsᵉbâ'âh". [Although this is far beyond the scope this work; and at the risk of causing additional controversy; the answer is that it is not a matter of capability, but a matter of authority. The truth, is that the instruction to man regarding the aforementioned kiboshing (kyboshing) of the earth, represents not the *granting* of authority, but rather the *transferring* of authority.]

The actual word translated as "hard" describing the "thing" that Elijah was asked for by Elisha, is used only four other times in the entire Old Testament and is:

"7185 qâshâh; a prim. root; prop. to *be dense*, i.e. tough or *severe* (in various applications): - be cruel, be fiercer, make grievous, be ([ask a], be in, have, seem, would) hard (-en, [labour], - ly, thing), be sore, (be, make) stiff (-en, [-necked])."[78]

Why is this important? The way that it reads, Elijah *seems* to be describing the difficulty of the *process* of granting Elisha a power equal to twice that of Elijah: "*You have asked a hard thing.*"

If this were the actual meaning and it was stated so today, it would read something like: "Giving you twice my power is a difficult thing for me to do, nevertheless..." But that is not what it seems Elijah is telling Elisha in this verse, and "difficult" appears nowhere in the definition of qâshâh.

It is not the actual process of *granting* Elisha the power that Elijah is describing as a hard thing or qâshâh, but the very *power* itself. Thus, if stated today it would read something like: "The *thing* you are asking for is literally a very dense, tough and severe thing; and translationally, a cruel, fierce and grievous thing." Elijah is actually warning Elisha about the other side of the actuality of this kind of power. It is the same as any dunamis and the corresponding weight or talantŏn. It is the same as the previously addressed "oracle" and "burden" each being correct translations of the same Hebrew word: massâ'.

By advising Elisha of this, Elijah is providing a means of what today would be referred to as "informed consent." When Elijah then tells Elisha that: "*Nevertheless, if you see me when I am taken from you, it shall be so for you; but if not, it shall not be so,"* he is giving Elisha the opportunity to either accept the *total* actuality of this power; or change his mind, simply by whether or not he watches the event.

Translations notwithstanding; no reference can be found which indicates that the word "nevertheless" actually appears in this verse. Thus, it seems that what Elijah is doing is informing Elisha, in a very frank manner, the *totality* of his request; and in a kind way is telling him to "take it or leave it."

But a more than fair argument exists, that despite the fact that we are told that Elijah *"went up by a whirlwind to heaven,"*—the "smart money" says: "He aint done yet."

———————

"Malachi 3:1 tells us:

> *"Behold, I am going to send My messenger, and he will clear the way before Me. And the Lord, whom you seek, will suddenly come to His temple; and the messenger of the covenant, in whom you delight, behold, He is coming," says the LORD of hosts."*[12.1]

"God is speaking here about what was to happen before the *first* coming of Jesus. This is entirely different than later in Malachi 4:5 which refers to the "great and terrible day of the Lord;"[12.2] with that passage likely being concerned with His *second* coming—a matter which is further detailed in the Book of Revelation. There is often conflation of these two separate events into one. But the first coming of Jesus, as a "laundryman's soap," although certainly great; was only terrible for two; those two being Jesus and the devil.

"God is telling us here that He will be sending a forerunner; a messenger sent before Jesus who was to "clear the way." But who is or was this messenger to be? Some believe that it was to be an angel. Perhaps this refers to Gabriel, as when he visited Mary. But that really doesn't make very much sense; as Gabriel visited Mary because he needed her permission for the "immaculate conception." That hardly represented clearing the way for anything; arguably not even the conception, as there was nothing to clear.

"Perhaps it was the time when Gabriel visited Joseph. But that also makes little sense, as he only wanted to let "Joe" know that Mary wasn't "cheating on him." After all, they did stone "adulteresses" back then; even though they (Mary and Joseph) were not yet; (and perhaps never actually were), married. Most people infer that the reason that there was "no room at the inn" is a euphemism for lack of funds. A better argument is that they were denied a "room" because they were not married.

"The Jewish people today believe that this messenger will be, (future tense used purposely), Elijah. They very much want Elijah to come; because they believe that this is necessary before the Messiah arrives, just as Malachi states; and they desperately want the Messiah. In fact; generally at the Passover Seder; a place and a glass of wine is set for Elijah; and the front door is symbolically opened and closed to admit him; welcoming him and facilitating his entry; should he choose to arrive at their home.

"But for Christians, the arrival of this messenger is not a matter of the future, but of the past. Since Jesus has already come the first time; and since God told us there would be a forerunner; then of course to Christians, the circumstances surrounding the arrival of this forerunner must necessarily be a historical fact, and not a future matter.

"The disciples of Jesus knew that He must have been preceded by a forerunner, but did not believe that they had any knowledge of the arrival of the forerunner. So they asked Him about this very issue.

"Matthew 17:10-13 tells us:

"And His disciples asked Him,
"Why then do the scribes say that
Elijah must come first?"

And He answered and said, "Elijah is coming
and will restore all things; but I say to you that
Elijah already came,
and they did not recognize him,
but did to him whatever they wished.

So also the Son of Man is going to
suffer at their hands."
Then the disciples understood
that He had spoken to them
about John the Baptist."[12.3]

"The use of "why then" here must be explained. Prior to this they had experienced a voice from heaven confirming that Jesus was the Son of God; but they also knew that Elijah was to come first. But none had seen Elijah, and therefore could not understand this discrepancy. Assuming the voice from heaven confirming Jesus was who He was; was in fact true, they sought resolution of this discrepancy; hence the "why then?" This was an inquiry as to why the scribes predicted a requirement, that the disciples believed had not yet happened. And Jesus explained to them that

Elijah had already "come and gone" and they had "missed it."

"Here the disciples and the scribes knew that this forerunner was not to be an angel; and they knew then, just as Jews believe today, that this forerunner was to be Elijah. And Jesus Himself commented on what happened to Elijah, and that the same was to happen to Him. And the last sentence confirms that the disciples knew that John the Baptist was Elijah.

Matthew 11:7-14 confirms this, as we are told:

> "As these men were going away,
> Jesus began to speak to the crowds about John,
> "What did you go out into the wilderness to see?
> A reed shaken by the wind?
>
> "But what did you go out to see?
> A man dressed in soft clothing?
> Those who wear soft clothing are in kings' palaces!
>
> "But what did you go out to see? A prophet?
> Yes, I tell you, and one who is more than a prophet
> "This is the one about whom it is written,
> 'BEHOLD, I SEND MY MESSENGER AHEAD OF YOU,
> WHO WILL PREPARE YOUR WAY BEFORE YOU.'
>
> "Truly I say to you, among those born of women
> there has not arisen anyone greater than
> John the Baptist! Yet the one who is least
> in the kingdom of heaven is greater than he.
>
> "From the days of John the Baptist until now
> the kingdom of heaven suffers violence,
> and violent men take it by force.
> "For all the prophets and the Law
> prophesied until John.
> And if you are willing to accept it,
> John himself is Elijah who was to come."[12.4"79]

Now all of this seems to work out well, because as previously cited, Elijah was taken into heaven "in corpus," or "ascended into heaven," via that "Chariot of Fire" while Elisha watched, and then got a "double portion" of Elijah's power.

And there is more:

> "Thus, all that God had to do was send the chariot of fire back and drop off Elijah, and all would be fine. This is not in any way an attempt to be flippant, as it just seems that the logical purpose for bringing Elijah into heaven in that manner; was to be able to return him as the forerunner. God knew He had additional plans for Elijah, and this would be a reasonable explanation. But the Bible clearly shows us that this is *not* in any way what He did.

This is a bit long, but Luke 1:5-20 tell us what God actually *did* do:

> *"In the days of Herod, king of Judea,*
> *there was a priest here was a priest named*
> *Zacharias, of the division of Abijah*
> *and he had a wife from the daughters of Aaron,*
> *and her name was Elizabeth.*
>
> *They were both righteous in the sight of God,*
> *walking blamelessly in all the commandments*
> *and requirements of the Lord.*
> *But they had no child, because Elizabeth was barren,*
> *and they were both advanced in years.*
>
> *Now it happened that while he was performing*
> *his priestly service before God in the appointed*
> *order of his division, according to the custom*
> *of the priestly office, he was chosen by lot*
> *to enter the temple of the Lord and burn incense.*
>
> *And the whole multitude of the people were*

*in prayer outside at the hour of the incense offering.
And an angel of the Lord appeared to him,
standing to the right of the altar of incense.*

*Zacharias was troubled when he saw the angel,
and fear gripped him. But the angel said to him,
"Do not be afraid, Zacharias, for your petition
has been heard, and your wife Elizabeth will
bear you a son, and
you will give him the name John.*

*"You will have joy and gladness, and many
will rejoice at his birth. "For he will be great
in the sight of the Lord; and he will drink no wine
or liquor, and he will be filled with the Holy Spirit
while yet in his mother's womb. "And he will turn
many of the sons of Israel back to the Lord their God.*

*"It is he who will go as a forerunner before Him
in the spirit and power of Elijah,
TO TURN THE HEARTS OF THE FATHERS
BACK TO THE CHILDREN,
and the disobedient to the attitude of the righteous,
so as to make ready a people prepared for the Lord."*

*Zacharias said to the angel,
"How will I know this for certain? For I am an old man
and my wife is advanced in years."*

*The angel answered and said to him,
"I am Gabriel, who stands in the presence of God,
and I have been sent to speak to you and to
bring you this good news.*

*"And behold, you shall
be silent and unable to speak until the day when
these things take place, because you did
not believe my words, which will be
fulfilled in their proper time."*[12.6]

"Zacharias was a holy man. He and Elizabeth were righteous in the sight of God; walking blamelessly in all commandments and requirements. The use of the term "walking" in the Scriptures generally means lifestyle, rather than ambulation. They were blameless, but it does not state innocent. Although these words are often used interchangeably, they are not synonyms. Blameless meaning cannot be blamed for wrongs; innocent at a minimum meaning you didn't do anything wrong, cause or mean to cause any harm. The word innocence is derived from the Latin "nocere;" as in the Latin "Primum non nocere." This is roughly translated as "first do no harm;" and is provided as a guide for physicians.

"Guilty and not guilty, in the legal usage, often have nothing whatsoever to do with what one did or did not do, but rather what can or cannot be proved. It would probably be fair to say that this couple endeavored to live a holy lifestyle, made some mistakes, but their hearts were in the right place. Elizabeth was now barren, likely had always been barren, as they had no children; and now they were both getting older. It does not seem that Zacharias would have been the type who would ever have introduced Elizabeth as his sister. (see Abraham and Abimelech).

"So now one day, Zacharias is performing priestly service according to all the customs, and he is chosen by lot to enter and burn incense. This is not actually stated, but there must have been more men wanting to enter and burn incense, as a lottery was used to determine who would enter that day. So then it was by "random" that he happened to be in the temple that day. But of course there is no such thing as random.

"While he is in this temple, an angel appears and tells Zacharias (who it seems is terrified) that his petition has been heard. Up to this point, it is not stated that they had been praying for a child, but they must have been.

The angel tells Zacharias that this son will be named John, and tells Zacharias a few other things as well.

"John "will drink no wine or liquor." A Nazarite or Nazarene was one who took special vows which could be for life, or for a fixed period of time. These vows usually included not drinking alcohol, and not cutting one's hair. Jesus was also a Nazarite or Nazarene. That is why when someone suggests that it is not known whether or not Jesus had long hair; this is false. We know that he did, because he had also taken these vows, which include the vow to not cut His hair.

"John will be filled with the Holy Spirit (Ghost) in the womb. This is important because when Mary is pregnant and meets Elizabeth, (who was Mary's relative), when Elizabeth was six months pregnant, there is a reaction from John within Elizabeth's womb. It is also important because it is when Jesus is later baptized by John, it is at that time that the Holy Ghost descends upon Him.

"Zacharias is then advised that it is his son John, who is to be the forerunner for Jesus in the "spirit and power of Elijah."

"This word "spirit" used in this passage can be a subject of much confusion. Many profess that this simply means that John would be like or similar to Elijah; but that John was not in fact Elijah; as in the "spirit of the law" as opposed to the "letter of the law." But the word "spirit" comes from the word "spiritus" which means breath. Since we know that man becomes a living soul when God breathes the breath of life into his nostrils, then the literal "spirit of Elijah" would then necessarily be the same breath that God originally breathed into Elijah's nostrils—by definition.

"Furthermore, the actual Greek word used for *spirit* in this passage is:

"4151 pneuma, from 4154; a *current* of air, i.e. *breath* (*blast*) or a *breeze*; by anal. or fig. a *spirit*, i.e. (human) the rational *soul*, (by impl.) *vital principle*, mental *disposition*, etc., or (superhuman) an *angel*, *demon*, or (divine) *God*, Christ's *spirit*, the Holy *Spirit*: - ghost, life, spirit (-ual - ually), mind."[12.7]

"The word used for *power* here is (the previously mentioned) *dunamis*,[12.8] or supernatural power, and not any form of dynamikós or natural power..."

"This is difficult to envision. An angel comes to Zacharias (obviously after he or they had been praying for a son), scaring the dickens out of him; tells him that his petition has been heard and that he will be given a son; including what to name him, and that he will be the prophesied forerunner.

"And what is Zack's response?

"How will I know this for certain? For I am an old man and my wife is advanced in years." The angel then tells Zacharias that he (the angel) is Gabriel, and warns him: "And behold, you shall be silent and unable to speak until the day when these things take place, because you did not believe my words, which will be fulfilled in their proper time."

"Zacharias was described as a priest. He knew full well the significance of the forerunner; this same forerunner for whom as stated, Jewish people today set a place, pour wine, and open the door.

"The way this reads, it sounded like he did not actually say that he did not believe it; but rather that he wanted insurance. But the *Interlinear Bible* version is: "By what shall I know this?"[12.9] Thus, a fair read is that Zacharias was actually asking for a sign. Since he commented on his age, it is likely he wanted a sign soon; or at least before his son reached adulthood.

"It would seem otherwise fair to ask the question as to why Gabriel not only insisted on Zacharias silence; but also made him physically unable to speak until after John was born and named.

"After all, back when Abraham's wife Sarah was told she would bear a son, and when they laughed because they did not believe God; neither God nor any angel on His behalf silenced them. Instead, God just named the child Isaac, which means "laughter" or "he laughs." So the question becomes: if Zacharias was asking for a sign; why then did Gabriel choose silence as this sign instead of something else?

"There is a reason why Gabriel caused Zacharias to be physically unable to speak. This reason is because even long before Newton, whose name was also to be Isaac; Gabriel understood F=MA. At this juncture, Zacharias simply could not be permitted to create or sow a negative F_T by speaking out loud F_A, with his doubt creating a negative F_R, rendering the total force negative. Remember Job?

"This was a "tight" time. There was no time for error correction. Back when Abram/Abraham took matters into his own hands by the comedy with Hagar, there was ample time for course correction. But here timing was critical; for among other reasons; Jesus and John were only to be about six months apart gestationally.

"Gabriel had advised Zacharias that his son John was to be "in the spirit and power of Elijah." The scribes of that time, as Jews today, believed the forerunner was to be Elijah. The disciples believed Elijah was to come first and had asked Jesus about it. Jesus had told them in Matthew 17:10-13, that "Elijah is coming and will restore all things; but I say to you that Elijah already came, and they did not recognize him, but did to him whatever they wished;" which resulted in the disciples understanding "that He had spoken to them about John the Baptist." Jesus also stated in Matthew 11:14; "And if you are willing to accept *it,* John himself is Elijah who was to come." And one additional fact is that John's mother's name was Elizabeth, which means "house of Elijah."

"Thus there is little possible doubt that John the Baptist was Elijah. If that were not so, then all of these people, including Jesus twice, are or were wrong. And if they are or were wrong, then there is a missing forerunner. But the problem is that Elijah did not return to earth as the adult male who had left in the whirlwind. (This event is possibly being reserved for the provision of the "witnesses" before the "great and terrible day," at some point during "end times.")

"Instead, he was born as the result of a "normal" pregnancy...

* * *

"The preceding shows there is no possible *reasonable* conclusion, other than that John the Baptist was Elijah reincarnated. But this tells us only that Elijah was reincarnated as John. This could have been a one-time event; as was the "immaculate conception;" because there is no reference or suggestion in the passages referenced thus far; that it had ever happened at any other time; or with or to anyone else.

"John 9:1-5 tells us:

"As He passed by, He saw a man blind from birth. And His disciples asked Him, "Rabbi, who sinned, this man or his parents, that he would be born blind?"

"Jesus answered, "It was neither that this man sinned,

> *nor his parents; but it was so that the works of God might be displayed in him.*
>
> *"We must work the works of Him who sent Me as long as it is day; night is coming when no one can work.*
>
> *"While I am in the world, I am the Light of the world."*[12.10]

"This passage is part of the story about Jesus performing a miracle in restoring sight to a blind man. As it reads, it shows the power Jesus had from the Father, and that it was the works of Him *"be displayed in"* this person.

"But there is additional revelation contained here that is very easy to miss. The disciples asked Jesus who sinned that he should be born blind. Now it might be easy to make the case that the parents had sinned, and the result was that the child was born blind. This argument could be raised today when children are born addicted to drugs, or when they are born with AIDS. Whether or not one agrees that using crack cocaine or sexual promiscuity constitute "sinful" behaviors, could arguably be argued. Nevertheless, a child can be born with a malady as a result of a parent's or the parents' behavior.

"The actual Greek word translated as sinned is:

> "*264* hamartano; perh. from *1* (as a neg. particle) and the base of *3313*; prop. to *miss the mark* (and *so not share* in the prize), i.e. (fig.) to *err*, esp. (mor.) to *sin*; - for your faults, offend, sin, trespass."[12.11]

"But it is the other possibility that the disciples raised, which contains the revelation. Most societies and religions acknowledge the fact that there are threshold ages with respect to knowing right from wrong; as well as threshold ages for responsibility for one's actions. This is seen in the ages for the Catholic First Communion and Confirmation. It is also evident with the ages required for bar-mitzvahs and bas-mitzvahs. There are also legal age requirements with respect to knowing right from wrong, or whether one should be "tried as an adult." The actual ages are not important here; but rather the concept that before a certain age, sin is not possible because the child is incapable of knowing right from wrong. So as a child, before reaching a certain age, this person or any person simply was incapable of sinning.

"But the fact is that the disciples did not ask Jesus if it was a sin of this person as a child that resulted in his blindness. Nor did they ask Jesus if it was possible that this man could have sinned, and that this resulted in him being born blind. What they actually asked was if it was because he sinned that he was (would be) born blind. There is a major difference. The only possible supposition for this question, of course being that it was their position that this man could have first sinned, and then been born.

"Since it is not possible for an unborn child to know right from wrong, there is no possible way this child could have sinned while in the womb. And even if he somehow could have known right from wrong, it is difficult to imagine what that sinful behavior could have possibly been. Furthermore, according to Genesis 2:7 man does not become a living soul until God breathes into his nostrils, which happens at the first breath; something which simply cannot physically happen while in the womb.

"Thus, what the disciples were actually asking Jesus, was if it was a sin from a time when this man could have sinned; which necessarily had to be prior to his birth. This means that the man would have had to have been old enough to know right from wrong, at some time prior to his birth. This also necessarily means knowing right from wrong prior to becoming a fetus, an embryo, a morula or a fertilized egg. There is no conclusion possible; other than they meant sinning in a prior life.

"Jesus did not respond by inquiring as to whether or not they had had hidden pocket flasks originally filled with water at the wedding; flasks which were very recently emptied. He did not inquire as to whether they had been having headaches lately. Instead he answered them, and the answer was neither. Thus, although today making an inquiry as to whether sin in a previous life could result in a malady in the next life would be considered as blasphemy; it most certainly was not such to Jesus at that time. Had this been so; His response would have been "as their folly deserved," as Jesus was known for "telling it like it is." Instead He considered it a legitimate question, and He answered "according to" it.

"There is no other reasonable conclusion other than Jesus and His disciples did not believe that reincarnation was a singular event; meaning one which had only ever occurred with the reincarnation of Elijah as John the Baptist.

Matthew 16: 13-16 tells us:

> *"Now when Jesus came into the district of Caesarea Philippi, He was asking His disciples, "Who do people say that the Son of Man is?"*
>
> *"And they said, "Some say John the Baptist; and others, Elijah; but still others, Jeremiah,*

or one of the prophets."

"He said to them, "But who do you say that I am?"
Simon Peter answered,
"You are the Christ, the Son of the living God."[12.12]

"Here Jesus is asking his disciples who it was that common people believed *He* was. The four answers that the disciples received from the people regarding who "He is" all had one thing in common. All of these individuals were deceased at that time; noting that the phrase: "one of the prophets," represents an unspecified number of possibilities—including those "under the altar" at some point in time.

"Thus, this idea of reincarnation was not limited to Jesus and His disciples, but also believed by the common people at that time. It was not arcane knowledge, but rather common knowledge; irrespective of the fact that it is generally considered at best heresy; more likely blasphemy, in today's "religious" circles..."[80]

And there is that matter of "appointed:"

"Hebrews 9:27-28 tells us:

"And inasmuch as it is appointed
for men to die once
and after this comes judgment,
so Christ also,
having been offered once to
bear the sins of many,
will appear a second time for salvation
without reference to sin,
to those who eagerly await Him."[12.15]

"The actual word for appointed is:

"606 apokeimai, from 575 and 2749; to *be reserved*; fig. to *await*: - be appointed, (be) laid up.[12.16]

"Taken in context, the subject under explanation has to do with why Jesus did not have to offer himself more than once. It has nothing whatsoever to do with reincarnation. It is stated merely to support the conclusion; which is what follows the word "so;" or one could substitute "therefore." A better translation for "appointed" would be "reserved" or "laid up." Laid up generally means stored or non-functional.

"This likely refers to spiritual death from sin, which means separation from God. No longer do men spiritually die or be separated from God because of sin, as salvation justifies those who accept this salvation. All of the Old Testament prophets and holy men did not have this option. These Jesus rescued at or after Calvary; depending upon ones perspective.

"As previously discussed, there is no actual spiritual "death;" if "death" here means non-existence; as we continue to exist somewhere forever, either heaven or hell. Physical death is merely a separation from the body, with neither ceasing to exist. In addition, if this is taken to mean that it is Divine will that men die only once physically, then it is arguable that Jesus sinned when He raised or resurrected Lazarus as well as others.

"*The Interlinear Bible* translation translates "appointed" as "reserved."[12.17]

"It is not clear as to precisely what it is that the "once" refers. It could refer to the "laid up/reserved," or it could refer to the "die." For the purposes of argument, if it is the die, and the die refers to "physical death" then it may very well mean that men dying once has been laid up; and now men physically die more than once. If it is the reserved/laid up to which the word "once" refers, and would be more consistent with the context; which is concerned with explaining why it is that Jesus only had to suffer once. If one takes the position that "Each human being lives once as a mortal on earth, dies once," is what is meant; and it is that concept or rule which was laid up; then either no one lives anymore, or it clearly proves physical rebirth.[81] [Excerpt from: *"MeekRaker Beginnings..."* Chapter 12: *"Reprise"* Reprinted by Permission]

And there is yet one more.
John 1:19-26 tells us:

*"And this is the record of John,
when the Jews sent priests and Levites
from Jerusalem to ask him,
Who art thou?*

*And he confessed, and denied not;
but confessed, I am not the Christ.*

*And they asked him, What then? Art thou Elias?
And he saith, I am not. Art thou that prophet?
And he answered, No.*

*Then said they unto him, Who art thou?
that we may give an answer to
them that sent us.
What sayest thou of thyself?*

*He said, I am the voice of one crying
in the wilderness,
Make straight the way of the Lord,
as said the prophet Esaias.*

And they which were sent were of the Pharisees.

*And they asked him, and said unto him,
Why baptizest thou then, if thou be
not that Christ, nor Elias,
neither that prophet?*

*John answered them, saying, I baptize
with water: but there standeth one among you,
whom ye know not;"*

*He it is, who coming after me
is preferred before me,
whose shoe's latchet
I am not worthy to unloose."*[82]

After all; given what ultimately happened to him, it may have been that John may have simply lied.

CHAPTER 5

"Religious" Commentary On Elijah et al.

It seems that many "authorities," ("fanumites"); take issue with that which seems so obvious—simply because they do not like it, and this is by no means new. There are reasons why they do not like it—reasons that have nothing to do with the acquisition of truth.   When truth and perceived practicality conflict; unfortunately it is truth that often becomes the sacrificial lamb. These "reasons" will be addressed later.

Rather than taking the scientific approach, and "going with" the explanation consistent with the maximum number of facts; instead *many* utilize *many* words, as generally *many* words are required in order to try to explain why what clearly *is*; somehow nevertheless *is not*.

Proverbs 10:19 (NAS) tells us:

"When there are many words,

> *transgression is unavoidable,*
> *but he who restrains his lips is wise."*[83]

The Bible is *lŏgŏs*, and designed to provide information. Once the precise original terminology can be determined, the result is supposed to be Apocalypsa, ("revealed things"); and not Apocrypha, ("hidden things"). The path should be from obscurity to clarity, and not the reverse. When *clarity* is deliberately obfuscated, the only remaining "clarity," is that something is *clearly* amiss.

It generally takes a lot of words to make the argument that the Bible does not mean what it actually states; but instead means something entirely different. Like attorneys buzzing around one or two key words in a contract; many "fanumites" labor likewise—lest someone, somewhere, at any time, believe differently than they. This can be especially effective, if some archaic Latin words or phrases are thrown in the mix—bringing to mind the "Ancient Hebrew" utilized by "the Duke and the King," in Mark Twain's: *"The Adventures of Huckleberry Finn."*

Proverb 18:17 (NAS) tells us:

> *"The first to plead his case seems right,*
> *Until another comes and examines him."*[84]

In furtherance of obtaining "the truth," it is the very purpose of this chapter to provide that *"another"* to that *"first,"* as proffered by the "fanumites."

Once again, Matthew 17:10-12 (NAS) tells us:

> *"And His disciples asked Him,*
> *"Why then do the scribes say*
> *that Elijah must come first?"*
> *And He answered and said,*
> *"Elijah is coming and will restore all things;*

"Religious" Commentary On Elijah et al.

> *but I say to you that Elijah already came,*
> *and they did not recognize him,*
> *but did to him whatever they wished.*
> *So also the Son of Man is going*
> *to suffer at their hands."*

Here Jesus is confirming that the prophesy about Elijah coming first had already happened, but that Elijah was not recognized.

This provides the context for the above conclusion contained in the very next verse.

As again, Matthew 17:13 (NAS) tells us:

> *"Then the disciples understood that He had*
> *spoken to them about John the Baptist."*

What is quite clear, is that the Elijah Jesus had spoken about in the previous verses, was in fact John the Baptist. This last passage merely confirms the fact that the disciples at that point, (then), *"understood"* that this was in fact so.

Searching "Matthew 17:13 commentary" on the internet; the following were the first results encountered on the very first page. What immediately follows, as well as all other "commentary," was randomly chosen from that which is contained in the "public domain."

The first is from "studylight.org" and attributed to John Gill ("Theologian" 1697-1771). These "comments" appear to be based upon the King James Version:

Gill states:

> ""*Then the disciples understood,*" .... By his saying that Elias was come, and by the account he gave of his ill usage, it was clear to them,"[85]

It is unclear what Gill means by "his ill usage." Likely this refers to the treatment of John the Baptist as stated by Jesus: *"did to him whatever they wished."*

Gill completely ignores anything unusual about Elijah having "come," with respect to possible reincarnation. Thus precisely what "it" was that was "clear to them," to Gill seems to be anything *except* reincarnation—or there would likely be some mention of it here by Gill.

Gill continues:

> "so that this observation, that according to prophecy
> Elias was to come before the Messiah, was no objection
> to Jesus being the Messiah; but on the contrary, since he
> that was intended by Elias was come, and had done his
> work and office, it was a confirmation of the truth of his
> Messiahship."[86]

It must be remembered why the disciples asked Jesus about this. In the passages immediately preceding Matthew 17:10-13, they had heard from a voice in heaven that Jesus was the Son of God; so the disciples knew who He (Jesus) was, and thus required no confirmation of this. Rather; they wanted to know why the scribes insisted upon a forerunner, yet they had seen no forerunner; i.e.; were the scribes wrong, (*"why then"*)?

Gill again then completely ignores anything unusual about the *form* in which Elijah "showed up;" but instead simply believes that this merely confirms Jesus' "Messiahship" by prophesy fulfillment—leaving of course a very large elephant in the room. This (Gill's) explanation would be the same if Elijah had merely been returned via the return of that chariot, rather than Elijah being John the Baptist.

And here is the "meaning" of the same Matthew 17:13, but according to Matthew Henry (Biblical commentator 1662-1714):

> "They understood that he spake unto them of John the
> Baptist. He did not name John, but gives them such a
> description of him as would put them in mind of what

"Religious" Commentary On Elijah et al.

he had said to them formerly concerning him; This is Elias. This is a profitable way of teaching; it engages the learners' own thoughts, and makes them, if not their own teachers, yet their own remembrancers; and thus knowledge becomes easy to him that understands.
When we diligently use the means of knowledge, how strangely are mists scattered and mistakes rectified!"[87]

It remains unclear as to precisely what Henry's comments have to do with Matthew 17:13 in the particular. Rather, this seems to be commentary regarding teaching and learning in the general sense—any difficulties in decipherability notwithstanding.

And what about that which we were told in another chapter of Matthew, specifically in Matthew 11:14; which was introduced in the previous chapter?
Again, Matthew 11:14 (NAS) tells us:

*"And if you are willing to accept it,
John himself is Elijah who was to come."*

Specifically, what is it that other "fanumites" have to say about Matthew 11:14?
For context, it must again be remembered what Jesus was saying in Matthew just prior to verse 14.
In furtherance of contextual accuracy, here is Matthew 11:7-13, which was introduced in the previous chapter. These verses are setting things up for the "bomb" contained in verse 14 above."
Matthew 11:7-13 (NAS) tells us:

*"As these men were going away,
Jesus began to speak to the crowds about John,
"What did you go out into the wilderness to see?
A reed shaken by the wind?*

> "But what did you go out to see?
> A man dressed in soft clothing?
> Those who wear soft clothing are in kings' palaces! "
>
> But what did you go out to see? A prophet?
> Yes, I tell you, and one who is more than a prophet
> "This is the one about whom it is written,
> 'BEHOLD, I SEND MY MESSENGER AHEAD OF YOU,
> WHO WILL PREPARE YOUR WAY BEFORE YOU.'
>
> "Truly I say to you, among those born of women
> there has not arisen anyone greater than
> John the Baptist! Yet the one who is least
> in the kingdom of heaven is greater than he.
>
> "From the days of John the Baptist until now
> the kingdom of heaven suffers violence,
> and violent men take it by force.
> "For all the prophets and the
> Law prophesied until John."

And here once again is that "bomb" that follows, and is contained in the very next verse, Matthew 11:14 (NAS):

> "And if you are willing to accept it,
> John himself is Elijah who was to come."

For this Matthew 11:14 (bomb #1114), following is some randomly chosen commentary, here from Albert Barnes (theologian, 1798-1870):

> "This is a mode of speaking implying that the doctrine which he was about to state was different from their common views; that he was about to state something

"Religious" Commentary On Elijah et al.

which varied from the common expectation, and which therefore they might be disposed to reject."[88]

On its face, this is largely correct. This is precisely why Jesus was "preparing the audience for the conclusion (bomb) contained in verse 14."

But as will be seen, Barnes continues, and then begins to "kind of flip it around."

> "This is Elias ... - That is, Elijah." Elias is the "Greek" mode of writing the Hebrew word "Elijah." An account of him is found in the first and second books of Kings. He was a distinguished prophet, and was taken up to heaven in a chariot of fire, 2 Kings 2:11."[89]

Here Barnes merely confirms the "ascension" of Elijah as witnessed by Elisha. There is no news here.

But Barnes then goes on:

> ". . . The prophet Malachi Malachi 4:5-6 (sic) predicted that "Elijah" would be sent before the coming of the Messiah to prepare the way for him. By this was evidently meant, not that he should appear "in person," but that one should appear with a striking resemblance to him; or, as Luke Luke 1:17 (sic) expresses it, "in the spirit and power of Elijah.
>
> "But the Jews understood it differently. They supposed that Elijah would appear in person. They also supposed that Jeremiah and some other of the prophets would appear also to usher in the promised Messiah and to grace his advent. See Matthew 16:14; Matthew 17:10; John 1:21.
>
> "This prevalent belief was the reason why he used the words "if ye will receive it," implying that the

affirmation that "John" was the promised Elijah was a doctrine contrary to their expectation."[90]

The text of that which Barnes' referenced at the end of the first paragraph above: *"in the spirit and power of Elijah"* (Luke 1:17), is contained in the instructions to Zacharias appearing in the previous chapter:

Here again is Luke 1:17 (NAS) in its entirety:

*"It is he who will go as a forerunner
before Him in the spirit and power of Elijah,
to turn the hearts of the fathers back to the children,
and the disobedient to the attitude of the righteous,
so as to make ready a people prepared for the Lord."*

And here is the same Luke 1:17, but KJV:

*"And he shall go before him
in the spirit and power of Elias,
to turn the hearts of the fathers to the children,
and the disobedient to the wisdom of the just;
to make ready a people prepared for the Lord."*[91]

And here is the same Luke 1:17, but NIV:

*And he will go on before the Lord,
in the spirit and power of Elijah,
to turn the hearts of the parents to their children
and the disobedient to the wisdom of the righteous—
to make ready a people prepared for the Lord."*[92]

According to Strong, the actual Greek word translated as "spirit" here in Luke 1:17 is:

"*4151* pnĕuma; from *4154*; a *current* of air i.e. *breath* (blast) or a *breeze*; by anal. or fig. a *spirit*, i.e. (human) the rational *soul* (by impl.) *vital principle*, mental *disposition*. . ."[93]

According to Strong, the actual Greek word translated as "power" in Luke 1:17 is the previously addressed Greek word for *supernatural* power:

"*1411* dunamis; from *1410*; *force* (lit. or fig.); spec. miraculous *power* (usually by impl. a *miracle* itself)..."[94]

The word *pnĕuma* is the Greek version of that which is contained in the previously referenced Genesis 2:7: "*And God formed man of the dust of the ground, and breathed into his nostrils the breath of life; and man became a living soul.*"

According to Strong, the Hebrew word translated as "soul" here in Genesis 2:7 is:

"*5315* nephesh; from *5314*; prop. a *breathing* creature, i.e. *animal* or (abstr.) *vitality*. . ."[95]

The use of "living soul" thus implies that this *nephesh* (Hebrew) is pnĕuma (Greek), or *rational soul*; when contained in a *physical* body or vessel.

As can easily be seen, Zacharias was not told that John would be in the spirit and power "*like* Elijah's, *similar* to Elijah's, or a *facsimile* of Elijah's." Rather he was told "*in the spirit* (pnĕuma) *and power* (dunamis) *of Elijah.*" Thus it literally was in the "soul and miraculous power" of Elijah.

Barnes' *first* reference at the end of the second paragraph: "see Matthew 16:14," is totally misplaced, (euphemism); in that Matthew 16:14 as cited in the previous chapter tells us: "*And they said, "Some say John the Baptist; and others, Elijah; but still others, Jeremiah, or one of the prophets;"* is a response to a question posed by *Jesus* as to who people thought *He* (Jesus) was; and not who *John the Baptist* was, as proved in the previous chapter.

Barnes' statement: "They also supposed that Jeremiah and some other of the prophets would appear also to usher in the promised Messiah and to grace his advent. See Matthew 16:14;" is thus also false, as Barnes' statement here is in no way supported by this same reference. Again, this verse, Matthew 16:14, has or had to do with who it was that people thought *Jesus* was; and not who might "usher" Him," or "grace his advent."

And with regard to Barnes' *second* reference at the end of the second paragraph, here regarding Matthew 17:10, cited in the previous chapter: *"And His disciples asked Him, "Why then do the scribes say that Elijah must come first;"* this clearly refers to the previously cited question to Jesus regarding the veracity of the belief of *"the scribes,"* regarding why *"Elijah must come first."*

Thus the purpose for Barnes referencing this same Matthew 17:10: *"And His disciples asked Him, "Why then do the scribes say that Elijah must come first;"* remains unclear. This passage clearly has nothing whatsoever to do with: "Jeremiah and some other of the prophets (*or anyone else*) would appear also to usher in the promised Messiah and to grace his advent."

Barnes' *final* reference in the second paragraph; regarding John 1:21; *"And they asked him, What then? Art thou Elias? And he saith, I am not. Art thou that prophet? And he answered, No;"* was addressed in the previous chapter. The same clearly being where John the Baptist had denied that he is Elijah. This will also be "re-addressed" shortly.

Barnes' statement: "But the Jews understood it differently. They supposed that Elijah would appear in person;" could be true or not true—depending upon which "Jews" it is to whom Barnes is referring. It is also unclear what Barnes actually meant by "in person."

With regard to this "in person" part of Barnes' statement, this could mean *reincarnated, resurrected*, or "dropped off by the chariot."

Resurrection is out, because as far as it is known, Elijah never physically died while on the earth, and there seems to be no Biblical or extra-Biblical evidence of anyone ever "physically dying" while in heaven.

There is no record of the chariot ever returning—although one day it might; and we also know that John the Baptist *did not* suddenly re-appear as a grown man.

Rather, it is in fact clearly known that John, (JTB), was contemporaneously "in-utero," as per the Zacharias "conversation" with Gabe, and the unborn baby's (JTB's) reaction to Mary's arrival. This leaves *reincarnation* as the only reasonable means for an "in person" appearance of Elijah as John the Baptist.

With regard to which particular "Jews" it is to which Barnes is referring; the *Sadducees* believed that the soul was not immortal; and they believed in no afterlife. It was the *Pharisees* who believed that the soul was in fact immortal, and believed in both an afterlife, and reincarnation.

So it seems that Barnes' position that the Jewish "surprise" was that Elijah in fact *did not* return "in person," could only apply to the *Pharisees*; as the *Sadducees* did not believe this was possible.

This "surprise" of course requires that Elijah/John was to be in the spirit and power *like* Elijah's, *similar* to Elijah's, or a *facsimile* of Elijah's; but not "in the spirit, (*pněuma*), and power, (*dunamis* or *miraculous* power) *of* Elijah;" as we are literally told in Luke 1:17. This reminds one of the episodes of "*The Honeymooners,*" where Ralph believes there is a surprise party for him upstairs in Norton's apartment. Norton then tells Ralph, that there is no party—*that's the surprise.*

Here Barnes' position: "This prevalent belief was the reason why he used the words 'if ye will receive it,'" implying that the affirmation that "John" was the promised Elijah was a doctrine contrary to their expectation;" means they (the Pharisees) expected the soul and miraculous power of Elijah as they were told, but instead they received a *substitute*.

Alternatively; the "*if you are willing to accept it,* (NAS);" or "*if you are willing to receive it,* (KJV)," in Matthew 11:14; could refer to the *Sadducees*, who did *not* believe that reincarnation was possible.

Thus here it would be the fact that John the Baptist *was* in fact Elijah reincarnated, that required acceptance.

Here Barnes' position with regard to the *Sadducees*: "This prevalent belief was the reason why he used the words "if ye will receive it," (actually: *"if you are willing to receive it"*), implying that the affirmation that "John" was the promised Elijah was a doctrine contrary to their expectation;" means they (the Sadducees) expected a *substitute*, but instead they received the soul and miraculous power of Elijah as they were told.

One other possibility is that the "willing to accept it" referred to both groups:

For the *Sadducees*; who did not believe in reincarnation; the "it" in "willing to accept it" was to accept both that reincarnation was a fact, and that John was Elijah reincarnated; and therefore the Messiah had arrived.

For the *Pharisees*; who already believed in reincarnation; the "it" in "willing to accept it" was that John was Elijah, and therefore the Messiah had arrived.

But which group is correct?

Is it the *Sadducees*; who believed that the soul was not immortal, and believed in no afterlife; who is/are correct?

Or is it the *Pharisees*; who believed that the soul was in fact immortal, and believed in both an afterlife, and reincarnation; who is/are correct? (Present tense utilized here, as nothing has changed.)

Perhaps there is some clue to this answer in the Bible.

Acts 23:6-10 (KJV) tells us:

> *"But when Paul perceived that the one part were Sadducees, and the other Pharisees, he cried out in the council, Men and brethren, I am a Pharisee, the son of a Pharisee: of the hope and resurrection of the dead I am called in question.*
>
> *And when he had so said, there arose a dissension between the Pharisees and the*

"Religious" Commentary On Elijah et al.

> *Sadducees: and the multitude was divided.*
> *For the Sadducees say that there is*
> *no resurrection, neither angel, nor spirit:*
> *but the Pharisees confess both.*
>
> *And there arose a great cry: and the scribes*
> *that were of the Pharisees' part arose,*
> *and strove, saying, We find no evil in this man:*
> *but if a spirit or an angel hath*
> *spoken to him, let us not fight against God.*
>
> *And when there arose a great dissension,*
> *the chief captain, fearing lest Paul should*
> *have been pulled in pieces of them,*
> *commanded the soldiers to go down,*
> *and to take him by force from among them,*
> *and to bring him into the castle."*[96]

It seems that today's *"great dissension"* has significant historical roots.

But again; is it the *Sadducees*; who believed that the soul was not immortal, and believed in no afterlife; who is/are correct? Or is it the *Pharisees*; who believed that the soul was in fact immortal, and believed in both an afterlife, and reincarnation; who is/are correct?

The *very next* verse (Acts 23:11 (KJV)) provides some insight with regard to this question.

Acts 23:11 (KJV) tells us:

> *"And the night following the Lord stood by him,*
> *and said, Be of good cheer, Paul: for as thou*
> *hast testified of me in Jerusalem,*
> *so must thou bear witness also at Rome."*[97]

It can be seen that in this very next verse following the *"great dissention"* in Paul's time, that God is telling Paul that Paul had

103

"testified" of God; and that Paul must once again *"bear witness"* to God—but this time in Rome.

What was it again that Paul had *"testified?"* *"Men and brethren, I am a Pharisee, the son of a Pharisee: of the hope and resurrection of the dead..."*

According to Strong, the actual Greek word translated as "testified" in the above Acts 23:11 is:

> *"1263* diamarturŏmai; from *1223* and *3140*; to *attest* or *protest earnestly*, or (by impl.) *hortatively*: - charge, testify (unto), witness."[98]

The actual Greek word translated as *"bear witness"* here in verse 11, is quite similar to the Greek word seen earlier with those *"under the altar"* and was translated as *"testimony."* There *"testimony"* was *"3141* marturia from *3144; evidence* given (judicially or gen.): - record, report, testimony, witness."

Here in Acts 23:11, the actual Greek word translated as "bear witness" is:

> *"3140* marturĕō; from *3144*; to *be a witness*, i.e. *testify* (lit. or fig.). . . ."[99]

So it seems that *"the Lord"* was so pleased with Paul's *diamarturŏmai*, that He wanted Paul to *marturĕō* the very same thing *"at Rome."*

Ergo; here in Acts 23:11, *"the Lord" confirms* that it is the Pharisees; who believe that the soul was in fact immortal, and believed in both an afterlife, and *"resurrection"* that were correct; and not the Sadducees; who believed that the soul was not immortal, and believed in no afterlife.

But the word spoken by Paul is translated as *resurrection*, and is not translated *reincarnation*.

The actual Greek word translated as "resurrection" in both verse 6 and verse 8 is:

"*386 anastasis*; from *450*; a *standing up* again, i.e. (lit.) a *resurrection* from death. . ."[100]

The translation of *anastasis* as resurrection is reasonably fair. But it must be noted that *"standing up again"* does not necessarily require the same body. Thus if no translation as "resurrection" were provided, *"standing up again,"* would be equally acceptable. This could also reasonably include the use of a *different* body (reincarnation), as well as the use of the *original* body (resurrection). It must also be noted that by definition, it is "from death" (physical death), to which *anastasis* clearly refers.

Following is Matthew Henry's, (author, 1662-1714), view of Matthew 11:14 ("Matthew on Matthew"), specifically: *"And if you are willing to accept it, John himself is Elijah who was to come."* (Get Ready!!!)

> "This is Elias, that was for to come. John was as the loop that coupled the two Testaments; as Noah was Fibula utriusque mundi—the link connecting both worlds, so was he utriusque Testamenti—the link connecting both Testaments.
>
> "The concluding prophecy of the Old Testament was, Behold, I will send you Elijah, Mal. 4:5, Mal. 4:6. Those words prophesied until John, and then, being turned into a history, they ceased to prophecy.
>
> "First, Christ speaks of it as a great truth, that John the Baptist is the Elias of the New Testament; not Elias in propria persona—in his own person, as the carnal Jews expected; he denied that (Jn. 1:21), but one that should come in the spirit and power of Elias (Lu. 1:17), like him in temper and conversation, that should press repentance with terrors, and especially as it is in the prophecy, that should turn the hearts of the fathers to the children.

"Secondly, He speaks of it as a truth, which would not be easily apprehended by those whose expectations fastened upon the temporal kingdom of the Messiah, and introductions to it agreeable. Christ suspects the welcome of it, if ye will receive it. Not but that it was true, whether they would receive it or not, but he upbraids them with their prejudices, that they were backward to receive the greatest truths that were opposed to their sentiments, though never so favourable to their interests. Or, "If you will receive him, or if you will receive the ministry of John as that of the promised Elias, he will be an Elias to you, to turn you and prepare you for the Lord," Note, Gospel truths are as they are received, a savour of life or death. Christ is a Saviour, and John an Elias, to those who will receive the truth concerning them."[101]

There is essentially nothing new here in Matthew Henry's commentary, but is provided to demonstrate "religious (fanumite) consistency" with regard to reincarnation.

The following is a recapitulation of that which was stated in a previous chapter, and was written long before even encountering Henry's "commentary" above.

"It generally takes a lot of words to make the argument that the Bible does not mean what it actually states; but instead means something entirely different. Like attorneys "buzzing around" one or two key words in a contract; many "fanumites" labor likewise—lest someone, somewhere, at any time, believe differently than they.

"This can be especially effective, if some archaic *Latin* words or phrases are thrown in the mix—bringing to mind the "*Ancient Hebrew*" utilized by "the Duke and the King," in Mark Twain's: "*The Adventures of Huckleberry Finn.*"

Likewise, again Proverbs 10:19 (NAS) tells us: *"When there are many words, transgression is unavoidable, but he who restrains his lips is wise."*

Note Henry's use here of the Latin: *"Fibula utriusque mundi*—(Noah) the link connecting both worlds, so was he (John) *utriusque Testamenti*—the link connecting both Testaments."

Precisely how Noah represented a link (utriusque) between two worlds (mundi) is not specified here. Neither is it specified what constitutes these "worlds."

However Henry may have inadvertently proved the *opposite* of his position by stating: "utriusque Testamenti—the link connecting both Testaments."

Fulfilling Old Testament prophesy in the New Testament is one thing. But the reincarnation of an Old Testament *person* into New Testament *times*, is another matter entirely—here perhaps "utriusque Testamenti"—*forte*.

As the reference for the "commentary" that follows, again Hebrews 9:27-28 (NAS) tells us:

> *"And inasmuch as it is appointed for men to die once and after this comes judgment, so Christ also, having been offered once to bear the sins of many, will appear a second time for salvation without reference to sin, to those who eagerly await Him."*

And precisely what does Barnes have to say about Hebrews 9:27-28? With regard to *reincarnation*, Barnes merely purports more of the same. But with regard to *physical death*, he raises some valid points:

> 1) "that death is the result of "appointment;" Genesis 3:19. It is not the effect of chance, or haphazard. It is not a "debt of nature." It is not the condition to which man was subject by the laws of his creation. It is not to be accounted for by the mere principles of physiology. God

could as well have made the heart to play forever as for 50 years. Death is no more the regular result of physical laws than the guillotine and the gallows are. It is in all cases the result of "intelligent appointment," and for "an adequate cause."

2) "that cause, or the reason of that appointment, is sin; notes, Romans 6:23. This is the adequate cause; this explains the whole of it. Holy beings do not die. There is not the slightest proof that an angel in heaven has died, or that any perfectly holy being has ever died except the Lord Jesus. In every death, then, we have a demonstration that the race is guilty; in each case of mortality we have an affecting memento that we are individually transgressors."[102]

Barnes first references Genesis 3:19 (KJV):

> "*In the sweat of thy face shalt thou eat bread,*
> *till thou return unto the ground;*
> *for out of it wast thou taken:*
> *for dust thou art,*
> *and unto dust shalt thou return.*"[103]

Barnes then goes on to explain the relationship between physical death and sin. This is Scripturally accurate. The monograph: "*Its Not Just a Theory,*" found in "*Wisdom Essentials,*" explains in great detail the relationship between health, longevity, and sin. This is done utilizing that which we are told in the Scriptures, along with scientific rules and evidence.

But with respect to Jesus being an exception to the "Holy beings do not die" rule, Barnes is incorrect. It must again be remembered that no one killed Jesus. Jesus "commanded his spirit" somewhat early in the crucifixion process, which is one reason why Herod was surprised that Jesus was "dead already." Had Jesus not done this, he likely would not have died no matter what they did to him. In this sense, Barnes is correct. This is the "flip side" of the relationship between sin and physical death—but here the absence of sin and the absence of physical death.

Barnes' citation of Romans 6:23 in the second paragraph, is totally misplaced; as this passage is concerned with "spiritual life," and not "physical life." [In fact, this particular passage, (Romans 6:23), appears at the beginning of the very first page of the monograph: *"It's Not Just a Theory"—"A Monograph Examining the Relationship Between Behavior and Longevity; According to Both Science and the Scriptures,"* immediately after the question "Is it true?" This "question" is provided as a "tease;" as Paul is speaking about "spiritual life," and not "physical life;" which is the very subject, ("physical life"), of the monograph.]

Regarding "religious commentary" on JTB's "big lie," here again is the actual passage.

Again, John 1:21 (here KJV) tells us:

> *"And they asked him, What then? Art thou Elias? And he saith, I am not. Art thou that prophet? And he answered, No."*

Following is Barnes' commentary on John 1:21:

> "Art thou Elias? - This is the Greek way of writing Elijah. The Jews expected that Elijah would appear before the Messiah came. See the notes at Matthew 11:14.

> "They supposed that it would be the real Elijah returned from heaven. In this sense John denied that he was Elijah; but he did not deny that he was the Elias or Elijah which the prophet intended Matthew 3:3, for he immediately proceeds to state John 1:23 that he was sent, as it was predicted that Elijah would be, to prepare the way of the Lord; so that, while he corrected their

false notions about Elijah, he so clearly stated to them his true character that they might understand that he was really the one predicted as Elijah.

"That prophet - It is possible that the Jews supposed that not only "Elijah" would reappear before the coming of the Messiah, but also "Jeremiah." See the notes at Matthew 16:14. Some have supposed, however, that this question has reference to the prediction of Moses in Deuteronomy 18:15."[104]

Barnes inclusion of: "See the notes at Matthew 11:14," arguably seems to be what in journalism is referred to as "circular reporting." Here this is an attempt to provide *credibility* to ones position; by citing one's own words, rather than the words of another. Barnes is not proffering the actual *passage* as evidence, but his own "notes" on the same as evidence. [When this is done merely as a *reminder* or *recapitulation*, this is not circular reporting; as there is *no* additional *credibility* is being sought by repeating one's own words.]

According to Barnes: "John denied that he was Elijah; but he did not deny that he was the Elias or Elijah which the prophet intended Matthew 3:3."

So it seems that Barnes' position is that in JTB *denying* that he was Elijah, JTB was *confirming* that he was the Elijah that was predicted, but he was not the same Old Testament Elijah. This will be revisited shortly.

Matthew 3:3 (KJV) tells us:

"For this is he that was spoken of by the prophet Esaias, saying, The voice of one crying in the wilderness, Prepare ye the way of the Lord, make his paths straight."[105]

Here in Matthew, it is confirmed (*"this is he"*) that John the Baptist is he who is spoken of by Esaias (Isaiah).

This reference to Isaiah contained in the above Matthew 3:3, is from Isaiah 40:3-4 (KJV):

> "*The voice of him that crieth in the wilderness,*
> *Prepare ye the way of the Lord,*
> *make straight in the desert a highway for our God.*
>
> *Every valley shall be exalted, and every*
> *mountain and hill shall be made low:*
> *and the crooked shall be made straight,*
> *and the rough places plain.*"[106]

The first sentence in this passage (in Isaiah verse 3): "*The voice of him that crieth in the wilderness, Prepare ye the way of the Lord, make straight in the desert a highway for our God;*" is that which is referenced in Matthew 3:3. But given that which follows in the second sentence of Isaiah, (verse 4), it is unclear as to which verse in *Malachi* it is to which Matthew 3:3 refers. And it must be noted, that the next verse in Matthew, (Matthew 3:4), is merely concerned with JTB's clothing, and what he eats.

Said second sentence in Isaiah (verse 4): *Every valley shall be exalted, and every mountain and hill shall be made low: and the crooked shall be made straight, and the rough places plain*" sounds much more like "end times," or "great and terrible day of the lord:" (Malachi. 4:5: *Behold, I will send you Elijah the prophet before the coming of the great and dreadful day of the Lord.*);[107] rather than "laundryman's (fullers) soap:" (Malachi 3:2: *But who may abide the day of his coming? and who shall stand when he appeareth? for he is like a refiner's fire, and like fullers' soap.*).[108]

And the truth is; that nothing described above in Isaiah 40:4 has of yet happened—either literally or otherwise; or at least there is no record of such.

This may present substantial evidence of two things:

Firstly; since as far as we know, Elijah was Elijah before he was "anyone else," it seems Isaiah 40:3-4 likely collectively refers to that which Elijah would do *in-toto*, including "post-chariot." Thus verse 3 refers strictly to Elijah as John the Baptist: *"The voice of him that crieth in the wilderness, Prepare ye the way of the Lord, make straight in the desert a highway for our God."* This is consistent with what is described in Malachi 3:2.

Secondly; as stated, many believe that Elijah, but here as "post-chariot" Elijah, will return in original "pre-chariot" *corpus* at "end times," as one of the "two witnesses." Thus verse 4 in Isaiah may refer to this "end times" event: *"Every valley shall be exalted, and every mountain and hill shall be made low: and the crooked shall be made straight, and the rough places plain."* This is consistent with what is described in Malachi 4:5. *"Behold, I will send you Elijah the prophet before the coming of the great and dreadful day of the Lord."*

Thus it reasonably seems that Isaiah 40:3-4 is concerned with both Elijah as John the Baptist, as the "forerunner;" *and* Elijah returning at "end times," in his original body as one of the two witnesses. Thus Matthew 3:3: *"For this is he that was spoken of by the prophet Esaias, saying, The voice of one crying in the wilderness, Prepare ye the way of the Lord, make his paths straight;"* refers only to the former.

With regard to Barnes' statement: "for he (John the Baptist) immediately proceeds to state John 1:23 that he was sent, as it was predicted that Elijah would be, to prepare the way of the Lord;" a careful examination is in order.

John 1:23 (here KJV) alone states:

> "He said, I am the voice of one crying
> in the wilderness,
> Make straight the way of the Lord,
> as said the prophet Esaias."[109]

But since all Bible verses should be analyzed in context, following is again John 1:19-27 (KJV):

"Religious" Commentary On Elijah et al.

> "And this is the record of John, when the Jews
> sent priests and Levites from Jerusalem
> to ask him, Who art thou?
>
> And he confessed, and denied not;
> but confessed, I am not the Christ.
>
> And they asked him, What then?
> Art thou Elias? And he saith, I am not.
> Art thou that prophet? And he answered, No.
>
> Then said they unto him, Who art thou?
> that we may give an answer to them that
> sent us. What sayest thou of thyself?
>
> He said, I am the voice of one crying
> in the wilderness, Make straight
> the way of the Lord,
> as said the prophet Esaias.
>
> And they which were sent were of the Pharisees.
> And they asked him, and said unto him,
> Why baptizest thou then, if thou be not that Christ,
> nor Elias, neither that prophet?
>
> John answered them, saying, I baptize with water:
> but there standeth one among you, whom ye know not;
> He it is, who coming after me is preferred before me,
> whose shoe's latchet I am not worthy to unloose."

Here John the Baptist is citing that which appears in Isaiah and Matthew 3:3, affirming that he is the one spoken about in Isaiah 40:3, (but he does not cite verse 4); and is confirmed as such in Matthew; but here in John, denied that he was Elijah.

Perhaps what we are told about these "interrogators," (they) in John 1:24 had something to do with John the Baptist's (JTB's) decisions, as the same tells us: "*And they which were sent were of the Pharisees.*" It must be remembered that it was: "*the Pharisees*; who believed that the soul was in fact immortal, and believed in both an afterlife, and reincarnation."

It seems that JTB could not win by telling the truth. The *Pharisees* would be the group most likely to believe that JTB was Elijah. And JTB handled it pretty well if he feared there was trickery afoot.

To better understand this, it seems prudent to look at a similar situation that took place with Jesus:

Mark 11:27-33 (KJV) tells us:

*"They arrived again in Jerusalem,
and while Jesus was walking in the temple courts,
the chief priests, the teachers of the law
and the elders came to him.
"By what authority are you doing these things?"
they asked. "And who gave you authority to do this?"*

*Jesus replied, "I will ask you one question.
Answer me, and I will tell you by what authority
I am doing these things. John's baptism—
was it from heaven, or of human origin?
Tell me!"*

*They discussed it among themselves and said,
"If we say, 'From heaven,' he will ask,
'Then why didn't you believe him?'
But if we say, 'Of human origin' ..."
(They feared the people, for everyone
held that John really was a prophet.)
So they answered Jesus, "We don't know."*

*Jesus said, "Neither will I tell you by what
authority I am doing these things."*[110]

First JTB tells them he is not The Christ. Why he said who he *was not*, when he when asked who he *was*; ("*Who art thou*"); is unclear. Perhaps he knew the fate of The Christ and did not want to "short circuit" the entire "Last Adam" process; so he figured he would "get rid of that silly notion" immediately.

Then when they "press him," he denies that he is Elijah, even though he must have known much, including that his mother's name was Elizabeth—which again means *"house of Elijah."*

Instead he then indirectly but essentially describes himself as Elijah, but according to Isaiah. JTB told them: *"I am the voice of one crying in the wilderness, Make straight the way of the Lord, as said the prophet Esaias."* (Isaiah states: *"The voice of him that crieth in the wilderness, Prepare ye the way of the Lord, make straight in the desert a highway for our God."*)

JTB likely feared what they would do to him if he admitted he was Elijah; and it would *not* merely be not setting a place for him at Passover Seder, and *not* opening the front door for him for millennia. The Biblical account of what was in fact ultimately done to him; shows us any such fears were not unfounded.

JTB concludes with all of that amphigory about the Baptizing, and then diverts matters to discussion of the greatness of The Christ.

But back to Barnes. Then there is the ultimate chutzpah by Barnes when he states: "while he (John the Baptist) corrected their false notions about Elijah, he so clearly stated to them his true character that they might understand that he was really the one predicted as Elijah."

So according to Barnes, it seems that we are to believe that although John the Baptist was *an* Elijah, he was not *that* Elijah, but rather some other Elijah of unknown etiology. And that *this* particular Elijah; although much more suitable to some men; somehow comports with the Scriptures, even though this ersatz Elijah did not comport with that which the Scriptures reasonably tell us.

Here their "imaginary friend" Elijah is necessary, because the true Elijah will force them to do that which they wish not to do.

A similar process was soon to be repeated by those Jewish leaders, and Jesus—as the long awaited Messiah...

CHAPTER 6

Why the Fuss?

Clearly; and for an incredibly long period of time; there are and have been organized, (and quite successful), efforts to derive meanings for certain Scriptural evidence for *anything—anything* at all. This includes many things that either simply make no sense, or are completely contradictory—and thus cannot possibly be true in any meaningful way.

If this is figuratively considered as *stretching*, or *increasing* the obvious dimensions of a thing to cover that which it reasonably and obviously *cannot* cover; then with respect to reincarnation, *compressing* seems to be the rule. That is; the deliberate *decreasing* the obvious dimensions of a thing to *not* cover that which it reasonably and obviously *does* cover.

Although there is much disagreement among the various western religious sects about many things; the *impossibility* of reincarnation is almost a "litmus test" for western religions in order to consider each other as "legitimate." "Legitimate" here can often also likewise mean "sincerely wrong." Religions other than one's own are "sincerely wrong" when they disagree, but their "errors" are considered "sincere"—*as long as they do not embrace reincarnation.*

Thus far, much evidence has been presented to show what the Scriptures have to say about subject of reincarnation. Likewise; some of the "religious efforts" undertaken in the attempt to prove that these passages mean something entirely different than proving the existence of reincarnation, have also been presented. It must be remembered that these "religious efforts" presented were not in any way "cherry picked" in furtherance of any position.

Rather; those presented were obtained as randomly as possible from true public domain sources. It is not unheard of for public domain sources to be "modernized," (modified); copyrighted, and then "re-modernized" over time; and thus these were avoided. The various "versions" of the Bible are likewise not immune to this process. [This has happened even with Strong's. This is precisely why *only* the original ©1890 edition was utilized here.]

Each of us must decide for ourselves if the obvious meanings of these Biblical passages are the truth; or if the various religious "experts" interpretations represent the truth. It seems that this is a binary, as if even so much as one passage reasonably proves reincarnation exists, that is sufficient.

Whenever various groups rally around one position despite major differences in other areas, an explanation is in order. Sometimes; as used to be the case with the first amendment—free speech and free exercise of religion; it was because this freedom in and of itself "trumped" any other disagreements. Or as is the case with the military, most reasonable people respect and back the military—*no matter what actions they are ordered to undertake.* Any reasonable argument is not with those who risk their lives to protect us, and *must* follow orders; but rather with the politicians; most particularly the president; who are formulating and *issuing* these orders to our military.

And given the Scriptural evidence, there should likewise be an explanation as to why there is essentially universal agreement among western religions that reincarnation does not exist, when there is so much else, (including transubstantiation), that is otherwise disputed. If it is said that one thing upon which the major western religions agree is that God exists; it can also be said that the only other thing upon which they largely agree, is that reincarnation does not—*no matter what the Bible may reasonably have to say about it.*

It is interesting that in today's world, there seems to be at least a partial similarity between the Scriptural passages regarding reincarnation, and those two groups of religious leaders, (Pharisees and Sadducees), who were alive at the time of Jesus. Specifically; what essentially is universal "religious" agreement that these same passages either have nothing to do with reincarnation or disprove it. Meaning that here the *Bible* is like the *Pharisees* with regard to reincarnation, as the *prima-facie* meanings are clear. And most *religions* today are like the *Sadducees*, utilizing extreme word parsing in a "lawyerly" manner, in order to arrive at the opposite conclusion.

This is also quite similar to what has become the situation with *salvation*; and for *predictable* and *understandable* reasons—but not necessarily for *good* reasons. So in order to understand the motives behind the ubiquitous religious doctrines of *negation* with respect to *reincarnation*; examining what various religious groups have done with respect to *salvation* would be illuminating.

No effort is being made here to attribute anything pernicious to religions(s) in the general sense. In addition; what is utilized is not what *others* might state about religion in general; or necessarily about any specific denomination. Rather; what is being utilized here, is what it is that said religious denomination(s) *themselves* are in fact stating about *themselves*—via official pronouncements, or their recognized authorities.

According to "thefreedictionary.com," a "papal bull" is:

> "a formal proclamation issued by the pope (usually written in antiquated characters and sealed with a leaden bulla)"[111]

It is not known if this term is in any way (etymologically) related to; i.e.; the source of; another term, (slang); that either *begins* with "bull," or is stated as a stand alone "bull;" that euphemistically refers to either likely inaccurate or false "information;" or "conversation(s)" of dubious value.

In order to understand the "fanumites'" AKA "religious folks'" "attitude" with respect to *reincarnation*, examining what the same has already and undeniably done with respect to *salvation* is quite illuminating.

Irrespective of intentions, if the Bible is considered as the main source or fountainhead of information regarding *salvation*; then that which in any way reasonably *contradicts* this source must necessarily be considered as falsehood by this very same test—and to the very same degree.

David Brin; scientist and science fiction author; is attributed with having stated:

> *"It is said that power corrupts, but actually it's more true that power attracts the corruptible. The sane are usually attracted by other things than power."*[112]

"Brin is speaking of power here in the general sense. [Although this is generally considered to relate to *governmental* power, which is one type or a subset of "power;" it is *power* itself in the broader sense to which he is referring.]

"Ephesians 2:8-9 tells us:

> *"For by grace are ye saved through faith; and that not of yourselves: it is the gift of God: Not of works, lest any man should boast."*[110.1]

"Strictly from the standpoint of *analysis*, it matters little whether one is a "Christian" or not. One not need be a Christian in order to understand what it is that "Christians" believe. *Knowing* what it is that Christianity actually states; is entirely different than *believing* that that which Christianity states is in fact true.

"The actual Greek word translated here in Ephesians as "grace" is:

"5485 charis; from 5463; *graciousness* (as *gratifying*), of manner or act..."[10.2]

"A fair definition of *grace*, is *receiving* something of positive value that *is not* deserved. This is in contrast to *mercy*; which is *not receiving* something of negative value that *is* deserved.

"Here we are told by Paul that we are saved by "grace" "through" "faith." This sounds suspiciously more like payment, rather than any type of grace. Meaning; *if* you believe, *then* your payment is salvation.

"Here it at first appears that the "work" is the faith that creates the imbalance; and the balance for this "work" is the granting of salvation. This of course would not be grace, and most certainly would then not qualify as any type of "gift." Rather; salvation would clearly be the result of "works;"—notwithstanding that any possibility of this cause-effect relationship existing, is clearly negated in the above citation as it clearly states: "*Not of works*."

"The key word here is: "through." Here "through" is:

"1223 dia; a prim. prep. denoting a *channel* of an act; *through* (in very wide applications..."[10.3]

"Thus the *balancing* of an existing imbalance by obtaining salvation; is not the result of any imbalance that may be *caused* by faith. Faith merely provides the *channel* by which salvation is obtained. The imbalance already exists and has existed since Calvary. Faith merely provides a *channel* for salvation; and in no way contributes to any pre-existing imbalance caused by faith; which is then resolved or balanced by the granting of salvation. When a channel is provided in a dam for water to escape, there are no pumps involved. There is no energy involved other than that required for the provision of the channel. The imbalance already exists, and the water will flow once the channel is provided. We are likewise told by Paul that salvation; like this water, will flow once there is a channel; and that faith provides that channel. Here faith in and of itself does not in any way "pay for" or create any *imbalance*, which salvation then balances—as the imbalance already exists. This is why salvation is both grace and a gift as it is "*not of yourselves: it is the gift of God.*"

"It is true that faith can create many imbalances in many areas, which can then be balanced many different positive ways. But salvation is not one of these.

"Similarly; we are told that salvation is: "Not of works, lest any man should boast."

"Works" is:

> "*2041* ĕrgŏn; from a prim. (but obsol.) ĕrgō (to *work*); to *toil* (as an effort or occupation) by impl. an act."[10.4]

"Erg is the root of the word ergonomics. An "erg" is a unit used for the measurement of energy.

"Thus we are told that there is no imbalance caused or possible by works or ĕrgŏn, whose balancing mechanism could possibly be salvation. Just as is the case with faith; works can also create many imbalances in many areas, which can then be balanced many different ways. But again, salvation is not one of these.

"It ain't bragging if you can do it."[10.5]
—Dizzy Dean

"This is quite true. It is not bragging if you can do it—but it *is boasting* if you can do it. "A boast" represents that which *is* (truth); while "a brag;" (braggadocio); represents that which is *not true* (falsehood).

"The actual word translated in Ephesians 2:9 as "boast" is:

> "2744 kauchaŏmai; from some (obsol.) base akin to that of auchĕō (to *boast*) and 2172; to *vaunt* (in a good or bad sense)..."[10.6]

"Thus when Paul tells us: "*Not of works, lest any man should boast;*" this confirms the falsity of any "works" related cause for salvation. "Any man" can surely *brag* about salvation being the result of his works; but of course this represents falsehood—because Paul tells us that he ("any man") can't actually *boast* about it, because he "cannot do it;" as salvation is unrelated to works.

"Ephesians 2:4 tells us:

> "But God, who is rich in mercy, for his great love wherewith he loved us,"[10.7]

"Mercy is:

> "1656 ĕlĕŏs; of uncert. affin.; compassion (human or divine espec. active)"[10.8]

"Titus 3:5 tells us:

> "*Not by works of righteousness
> which we have done,
> but according to his mercy he saved us,
> by the washing of regeneration,
> and renewing of the Holy Ghost;*"[10.9]

"Here in Titus, Paul is reaffirming that not by any works; even works of *righteousness*; are we saved, but "according to his *mercy.*"

"The introduction of *mercy* here is also actually:

> "*1656* ĕlĕŏs; of uncert. affin.; *compassion* (human or divine espec. active)."[10.10]

"Earlier in Ephesians, it was *charis*, translated as "grace;" which was a causative factor. Here in Titus, the same is so for mercy. Thus salvation is described as both *grace*, i.e.; receiving something of positive value (salvation) that is *not* deserved; and also *mercy*; i.e.; *not* receiving something of negative value (eternal separation from God) that *is* or would otherwise be deserved. [Note the "renewing of the Holy Ghost" included at the end. This subject will be addressed later.]

"A fair argument can be made that the "gospels" (Matthew, Mark, Luke and John) are about Jesus, or the second part of the Trinity; and Book of Acts is about the Holy Ghost or the third part of the Trinity.

"What is a "mortal sin?"

"According to Colin B. Donovan, STL, from *etwn.com*:

> "Mortal sin is called mortal because it is the 'spiritual' death of the soul (separation from

God). If we are in the state of grace it loses this supernatural life for us. If we die without repenting we will lose Him for eternity."[10.11]

"Here Donovan seems to be stating that mortal sin will alter the "state of grace;" i.e.; salvation by justification; to that state which was prior to obtaining said "state of grace." This seems to be a variant of the common definition of *justification*. Justification is often considered to mean: "just as though one never sinned." Here Donovan seems to make a similar argument with respect to the commission of a mortal sin. According to Donovan, it seems that mortal sin is: "Just as though one never received salvation."

"Thus by only minor extension, although works cannot in any way *provide* salvation; it seems that according to Donovan, certain works can *remove* salvation or this "state of grace."

"However Paul just told us that it is *faith* and not *works* which provides the *channel* for salvation; and that salvation is unrelated to works. Given this *channel* provided by faith, salvation will flow of its own accord, without any additional action. Since it is faith alone that opens this channel and not works; it must be asked as to the mechanism whereby this channel can be *blocked* by works. The answer is that it cannot, as we are told that no relationship exists between works, and the establishment of this channel for salvation/justification.

"However; Donovan provides an "out" for the commission of mortal sin—*repenting*.

"According to Donovan, "repenting" is:

> "receiving the Sacrament of Penance we are restored to His friendship. Catholics are not allowed to receive Communion if they have unconfessed mortal sins."[10.12]

"The root or the "pent" part of *repent* is the "Latin *penitire*, to regret."[10.13]

"But the word is not "pent" but rather *repent*. This could reasonably be defined as not to regret, but rather to *regret again*. The word repentance does not generally mean to receive any type of Sacrament; and neither does it generally mean to make any type of formal confession to any third party.

"According to "*aboutcatholics.com:*"

> "'Mortal' means death; they are sins that cause death to the soul. Mortal sins completely sever one's relationship with God and the sacrament of Penance and Reconciliation (commonly called Confession) is necessary to restore this relationship."[10.14]

"So it seems that although according to Paul, salvation cannot be obtained by any type of works; righteous or otherwise; according to others, it somehow can nevertheless be *removed* by works; if and when said works constitute a *mortal* sin. If merely for the purposes of discussion, this is stipulated to be true; it must be asked as to what the change in status is? Meaning; what is the difference between one who is unsaved; and one who is or "was" saved, but then his "works" were such that a commission of a mortal sin occurred?

"Paul tells us that salvation has nothing to do with works, but only faith. There is no cause-effect relationship between works and salvation. Rather; it is *faith* that opens this *dia* or channel, whereby salvation is then delivered. Like merely opening the front door, and there is an automatic pizza delivery at no cost—because a lifetime of pizza has already been paid for. All that is required is an opening for delivery.

Why the Fuss?

"Paul also tells us that salvation does not represent any type of payment or "karma;" but rather is a gift of grace or mercy or "compassion"—depending upon one's perspective. The availability of salvation is like potential energy, which requires only a *dia* or channel; here the channel provided by faith, and faith alone.

"So if one is unsaved, all that is required is this dia or channel; which is created by faith, and faith alone; and whose existence is completely unrelated to any works. This is Paul's position.

"But others claim, that although this may be true; works that fit into the "mortal sin" category, can remove this salvation. And according to this same theory, maintaining this dia or channel with faith, is now insufficient to maintain or restore said saved status. Presumably, mortal sin now blocks this dia or channel, and despite the fact that faith alone originally provided this dia or channel, said blockage cannot be removed by faith alone—unlike the "original" blockage. Instead: "Penance and Reconciliation (commonly called Confession)" is necessary to "reopen" this channel, or "restore this relationship."

"What is "commonly called confession," consists of the *works* of seeking out and "confessing" one's sins to a third party, and thus not directly to God. Said third party then advises as to what the penance for this mortal and other sin commission is to be—and these *works* usually consist of some level of repetitive prayer. Once these *works* are all completed, the presumed blockage is removed, the "petitioner" is "good to go" in the salvation department—at least until next time.

"It remains unclear as to the logic behind the theory regarding precisely how it is that although faith alone, and not any works, is sufficient to *provide* this *dia* or channel; but nevertheless, somehow works are required in order to maintain or *restore* this channel. It also remains unclear as to how it is; that although God provides salvation the first time, any future provision of salvation (assuming it actually can be lost by works) cannot be provided by God alone; but rather now requires a man to assist Him. It is likewise unclear as to why it is that *initial* gift of salvation is completely unrelated to works; but any *"subsequent"* "re-provision" of salvation requires works, and thus must be and is paid for.

"This theory also seems patently unfair. According to Paul, even those such as Hitler, Stalin, Tojo and others; even if locked in a bunker alone; were *alone* capable of receiving salvation in the last seconds of their life, simply by faith. But one who had already received salvation by faith, and was also alone and locked in the same or a similar bunker; would be in big trouble, had they committed any sin characterized as mortal *after* being saved. In the absence of any third party, how could these purported required works take place?

"Donovan goes on to cite 1 Cor. 6:9-10 in support of this."[10.15]

"Cor. 6:9-10 tells us:

> *"Know ye not that the unrighteous shall not inherit the kingdom of God? Be not deceived: neither fornicators, nor idolaters, nor adulterers, nor effeminate, nor abusers of themselves with mankind,*
>
> *Nor thieves, nor covetous, nor drunkards, nor revilers, nor extortioners, shall inherit the kingdom of God."*[10.16]

"This sounds quite supportive of Donovan's position—unless and until the very next verse (1 Cor. 6:11) is read.

Why the Fuss?

"1 Cor. 6:11 then tells us:

> *"And such were some of you: but ye are washed, but ye are sanctified, but ye are justified in the name of the Lord Jesus, and by the Spirit of our God."*[10.17]

"According to Fox News in March of 2008:

> "After 1,500 years the Vatican has brought the seven deadly sins up to date by adding seven new ones for the age of globalization... The new deadly sins include polluting, genetic engineering, being obscenely rich, drug dealing, abortion, pedophilia and causing social injustice."[10.18]

"The two most interesting new "mortal" sins seem to be "being obscenely rich" and "causing social injustice;" as these; unlike sins such as murder or adultery; are not binaries.

"It is unclear as to the difference between "being rich" and "being obscenely rich." Likewise it is unclear as to *who* it is that makes this determination, or precisely *how* this determination is made. The threshold for the aforementioned mortal sins murder and adultery are clear. Without some type of corpse, there can be no murder. And with respect to adultery as commonly understood, there has to be—well there either is or is not binary evidence. But being "obscenely rich" as opposed to just "rich" is not a binary, but rather an "analog," as well as a *subjective* determination.

"In the absence of clear and objective standards adjusted for inflation; the average person simply cannot determine if or when they cross the threshold from merely being rich, to "being obscenely (offensively) rich." And it must be asked offensive to whom?

"It should be noted that with respect to the *love* of money, 1 Timothy 6:10 tells us:

> *"For the love of money is the root of all evil: which while some coveted after, they have erred from the faith, and pierced themselves through with many sorrows."*[10.19]

"But it should also be noted that with respect to the very money itself, Ecclesiastes 10:19 tells us:

> *"A feast is made for laughter, and wine maketh merry: but money answereth all things."*[10.20]

"Thus this mortal sin of "being obscenely rich," (having an obscenely large amount of money), means that someone committing this new mortal sin; simultaneously and necessarily then also has an obscenely large amount of answers—at least according to Ecclesiastes. It should be remembered from Chapter One "obscene" generally means offensive; so "obscenely rich" is likewise "offensively rich;" but offensive to whom?

"It is also unclear as to the remedy for "being obscenely rich." This is not a singular event that has a definable ending, such as murder or adultery as commonly understood. One can "repent" in both the literal and "Sacramental" sense, to a *fait accompli*. But being "rich;" irrespective of the level of obscenity; is an ongoing issue. If one gives his wealth away for good reason, this would result in only a temporary diminution of the level of wealth to that which is considered below the "obscene" level. Once karma, or F = MA and equal and opposite reactions occur, the level of wealth will once again pierce this "obscene" threshold resulting in an even higher degree of "obscenity;"—perhaps an even greater "mortal sin." It seems that the only true way to avoid continual commission of this mortal sin; would be to give away some portion of the wealth for reasons that are not good, thereby incurring negative karma or loss.

"It also must be asked how this new mortal sin comports with Deuteronomy 28:2?

"Deuteronomy 28:2 tells us:

> "And all these blessings shall come on thee, and overtake thee, if thou shalt hearken unto the voice of the LORD thy God."[10.21]

"It seems that hearkening "unto the voice of the Lord thy God," could easily result in blessings which will result in a level of wealth well beyond the "obscene" level. Here God would have to be careful as to make certain that the level which will "overtake thee," consistently remains below the *man determined* "obscene" level—else it would be God Himself who would become an "accessory before the fact" to the commission, and continued commission of this "mortal sin."

"The new mortal sin of "causing social injustice;" is even more difficult to understand. It seems that the "woe to(s)" contained in Isaiah and elsewhere "cover" those who are in power—irrespective of the seemingly consistent ignoring of this admonition by the same.

Here it seems that this "causing social injustice;" mortal sin is not limited to those who violate their fiduciary responsibilities to those who trusted them, and willfully granted them the same. Rather; it seems that this sin can be committed by anyone at any time.

"Is it "causing social injustice;" to get the best price possible on a new car? After all, there are ramifications to the seller for the buyer willfully paying the seller less than one can. Is it "causing social injustice;" to drive a vehicle that others cannot afford? Is it "causing social injustice;" to not feed the hungry?

"After all, Matthew 25:40 tells us:

"Verily I say unto you,
Inasmuch as ye have done it unto one
of the least of these my brethren,
ye have done it unto me."[10.22]

"But the person who does not *feed* the hungry, did not *cause* them to *become* hungry. Assuming that hunger falls into the "social injustice" category, the causative factor lies outside of the person who encountered the hungry person. Rather it is the failure to provide a *remedy* to the pre-existing seeming injustice of hunger to which this passage refers. Can it be stated that *failing* to *remedy* "social injustice" is the same as "causing social injustice?" And how can it be determined that the state of hunger is in itself a "social injustice?"

"It must also be remembered that 2 Thessalonians 3:10-12 tells us:

"For even when we were with you,
this we commanded you,
that if any would not work,

Why the Fuss?

neither should he eat.

*For we hear that there are some which
walk among you disorderly,
working not at all, but are busybodies.
Now them that are such we command
and exhort by our Lord Jesus Christ,
that with quietness they work,
and eat their own bread."*[10.23]

"Here it seems that the state of hunger is not any type of social *injustice*, but rather *justice*—at least according to Paul. Choosing to be one of the "busybodies," instead of working, is choosing non-productivity. Is it social justice to consume the efforts of others because of this choice—assuming it is a choice? Meaning; that one is capable of some level of productivity; but chooses not to work, and instead chooses to be a busybody; and then relies upon consuming the fruits of the labors of others in order to survive. How is this justice to the worker?

"It seems that that "causing social injustice" can also be pretty much what anyone determines it to be. And this is especially serious here, in that it is a mortal sin that is the penalty. How can a "lay person" reliably decide what constitutes violations of such a serious nature? One best then rely upon and trust others as experts to decide what constitutes this sin, and then behave accordingly. Does this sound a bit familiar?

"While conducting research for this tome, interviews were conducted with one who was taught Catholicism by Dominican nuns many years ago. This person; (hereafter "he"); recounted other behaviors taught as "mortal sins" at that time. One was failure to attend church on Sunday or any "Holy Day of Obligation." Eating meat on any Friday was another, although this was later changed.

"He was also taught that receiving Holy Communion on nine consecutive "First Fridays," would guarantee that he could not die without a priest at his side. As a child he did in fact do this; and then made a lifelong commitment to *stay away from priests*.

"No efforts are being made here to in any way disparage any religion or religious beliefs. To the contrary, religions have been instrumental in disseminating the knowledge about the availability of salvation—irrespective of any deviations from what was originally taught.

"But although the *ends* of religion and statism *may* sometimes be entirely different, there seem to be striking resemblances in the *means*—if it can be stipulated that each is primarily concerned with a different realm.

"The *statists* are concerned with that which is in the material realm. More likely than not, they do not in any way seriously believe in any type of existence in any other realm. They promulgate very serious penalties here and now if one does not behave in a manner to *their* liking. The use of *their* here is in contradistinction to "just" laws, where there "their liking" means with the agreement of the citizenry.

"The *"religious folk"* are concerned with not merely the material realm, but also eternal existence in another (the immaterial) realm. They promulgate penalties in this immaterial realm if one does not behave on a manner to *their* liking in this realm. But here "their" liking is supposed to be based upon a higher authority; i.e.; to *God's* liking, as per His written word. And some of this is in fact quite commendable. Proffering obedience to The Commandments; of which there are not and never were ten; represents good instruction.

"However even God Himself; at least in Exodus 20; did not require *obedience*, but rather only that we *shâmar*; or *keep* these Commandments. "Keep" or *shâmar* does not mean obey, but rather to guard them as though surrounded by a hedge of thorns. One "keeps" one's car in a garage for protection.

"Men are asked to *keep* these Commandments at the ready when "decision making time" arrives; and incorporate these as instructions into the same. God did not engage in interference of man's free will even to the extent of requiring *obedience* to His Commandments—at least at the time He announced them.

"There is that "mess" afterwards with "Hebrew slaves" and such; but the authenticity of this is highly suspect. Man is free to obey or disobey His Commandments, and will receive a return in accordance with his choices.

"But religions often do that which even God himself would not do. Religions often attempt to not *influence* behavior by the provision of knowledge; but *coerce* behavior by promulgating severe penalties in the thereafter, for failure to engage in the type of "works" religions prefer in the here and now. This is compulsion at best, manipulation at worst; and although the *ends* of upright behavior are commendable, these *means* are not of God. Religions often create "clear and present dangers" to salvation, when no such danger can reasonably even be *derived* from His Word.

"Sometimes this is done with best of intentions, and sometimes not. There are those who truly care so much, that these types of judgmental errors occur. But it must be asked that if these intentions were used as pavement; where would the road lead? Intentions alone were insufficient to prevent higher incidences of illegal drug use by those who completed the "program." [Deliberately lying to these participants because of an over zealous desire to help; had the predictable opposite result.]

"Most believe that "judgment day" is where or when that immaterial part of man is to be judged. A more compelling argument is that "judgment day" is not when a man is judged; but rather where or when man *receives* his judgment—with the actual judging having occurred prior to this. This judgment is a binary. Either that immaterial part is to be reunited with its source, or it is not."[13] [Excerpt from: *"Statists Saving One"* Reprinted by permission.]

As previously stated: *"Irrespective of intentions, if the Bible is considered as the main source or fountainhead of information regarding salvation; then that which in any way reasonably contradicts this source must necessarily be considered as falsehood by this very same test—and to the very same degree."* We much each decide how well, (passed their own test), many Western religions have done with regard to this.

With regard to the aforementioned salvation "binary," what if possibly another possibility existed? What if it became "common knowledge" (*doxa*), that the God of "second chances" provided an alternative to eternal separation via *reincarnation—whether this* "common knowledge" were *true* (epistémē), *or not*? Here the "or else" utilized by many religions in order to obtain behaviors to their liking by the threat of conditions in the afterlife, would suffer substantial diminution. As a result, many religions would lose much of their power.

This would be so, irrespective of whether or not it was *actually true* that reincarnation does in fact provide an alternative to eternal separation from God. It would be necessary only that this was *believed* to be so, that would diminish the efficacy of the "lose your salvation" weaponry.

This is not raised in any attempt to either suggest or not suggest that reincarnation provides any such alternative. Rather; this is raised in order to try and determine *why* religions behave the way that they do with regard to this particular subject (reincarnation). It is clear that with respect to *salvation*, many religions proffer that which is clearly inconsistent with their own admitted source of these same profferings (The Bible); and this fact was just more than reasonably proven.

Why the Fuss?

If one knowingly provides falsehood, this is lying; and good intentions provide no excuse. If ignorance is the reason, this is also quite problematic; as each and every one of these religions claims it is *they* who are the most informed (least ignorant), and greatest repository of this very knowledge known to exist on earth.

As the predictable and desired result of promulgating these falsehoods, today most believe that admission into heaven depends upon that which is done and not done while alive on earth (works). Thus it follows that the *weighing* or *judging* the actions and inactions takes place on the aforementioned "judgment day." Then; through some undisclosed and less than arcane means of judgment; one is either admitted into heaven, or rejected and instead "sent" to hell.

Since the Bible states no such thing, it must be asked whence this came? Even so much as *one sin* disqualifies one from heaven—at least that is what the Bible states. It is a simple matter of *contamination*, and a "reverse quarantine;" where here instead of forbidding an *exit*, it is *entrance* that is forbidden. The *only* way the effects of this contamination can be remedied is justification, or "just as one never sinned;" and the Bible is clear in this regard. The level of sin and resultant level of contamination is irrelevant with respect to admissibility, as it is a binary. One does not have to believe this is true, but one cannot *reasonably* deny that this is what the Bible teaches us.

But if a "petitioner" were to understand this, then only education and not coercion could reasonably be utilized to affect behavior. Once it is clear that it is the fact that: "you are going to *hell* no matter what it may be that you do or do not do, (works), *without* justification/salvation;" or it is the fact that salvation provides that "you are going to *heaven* no matter what it may be that you do or do not do (works) *with* justification/salvation;" then only *earthly karma* can be affected by behavior. It is this variable *earthly karma* that is determined by behavior, and not the binary of salvation.

Thus if it is *manipulation* that is desired, the common belief in a "works based" admission to heaven provides a much better means of controlling behavior. The problem with this; is that not only does the Bible not tell us that this is true; but in fact tells us that this is *not* true. Thus the "whence" of this non-OSAS (once saved always saved) doctrine is *man*, and not God's word. Thus "man's word" then in fact necessarily contradicts the word of God—*no matter what level of parsing of His Word is attempted.*

The *acquisition* of salvation is a simple matter—if it is the Bible that is relied upon for the instructions. It is true that making salvation *available* was a complicated (entwined), and complex (many parts) matter. This process began with the First Adam, and was completed or "finished" with the Last Adam; i.e.; Jesus. But to acquire salvation remains a simple matter—any and all man caused complexities notwithstanding.

It also seems that many religions in certain ways are even afraid of *salvation*, at least in the sense of how it was presented by Jesus. According to Jesus, salvation is free and has nothing to do with works; and all that is required to obtain it is to accept it. Yet many if not most major religions seem to ignore this, and nevertheless maintain a "works based" view of salvation.

John 10:27-28 (KJV) tells us:

> *"My sheep hear my voice, and I know them,*
> *and they follow me:*
> *And I give unto them eternal life;*
> *and they shall never perish,*
> *neither shall any man pluck*
> *them out of my hand."*[114]

If an "OSAS denier" were asked how their view of works based salvation comports with these passages, the response would likely go something like this:

> "This type of thing happens all the time with those who are not of our one and true religion. Of course Jesus is talking about two groups of people here. You notice that Jesus makes the distinction between those in His *"hand"* and *"any man."*

"Thus He is specifically excluding those in his "hand" from "any man." It is true that no "other man" can pluck them from Jesus hand. But by excluding those already in His hand from this group, He is clearly saying that those in His hand can do it to themselves."

"Although "any man" generally means "any man;" here in this usage any man does not actually mean any man; but rather, means any man *except* those already in Jesus' "hand.""

"Come to our Bible study and we will show you how to correctly read the Bible."

With respect to the *earthly* effects of sin, salvation is essentially irrelevant. The earthly "equal and opposite reaction;" i.e.; *karma*; is largely unaffected by salvation. Do a lot of "bad stuff," and a lot of "bad stuff" will be done unto you—even with "saved folks." There is a relationship between the amount of *earthly* sin, and the *earthly* repercussions of said sin.

But salvation; at least according to Jesus; is an absolute and cannot be achieved by works. He alone paid the required price for *salvation*, which is the desired result of *justification*; and since there was a price paid "according to the rules," this was a *redemption*. There are no "co-pays" of any type required.

Yet many religions maintain that some level of "works" is required in order to gain or maintain salvation. Thus although salvation is a binary as explained by Jesus, nevertheless many Christians proffer it as an "analog."

Contamination of the immaterial part of man by sin is a binary, and thus as a binary remains unaffected by "how contaminated" any given person may be.

Salvation is likewise a binary making the *amount* of sin *irrelevant*, or "just as though there was never any sin."

Using "works" as some type of ransom payment for everlasting life is not only wrong; but represents attempts at *manipulation*—

irrespective of how noble one may believe the motivations for the same may be.

"Works based" salvation is also *unreliable*, as outside of what the Bible tells us; who is to say? If consuming alcohol were in and of itself sinful; then it must be asked why it was that Jesus turned the water into wine? It must be remembered that He did this because they had "ran out" of wine at the wedding. This means that they had already consumed what they had, and He nevertheless provided more. Does this then make Jesus an "accessory" to sin "before the fact?" If instead of a sin, this were a crime; in many jurisdictions this would make Jesus just as guilty of the crime as the perpetrators.

The way to obtain "upright" behavior; is *education*, and not *manipulation*. God utilizes the former; and the enemy utilizes the latter, both *directly* and *indirectly*.

The *existence* of the phenomenon of reincarnation, and the *purpose(s)* of reincarnation; (assuming that reincarnation is an actuality); are two entirely different matters. It is true that any purpose(s) of reincarnation *pre-supposes* the existence of the phenomenon, but that is not the point. Other than fulfilling prophesy, it is not particularly clear as to why it was that *Elijah* was the one to be the forerunner; as opposed to simply why there was to be a forerunner.

And it is even more of a problem; as there is no evidence, unlike John the Baptist; that Elijah ever physically died. Whatever happened to him after he "got on the bus" remains unknown. The "smart money" bets that the chariot will in fact be returning him again, but this time as an adult (witness) during "end times."

"If reincarnation is a fact, is everyone reincarnated?" This is an interesting question, but irrelevant with respect to the existence of reincarnation, unless the "if" has been met. "If not, then who gets reincarnated and why?" Here again it would be the *purpose*, rather than the *existence* of the phenomenon under discussion.

Those who most vociferously proclaim "God can do anything!;" insist; and with at least the same degree of vociferousness proclaim: "He cannot do reincarnation... Wait... it's not that He can't do it, he just doesn't do it." This is despite the fact that a *reasonable* read of His Word that *reasonably* explains the most facts, say it is likely He already did. And not only that He did; but He made certain that we were told that He did. This applies not only to *resurrection*, but *reincarnation* as well.

One must decide if the Bible is to be taken literally, or if one is free to engage in fanciful interpretations based upon some perceived need(s)—needs other than the sincere hope; (desire plus expectation); for the acquisition of wisdom, via the assiduous acquisition of knowledge.

CHAPTER 7

On the Nature of the Matter

As is the case with most subjects; distinctions must be made, and very specific terminology must be utilized; in order to adequately and precisely understand any phenomenon.

The general term "reincarnation" can be broken down into three parts. The "re;" the "in;" and the "carnation." The "re" generally means to do something *again*. The "in" of course means *in*, or *within*; and the "carnation" refers to a process concerning *flesh*. The words carnage, carnal, and even the flower "carnation" all related to "flesh." Thus both *incarnation*, and *reincarnation*, respectively refer to the process of the *introduction*, and *reintroduction*, of something into the *flesh*.

Again, in Genesis 2:7 (KJV) we are told:

> *"And God formed man of the dust of the ground, and breathed into his nostrils the breath of life;*

and man became a living soul."

Clearly this literally represents an *incarnation*. God first forms the body, and then introduces this "breath of life;" and a "living soul," (nephesh), is the result. It must again be noted that the term "living" here refers to that "dual" condition of a soul contained in a physical body or vessel.

A soul that is not contained in a physical body is a *ghost*. And although all ghosts are "spirits" in the strict sense of being "breath-like" or immaterial; not all "spirits" are ghosts. A ghost is designed to reside in a physical body.

We are told here in Genesis how God *formed*, (not *created*), this particular physical body. This body did not exist prior to its formation, and neither was anyone else involved in its formation. Rather, the pre-existing matter utilized by Him alone was merely "dust" or *'âphâr* (H).

Although this is a description of how Adam was brought into existence, and not the original created hosts; who were *created* from *nothing* material (*bârâ*); this same rule applies today. The material vessel is first formed, and then God imparts His "breath" into the vessel. This condition of "life" begins with the first breath, and ends with the last. Again; this "breath of life" *enters* man with the first breath, and *exits* with the last.

Some distinctions need to be made regarding "breath of life" as used here in Genesis 2:7. Often "breath of life" is utilized to indicate the immaterial part of man (soul); and in certain usages this is sufficient. However that which is *total* immaterial part of man when physically alive, consists of at least two parts: One is the aforementioned "soul" or "I am," which is contained in the physical vessel, and without such containment physical life or connection ceases. Another is the *vital life force*, which maintains the physical vessel, without which the vessel becomes incapable of this containment.

What "remains" materially after the "breath of life" exits, is referred to as *remains*. Unlike in the condition of *life*; where this *immaterial* or *supernatural* force or forces known by various names such as: the vital life force, Chi or Innate Intelligence, cause the body to essentially defy natural law; these *remains* are strictly subject to *material* or *natural* laws.

And any material objects that were accrued while living, are often referred to as *effects*. Here the *cause* for their acquisition was the living being; with one of the *effects* of this cause, being said material objects acquired. This seems to be more than a euphemism; as it seems that to refer to these as *possessions*, would requires a possessor, here being a *living* being as defined above.

There are some occasions *after* the exit of this "breath of life," when the condition of the body can be improved to the point where the "breath of life" can again be contained in it. This improved condition can be achieved *materially*, such as in an emergency room setting. Or it can be achieved *immaterially*, as per the stories in the Bible—despite the fact that this immaterial cause is usually misunderstood, simply referred to as "miraculous;" and then summarily dismissed. Miracles by definition must violate natural law(s).

There are also *transitional* states. One is the so called "near death" experience. This transitional state is where the "breath of life" is either about to exit, but does not; or exits, but not completely; or exits, and returns. Very little is actually *known* about these actual phenomena, as opposed to the *recollection* of any perceived concomitant "events."

It seems that these stories are always necessarily recounted by *living* beings, where the "breath of life" either did not leave, or only left temporarily and then returned. This is for good reason; as it must be asked by what process *can* one who experienced this same transitional state; but here where the "breath of life" exited and remained so; and yet somehow be able to "materially" recount what happened? [Barring necromancy, or some other "mancy," it seems that some type of an affirmative position on reincarnation would be required in order to provide any such latter process.]

Thus while "alive," man has both a *material* and an *immaterial* component. One is *indirectly* of God (material) and the other is *directly* of God (immaterial)—often described as *body* and *soul* respectively. The material part is subject to the laws of the material realm, unless acted upon by an immaterial force, such as the aforementioned "Vital Life Force." And the immaterial part is subject to the laws of the immaterial realm.

How do we even *know* that this immaterial realm exists? The key term here is to *know* (epistémē), rather than to merely *believe* (doxa). The answer is that simply as a matter of logic—it "cannot not" exist.

Genesis 1:1 (KJV) tells us:

> "In the beginning God created the heaven(s) and the earth."[115]

It must be remembered that the word here translated as "created," is the Hebrew word *bârâ*; meaning to bring into existence from *nothing* or "no (material) thing." This is again in contradistinction to *yâtsar*, generally translated as *formed*; which of course then requires *something* material with which to *yâtsar* or form.

As previously indicated, the latter was the case with Adam, as Adam was not brought into existence via bârâ; but rather was *formed* (yâtsar) from 'âphâr, generally translated as "dust." Again it is from this pandemic misunderstanding of the *process*, that the purported conflict between the scientific and Scriptural age of the earth arises—Adam was *formed*, and thus could not be one of the original *created* hosts. The use of matter in a process precludes the requirement of not using matter in this same process, and the reverse.

Here in Genesis 1:1 we are told about the creation of the universe, or the *material* realm. If one could have been an observer to the events described in Genesis 1:1, one would have witnessed what is generally scientifically referred to as the "Big Bang."

Some translations translate "heaven" in the singular. This translation presents a problem, because God could not have resided in a yet to be created realm prior to the creation of that very same realm.

The use of the term "heaven" in the *singular*; generally refers to the *immaterial* realm where God resides; e.g.; the "heaven" in "Who art in heaven;" which again refers to the *immaterial* realm. The use of the *plural* of heaven: "heavens," generally refers to the space between the celestial bodies, and thus is contained (as "space") in the *material* realm.

From man's perspective in the *material* realm; where there is time, space, and matter; there had to be a *cause* for the creation of the heavens and the earth; ("Big Bang" or Genesis 1:1); that *preceded* this creative event. From the perspective of the *immaterial* realm, from where this cause necessarily must have emanated; the same realm where there is no time, space, or matter; any type of sequencing is extremely difficult; if not impossible; to comprehend.

Thus "heaven" refers to the *immaterial* realm where God resides, and where He resided before He created the *material* realm, (Genesis 1:1/Big Bang). As stated, He could not have resided in a realm that did not exist prior to its existence via creation. Ergo: there is and was an immaterial realm that existed prior to the existence of the material realm. [See Monograph *"Inevitable Balance"* contained in the pentalogy: *"Wisdom Essentials"* for an explanation in much greater detail.]

Most religions speak of, and are very concerned with "afterlife." This is what happens *after life*; with life again being defined here as that dual condition, or the unity of body and soul. Afterlife is that *severed* condition; and that which happens to the *immaterial* portion *after* it is no longer contained within the physical vessel.

But again when speaking of the realm that has no time; that realm; by definition has "no time." This is not meant as any type of tautology, but rather as a reminder. If there is no time, then one could just as easily inquire as to "beforelife;" or that condition of this immaterial portion *before* it is "*breathed into his nostrils. . . and man became (becomes) a living soul.*" *Physical* (material) nostrils are required before they can be "breathed into." It seems that the only "time" that "time" affects this immaterial portion, is when it is contained in the physical vessel. "Beforelife" is rarely spoken about by conventional religions.

Outside of the "always was and always will be" belief regarding God—which is true, and cannot logically be false in a realm with no time; in major Western religions there is little or no serious mention of man's status *before* he is in that dual condition of life.

There is that "creation of new souls" theory, which clearly had to be true at some point in "time," and may remain so. However this in no way precludes what those proponents of reincarnation believe—that an afterlife can and sometimes does *become* a beforelife in a cyclical manner. When the immaterial part exits the physical body, it is in both an afterlife state, as well as a beforelife state; *if* it is awaiting entrance into another body, thereby beginning the dual "life" status once again.

We are told both that the "soul" part is introduced, and we are told *how* it is introduced. Genesis 2:7 provides no conclusive information as to whether or not this "soul" part; unlike the formed vessel; existed separately, or as a part of God prior to being breathed into the vessel's nostrils. This is likely because Genesis 2:7 is a *process* related passage, the significance of which is generally missed. Most erroneously believe that this is merely a recapitulation of the creation of man. But as previously discussed, this represents the first clear act in the redemption of *man*, (as opposed to the redemption of the earth); and it is known from all the well documented "begats," that this event, (the formation of Adam), occurred less than ten thousand years ago.

This must be clarified: The original *created* hosts were created to redeem the *earth*, and were in fact instructed to do so by God Himself, as previously cited. These hosts needed no redemption prior to their creation. But once "alive," they became subjected to the 24/7 attacks of the enemy—that very same entity from which the earth was to be redeemed, and none failed to sin. Thus the *formation* of Adam was the first clear act to redeem the hosts; i.e.; "redeem the redeemers."

This *first Adam* was the initial act in the process of obtaining the "Last Adam" (Jesus). The acceptance of this redemption is voluntary. But with respect to that *process* that resulted in the *availability* of or for the redemption of man—"It is finished."

It is likely that this soul part, or "breath of life" as per Genesis 2:7, *existed* prior to its introduction into the vessel. This is because we are provided no information in Genesis 2:7 as to its origin, other than at that "time" it must have been contained within, or connected to God, when He introduced it into the vessel. And again we are faced with the "time, but no time" material/immaterial paradox.

God had no beginning, so it seems He either caused this "breath of life" or soul, to "come into existence at that time;" or "He had it within Him all along." We are not told anything about this actual "soul" process, like we are told with the *formation* of the physical body. This is likely either because there was none, or because the human mind is not *designed* to, or even *able* to, comprehend it. And since there is no time in the immaterial realm, this soul can have no beginning or end, thus it seems any "intra-immaterial" *duration* is not possible.

As previously discussed, this same process occurs today, except that the formation of the vessel occurs a bit differently. It is *normally* man, (and woman), through the exercise of free will that initiates the formation of the vessel. Then the soul enters the body with the first "breath." Whether it is actual "positive pressure" from God, as we are led to believe in Genesis 2:7; or "negative pressure" caused by contraction of the "bell shaped" diaphragm of the newborn increasing thoracic cavity volume; or both; or "x;" is not clear.

It should be noted that the nerves supplying the diaphragm are *not* called "diaphragmatic nerves," with "diaphragm" roughly meaning *partition*. This would be a *structurally* derived name.

Instead; these nerves are called "phrenic nerves;" with the same being a more *functionally* derived name.

Following are some Biblical Greek "relatives" of "phrenic," according to Strong:

"5426 phrŏněō; from 5424; to *exercise* the *mind*, i.e. *entertain* or *have* a *sentiment* or *opinion*; by impl. to *be* (mentally) *disposed* (more or less earnestly in a certain direction); intens. to *interest oneself* in (with concern or obedience)..."[116]

"5427 phrŏnēma; from 5426; (mental) *inclination* or *purpose*..."[117]

"5424 phrēn; prob. from an obsol. phraō (to *rein* in or *curb*; comp. 5420); the *midrif* (as a *partition* of the body), i.e. (fig. and by impl. of sympathy) the *feelings* (or sensitive nature; by extens. [also in the plur.] the *mind* or cognitive faculties): - understanding."[118]

"5420 phrassō; appar. a strength. form of the base of 5424; to *fence* or inclose, i.e. (spec.) to *block* up (fig. to *silence*): - stop."[119]

Thus the relationship between the "will, intellect, and emotions;" (common, but incomplete definition of soul); and breathing or *inspiration* can be seen here. [As also can be seen, the use of "inspiration" or "inspired" figuratively as in: "I was inspired to do x;" can be much more literal than figurative.]

Most religions are primarily concerned with *afterlife*. But again; given what seems to be necessarily true; there is also the concept of *beforelife*; if it is again stipulated as per Genesis 2:7, that *life* here means "physical life," when the soul contained within the body or vessel.

Thus there is *physical life*, when the soul is *contained* in the body. This begins with the first breath, and ends with the last breath. There is *afterlife*, which begins when the soul *exits* the body. And there is *beforelife*, which is the status of the soul before it is contained in a vessel or body.

It is extremely difficult to in any way reasonably comprehend *before* and *after*—if and when one is concerned with one realm that includes time, and another realm that does not. Nevertheless, if science is correct with respect to what it was that was created at the time of the "Big Bang," this is the actuality.

Here again is the diagram:

Material

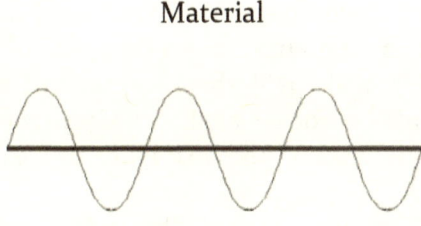

Immaterial

Again, it is stipulated that the *horizontal* line here refers to the division between the material and the immaterial realms, with the material being *above* this line, and the immaterial *below* this line; and it is also stipulated that "time" on the material realm runs from left to right. And for the purposes of this discussion, here the curve above this line represents; among other things; the overall *condition* of the physical vessel (the body or *soma*) with respect to this *time*.

And once again, the first "curve's" "I am" begins or began when this wave begins at/intersects the horizontal line, which is what is seen on the left. This represents physical *birth*. This type of "I am," represents the time that the "soul" is first introduced and contained in the physical body; with total "physical life" or "incarnation" (*literally—in the flesh*), represented by the entire "positive" half of the wave above this horizontal line; i.e.; one *lifetime*, "life-time."

With the *curve* theory as discussed in an earlier chapter, "beforelife" is one of two possibilities: One is a matter of no existence of a given "I am," with this "I am" then coming into existence only when there is physical existence, (the use of "first introduced" is avoided for obvious reasons), at birth. Or alternatively, an "I am" that does in fact (pre)exist but only as a direct or attached part of God, which He then at some point breathes into a physical vessel for the first and only time.

With the *curve* theory, once the peak of the wave is reached, and "negative slope" begins; the trajectory *below* the horizontal line is different than in this diagram. Its trajectory instead becomes forever downward (negative slope continues) and this is non-sinusoidal, and thus different than on the "graph." Here there is an *afterlife*, but never again will the trajectory of this line become positive or upward; i.e.; never again will it intersect or rise above the horizontal line; again perhaps with the exception of "end times."

However with the *wave* theory, "beforelife" can also include a previous incarnation. This does not in any way *preclude* the initial incarnation as with the *curve* theory; but neither does it preclude the introduction of an "I am" that had been previously "breathed" into another and different set of "nostrils." This then necessarily acknowledges the possibility of a "beforelife" that includes the human experience—whether all, some, or none of the details of "previous personalities," or previous human experiences are "known;" i.e.; "readily recoverable." Here with the *wave* theory, the "wavelength" of the wave may vary with regard to material time; (how long in between incarnations); but it nevertheless remains a "wave."

This of course necessarily changes the view of *afterlife*.

With the *curve* theory, it is clear that the immaterial part of man remains solely in the immaterial from the point of downward intersection with the horizontal line and onward; (forever remaining below the horizontal line)—with one possible exception as previously noted. One may believe this represents hypocrisy, or a schizophrenic belief, because of Jesus, Lazarus, and others. However; those were *resurrections*, as the very same physical vessels were utilized.

But with the *wave* theory, the immaterial part of man *may or may not* remain solely in the immaterial from the point of downward intersection with the horizontal line and onward. ["Remaining in the immaterial" in this usage, refers to a soul not "contained" in a physical body or "alive." This must be noted, as it is unclear that this immaterial part; whether contained in a physical vessel or not; ever actually leaves the immaterial realm.]

It must be noted that "under the altar" and "Abraham's Bosom" (kŏlpŏs); at first blush; seem to represent a "place" or "places" other than heaven or hell. The latter, (kŏlpŏs), is or was clearly designed for many, including those such as Abraham, who were unable to obtain salvation while physically alive. "Under the altar" may be the very same "place" as "Abraham's Bosom," (kŏlpŏs); and may be for the same reason; or it may be a different "place" for the same or for a different reason or reasons.

Here is where justification/salvation/redemption becomes an issue. Once that immaterial part of man becomes contaminated through sin, it cannot return to the source—lest the source also become contaminated.

In order to return to its source, a means by which man's sin could become irrelevant; or "just as though he never sinned;" is or was required. Whether one believes that this has already happened, (Christianity); or believes that it will happen at some point in the future, (Judaism, Islam, etc.); in no way changes this need.

Absent this, man's immaterial part cannot return to the *immaterial*, (there is no "place" for it); and absent a material or physical vessel, it no longer has a means by which to exist in the *material*. Thus this immaterial part is "stuck" between the two worlds or realms, existing in *neither* "world;" or perhaps the correct spelling of, and the true meaning of the *nether* world.

"Abraham's Bosom" (kŏlpŏs) is contained within this neither or nether world, but it is the "air conditioned" section. [See: "*OSTIUM AB INFERNO*,"—*Lazzaro, L'uomo Ricco, e il Seno* (*Lazarus, the Rich Man, and the Bosom*)]. And it is possible that "Under the Altar" is another "place"—assuming of course that these are not merely different names for the same "location."

It would be highly speculative to claim that reincarnation provides a third means of, or "place" for, those who remain "contaminated" by sin, to "try it again"—but of course "highly speculative" is not synonymous with "not true."

With the *wave* theory, this immaterial part of man is considered to be more like someone who lives part of the year in one location; and then moves to another location for the rest of the year, when the seasons become cold.

However; this analogy is somewhat flawed because of "conditions on the ground." Since the *immaterial* realm "has no place for" any evil or wickedness, it is a "pleasant locale." But man, when in the *material* realm; again is by design a fighter; which again is why God Himself called man that which is translated as "hosts" in English, and which again is originally *tsâbâ'* in Hebrew.

Thus the primary purpose of man's existence in the material, is *bellum gerere*; or to *wage war*, and is not for pleasure. Because of this, the "TDY" (temporary duty), of the dual condition of "physical life" is often at odds with man's immaterial nature, (image and likeness of God), and thus is often unpleasant.

Although a detailed analysis is beyond the scope of this work, the purpose of this war is *redemption*; but not man's redemption, as that is God's unique capability. After all; man *was* in fact instructed by God Himself in Genesis, to "put the *kibosh* on" (English); or *kâbash* (Hebrew) the earth.

This lack of understanding of man's designed purpose leads to many suppositions about the same, with seemingly endless disappointments. C. S. Lewis is reputed to have been "angry with God for not existing" at one point in his life. If it is stipulated that the purpose of the existence of man is somehow not *tsâbâ'* as God Himself clearly stated; but rather *enjoyment*, as many today believe; grave disappointments are inevitable.

Decisions must be made regarding whether it is the *curve* theory or the *wave* theory that best represents the truth.

Specifically; does the line in the graph when at the "peak," attain a permanent downward trajectory at physical death, never to rise upward again before "end times" (*curve* theory)?

Or does the line again attain a positive trajectory at some point in time, and eventually rise above the horizontal at some future point in time (*wave* theory) if and when it enters a new and different vessel?

There are believed to be three possible categories of reincarnation or quasi-reincarnation:
The first category of reincarnation is termed *metempsychosis*. This word can be broken down literally as metem-psych-osis. The "Metem" or "met" roughly meaning a *change in*, or in the *middle*. The "psych" refers to the *soul*; with "*osis*" being a suffix usually meaning an "abnormal condition of."
"*Merriam-Webster.com*" provides the following:

> "Definition of *METEMPSYCHOSIS*: the passing of the soul at death into another body either human or animal... from meta- + empsychos animate, from en- + psychē soul"[120]

This definition provides a little additional insight, and may also be a bit misleading; depending upon precisely what is meant by the use of the term "animal" in this definition.
In addition, "passing of the soul at death into another..." is also misleading, as there is no prerequisite suggestion of immediacy ("at death"); or any other length of "time" that the "wave" on the graph remains beneath the horizontal line. This "time" may be zero, or it may be some other length of "time" as measured on the material realm.
"*Metempsychosis*" is the term generally recognized to represent that category of reincarnation which maintains the view that reincarnation is kind of a one way street; meaning that there is no possibility of regression. The term "regression" as used here does not mean the "regression" process that involves an individual attempting to find out about past lives, (this will be addressed later); but rather "regression" here meaning to be reincarnated to a "lesser state."
The tenets of this view (metempsychosis) include that whatever the status of a life form in a given incarnation; this represents the highest level of existence ever yet attained by that being. One cannot go backwards, as say a human being reincarnated as a cow or a snake. Thus when someone at a cocktail party claims that he or she was once some famous, wealthy, or extremely talented person in

another life; this is highly unlikely or even impossible according to the tenets of metempsychosis. Whatever they currently are represents the highest level at which they have ever been, according to this (metempsychosis) view. Of course, it is often difficult to objectively determine precisely what constitutes "highest."

"Transmigration of Souls" is another "category" of reincarnation. The term is not migration but rather transmigration. Here the "soul path" if you will, is considered to be "two way" in terms of "attainment." In this category, the direction of the soul is generally believed to be related to *karma*, and with this view; one can return as either higher or lower status, including the *type* of life form. Depending on karmic factors, one is here believed to be able to return as a "reward" or "punishment" for their behavior in his or her past life or lives. This apparent conflation of metempsychosis and Transmigration of Souls is likely why the "either human or animal..." is contained in the previous definition, as this covers both viewpoints/theories.

The question that the disciples asked Jesus about the blind man; "*Master, who did sin, this man, or his parents,*" tends to lead one to believe that this question relates to the Transmigration of Souls view.

John 9:1-3 (KJV here) tells us:

"And as Jesus passed by, he saw a man which was blind from his birth. And his disciples asked him, saying, Master, who did sin, this man, or his parents, that he was born blind?

Jesus answered, Neither hath this man sinned, nor his parents: but that the works of God should be made manifest in him."[121]

When Jesus answered "neither," this could be construed either as an outright negation or rejection of this (transmigration of souls) view; or, that it just did not apply to this particular situation.

When Jesus gave the reason: *"but that the works of God should be made manifest in him,"* this could be construed as support of the metempsychosis; as it does not seem likely that this man had ever been involved in such a great event as to be recorded as a party to a miracle of Jesus. On the other hand, it could also be that this man was never reincarnated, indicating that the question was irrelevant with respect to this man.

Both *Metempsychosis* and *Transmigration of Souls* require that the soul returns and resides in a different, generally a new body, and generally at the time of birth. When the soul returns to the *same* body, this arguably represents the third, but a different type of reincarnation known as *resurrection*.

This word *resurrection*, contains the suffix "rection" which refers to being "erect." As previously discussed, this is seen in the term "insurrection," and essentially means to rise up. So the word "resurrection" can reasonably be defined as to be "erect again," or "rise up again." Thus, there is an implied requirement that this person or body must have been erect at one time—else how could they become "re-erect" or resurrected?

Jesus was resurrected, as it seems were all those who came out of the graves after the crucifixion.

Matthew 27:52 (KJV):

> *"And the graves were opened; and many bodies of the saints which slept arose,"*[122]

There is a belief that the original reason for embalming a corpse, was because many years ago (and likely even today), certain cultures believed that they would ultimately be *resurrected*, and took measures to preserve the body for that day. This is to be distinguished from the mere application of makeup for a viewing.

It is also likely that this could also be the reason for the elaborate burial procedures for kings in ancient cultures. It is not revealed what, if any, body preparation may have been done to those in the graves who were resurrected at the time of the crucifixion. It could have been *none*, as is the case with Judaism today. And the identities of those who were interred is not known. Neither is it revealed how long these bodies had been interred. Thus there likely was a substantial amount of *dunamis* or supernatural power involved—and not just for the resurrection part; but in the required "reconstructive" changes to these physical vessels.

It has been shown how most western religious leaders today, (and even centuries ago), will reject and avoid any discussion of reincarnation—even to the point of absurdity. In fact, again in referencing *Strong's Exhaustive Concordance*, the word reincarnation does not seem to appear anywhere in the King James version of the Bible. This cannot be cited as a quote here, because Strong does not actually make that statement; but rather, the word simply does not appear in the concordance. Nevertheless, the passages cited in the previous chapters are what they are, and state what they state.

As is generally the case with most types of conflation and confusion; the conflating and confusing of that which is temporary with that which is permanent, represents a significant obstacle to the attainment of wisdom.

CHAPTER 8

"The Force"

Clearly there is some type of "force" involved in miraculous phenomena, whether said miracles manifest as a virgin birth, resurrection, and/or likely reincarnation—assuming of course that reincarnation is an actuality.

What these phenomena have in common, is that each disobeys natural law. Discarding the *doxa*, (possible or probable knowledge); and obtaining *epistémē* (certain knowledge); is key in understanding the *nature* of this force, as well understanding its *purpose*.

What is a force? There are many possible definitions for this word; ranging from compulsion, through Newton's F=MA. But here the word "force" will be used in a much simpler and a much more broad manner. Here "force" will be stipulated to simply mean: *"the ability to cause change."*

A fair argument could be made as to whether this ability exists prior to the implementation of the same. Stated another way: by this definition, does one who say has the ability to lift an automobile engine, have "force" prior to lifting or attempting to lift said engine? In the classical sense of F=MA, the answer is probably no. But here we will also consider force to be *capability*—whether implemented or not.

There are many types of *material* forces, or abilities to cause material changes; and many of these are well *known*, irrespective of how well these are actually *understood*. Electrical *voltage* is technically EMF or electromotive *force*. This is the ability to change the location of electrons (electro); by movement (motive); by this force (force).

There are also *immaterial* forces able to cause *material* change, and these; although not necessarily less *known*; are perhaps less *recognizable* as such. Just tell one's mother or spouse that you now know they are a lousy cook; because when you went into the military, you were the only one who liked the food; and witness the changes that take place. This not because of the material sound, but the immaterial content.

The one thing that these types of forces, (material forces, and *some* immaterial forces), have in common; is that they *obey* natural law.

What about a force that could *disobey* natural law? Here a distinction should be made between a force and "The Force." Hold these thoughts.

The drastic alterations of the requirements for *salvation* by many of the mainstream religions have been addressed. It is unclear how many people never obtain salvation because of all of the behavioral requirements placed upon it by same—*with virtually none of said requirements appearing anywhere in the Bible.*

"If you wanna be saved like me, then you "haf-ta" (gots-ta) act like me," is a man made requirement; and is antithetical to what the Bible instructs us. But in order to successfully manipulate human behaviors, some serious "or else" is required; and clearly salvation; or lack thereof; is a pretty good one. It is difficult to imagine the *karmic debt* incurred for lying to people about what is necessary in order to be saved.

If this sounds like hijacking Christianity, a fair argument exists that this is so. But this is not actually so. This is because despite the fact that they are generally considered as the same thing (salvation and anointing); because in a sense, both were provided by the same person (Jesus); *salvation* and *anointing* are not the same thing.

Despite this incessant conflation; *literal* salvation is not an actual part of *literal* Christianity, although it is related. Most particularly that "believing" in Jesus, is a requirement or pre-requisite, with respect to the *quantity* of dunamis or supernatural power available; as will be seen.

In support of this, as previously stated; "Matthew, Mark, Luke and John;" are largely about Jesus; about a *person*. The book of "Acts," is largely about the "Christ;"—hence this name ("Acts"), is referring to *action* and not a person.

Conflation and confusion are common in Biblical "commentary;" but must be strictly avoided in analysis.

Similar, although unrelated, confusion is seen with that which Noah built. Today there is available for touring; that which is a purported replica of what it was that was built by Noah. Common knowledge (*doxa*) is that Noah built a very large and fine ship.

The problem is that Noah was not asked to build, and did not build any type of "ship." Noah was asked to build, and in fact built a very large box.

The actual Hebrew word for what Noah in fact did build is:

"8392 têbâh; perh. of for. der.; a *box*: - ark."[123]

An "ark" is actually a box; and today, "Noah's Ark," is only considered as a boat or ship because of the belief that Noah built a boat or a ship—which he did not. One main difference between a ship and a large box; is the ability of a ship to *navigate*. Thus it was not Noah who determined the ultimate destination of this *têbâh* or box.

Jesus was actually named Yeshua. A fair translation of this is: "YHWH; (the previously discussed Tetragrammaton or ineffable name of God in all of its various spellings); is salvation." This is as opposed to double dose *receiver* Elisha, which roughly translates as: "God is salvation." And of course Elijah; the double dose *giver* must also be mentioned here; as Elijah translates roughly as: "God is YHWH."

This is also seen when God delivers the Commandments; as "I am the Lord your God" is actually: I am "YHWH your ĕlôhîym." This was more important at that time than it may seem, because of many beliefs in various false gods. To say that "god is salvation" could refer to any "god;" but the use of the tetragrammaton, or the ineffable name of God, could only refer to one—The Living God.

The naming of Jesus, actually *Yeshua*, had to do with the provision of salvation, as stated. He was given quasi-surnames such as Jesus of Nazareth, Jesus the carpenter's son, etc. But today he is correctly known as Jesus *the* Christ. Christ was not His surname, thus "Jesus Christ" here without the definite article "*the*;" represents an incorrect usage. This use of this definite article is important, as will be seen.

Both *Christos* and *Messiah* roughly mean "anointing," or "anointed one." Thus "Jesus the Christ" means: "Jesus *the* Anointed One."

But it seems that although Jesus was born *to be* The Anointed One, He was not *born* The Anointed One, as we are told the following in Luke 3:21-22 (KJV):

> *"Now when all the people were baptized,*
> *it came to pass, that Jesus also being baptized,*
> *and praying, the heaven was opened,*
> *And the Holy Ghost descended in a*
> *bodily shape like a dove upon him,*
> *and a voice came from heaven,*
> *which said, Thou art my beloved Son;*
> *in thee I am well pleased."*[124]

Here Jesus receives the *anointing* of the Holy Ghost, thus becoming not *an* anointed one, but *The Anointed One*.

This also appears in Matthew 3:13-17 (KJV):

"The Force"

"*Then cometh Jesus from Galilee to Jordan
unto John, to be baptized of him.
But John forbad him, saying,
I have need to be baptized of thee,
and comest thou to me?*

*And Jesus answering said unto him,
Suffer it to be so now: for thus it becometh
us to fulfil all righteousness.*

*Then he suffered him. And Jesus, when he
was baptized, went up straightway out of the water:
and, lo, the heavens were opened unto him,
and he saw the Spirit of God descending
like a dove, and lighting upon him:
And lo a voice from heaven, saying,*

*This is my beloved Son,
in whom I am well pleased.*"[125]

Here in *Matthew*, we are told that Jesus went *"out of the water,"* prior to receiving the anointing of the Holy Ghost.

And Mark 1:8-12 (KJV) tells us:

"*I indeed have baptized you with water:
but he shall baptize you with the Holy Ghost.*

*And it came to pass in those days, that Jesus
came from Nazareth of Galilee, and was baptized
of John in Jordan. And straightway coming
up out of the water, he saw the heavens opened,
and the Spirit like a dove descending upon him:*

*And there came a voice from heaven,
saying, Thou art my beloved Son,
in whom I am well pleased.
And immediately the spirit driveth*

him into the wilderness."¹²⁶

Here in *Mark*, the "*you*", and the "*he*" should be reconciled.

John the Baptist is first speaking to (you); those, (not Jesus); whom he (JTB) had already baptized, telling them that he (JTB) had baptized them with water, but another (he—Jesus) would (*shall* and not may or might) baptize them with the Holy Ghost. The inclusion of the non-capitalized "he" in the above; "*he shall baptize you;*" translation causes confusion.

Thus there is a two-fold process revealed here for both those who were baptized, and Jesus. Those who were first baptized with *water*, will be baptized with the *Holy Ghost* in the future, by He who is, (at that later (*will*) time, but is not yet at *this* (the time this was actually stated) time), *The* Anointed One. After being baptized by *The* Anointed One, each of these "baptizees" would then become "*an* Anointed One."

Jesus is then baptized by JTB with water, leaves the water, and *then* receives the anointing of the Holy Ghost, and becomes "*The* Anointed One."

John 1:29-33 (KJV) adds a bit more:

*"The next day John seeth Jesus coming unto him,
and saith, Behold the Lamb of God,
which taketh away the sin of the world.*

*This is he of whom I said, After me cometh a man
which is preferred before me: for he was before me.
And I knew him not: but that he should be
made manifest to Israel, therefore
am I come baptizing with water.*

*And John bare record, saying, I saw the Spirit
descending from heaven like a dove,
and it abode upon him.*

And I knew him not: but he that sent me

"The Force"

> *to baptize with water, the same said unto me,*
> *Upon whom thou shalt see the Spirit*
> *descending, and remaining on him,*
> *the same is he which baptizeth with the Holy Ghost"*[127]

John the Baptist or JTB, (not John the author of the passage), immediately knows when he sees Jesus, about the salvation available by or from or through *"The Lamb of God."* This is consistent with the role of "savior," something of which Jesus was already capable, as per Jesus' birth.

John *then* testifies (*"bare record"*) that he saw the *"Spirit descending, and remaining on him."* JTB did not previously know Jesus, (twice—*"I knew him not"*). But despite the fact that JTB did not know *Jesus*, JTB knew the *"Lamb of God"* when He arrived.

The first *"I knew him not"* seems to best refer to Jesus' role as savior, which JTB seemed to already know, without actually *knowing* Jesus—perhaps from when Mary visited Elizabeth while John was "in-utero,"—perhaps not.

But the second *"I knew him not"* clearly refers to JTB not knowing that Jesus was the one who would *baptize* others with the Holy Ghost, until JTB saw the event.

As then JTB states: *"but he that sent me to baptize with water, the same said unto me."* So it must be asked who it is that is represented by this *"he?"* Was this (*"he"*) the *Pharisees*; or was it the *Sadducees* who sent John to *"baptize with water?"*

The answer to this question is contained in verse 6 of this same chapter in John, (author); about John, (the Baptist):

> *"There was a man sent from God,*
> *whose name was John"*[128]

Here we are told that it was God (He) that had sent him (JTB); and also that God had said something to him about the circumstances surrounding the soon to be empowerment of The

Christ. And what God had said to him, was: "*Upon whom thou shalt see the Spirit descending, and remaining on him, the same is he which baptizeth with the Holy Ghost.*"

It cannot be overemphasized that God did *not* tell JTB: "When you *recognize the 'Lamb of God,'* the same is he which baptizeth with the Holy Ghost."

Jesus had the capability to be savior from birth. He could have changed his mind when He was attacked at Gethsemane, and not gone through with the process. Jesus was *born* with the capability to be the savior, unlike any other man. But Jesus could not have been the one to "baptize with the Holy Ghost," until after this (*the Spirit descending, and remaining on him*) event.

Thus it seems reasonably clear that when Jesus arrived, John knew Jesus was the "Lamb of God," who would provide salvation to the world, although John did not know *Jesus*. But it is more than arguable; that John did *not* know whether or not it was to be Jesus who was the one John would see the "*Spirit descending, and remaining on him.*"

Once John baptized Jesus, it seems Jesus walked out of the water. One might ask why He did not walk out of the water by walking *on the water*?

The answer, is that He did not obtain this *dunamis* or supernatural power until *after* He left the water. John may or may not have been surprised that Jesus was the one who was to become, and in fact in John's presence *became* "The Christ."

It is clear that Jesus is; (or at least is a major part of); the *second* part of The Trinity. He was born the "Lamb of God," or "Redeemer." This (Lamb) of course being the fulfillment of that which happened at the first Passover. The first Passover utilized blood for the prevention of "physical death," or separation of the body and soul; and much later Jesus' blood would be able to prevent "spiritual death," or separation of the soul from its source (God).

But He did not *become* "The Christ," until He was anointed by the *third* part of The Trinity; i.e.; the Holy Ghost, as recounted in these passages.

"The Force"

As previously stated, a fair argument could be made that the "books" of Matthew, Mark, Luke and John; AKA the "gospel(s)" or the "good news;" is primarily about Jesus, or the *second* part of The Trinity; and the "book" of Acts is primarily about the Holy Ghost, or the *third* part of The Trinity.

But Christian religions are self-named *Christian*—they do not call themselves "Jesusites." Thus this very nomenclature strongly suggests that at least initially, it was the *Christos* or the Anointing of the *third* part of The Trinity, and the resultant supernatural power with which they, (Christians), *then*, (at that time long ago), were primarily concerned; and that likewise "true Christians" *today* should be primarily concerned. That which is described in the "Book of Acts," reasonably proves this.

If it can be stipulated that the word mysticism does not mean what it is commonly believed to mean (doxa); but in fact means: "The ability to experience God while *physically* alive on the earth;" then true Christianity is true mysticism.

Nevertheless; instead today most "Christian" religions are primarily concerned with the *Second Part*, (Jesus); and are not concerned with the *Third Part*, (The Holy Ghost); in any meaningful way. In fact, they essentially ignore this Third Part, except cursorily; and they have largely chosen to rename this Third Part: "The Holy *Spirit*."

Again; although both ghosts and spirits are each *spiritual* in the literal sense, with the Latin *spiritus* essentially meaning breath or breath-like as previously indicated; a *ghost* and a *spirit* are not the same. Lacking matter, it could be reasonably said that the entire *immaterial* realm; (*heaven*, but not *the heavens*); "metaphorically" is *spiritual*, or "breath-like."

But as previously stated, a *ghost* is something that is *designed* to reside in a physical body, while "a spirit" can represent any immaterial thing, including that which is capable of thought. It is often said that God is "a spirit." One individual *evil spirit*; e.g.; a demon; is also "a spirit." An angel is also "a spirit, and a spirit that is in fact "holy;" albeit that an angel is merely "*a* holy spirit," and not "*The* Holy Spirit. And absent the *indefinite article* "a" preceding it; "spirit" can also describe that which emanated or emanates from

God that created and/or maintains the existence of the entire material realm, as well as a myriad of other things.

The relatively recent diminution of the stature of the Holy Ghost to the "Holy Spirit;"—even if still including the definite article *"the,"* changes both the understanding and perceived purpose of this entity. [The use of *diminution* here and hereafter, refers to the *reality* or *perception* of the Holy Ghost, which can be changed by man; but in no way refers to the *actuality* of the Holy Ghost, which cannot.]

The Holy Ghost; being a *ghost* and not merely a "spirit," albeit a Holy one; it is designed to reside within us, but only with our legitimate informed consent. The Holy Ghost *will not* reside within us absent this consent; which in order to be legitimate; must be based upon *truth*. And the *main purpose* of this, is the provision of *dunamis*, or *supernatural* power/capabilities in various forms—which are very often erroneously referred to as "gifts."

As stated, demons are also "spirits," albeit *not* Holy ones; and they also *desire* to reside within us, but this is *against* their original design and thus is *against* Gods will—hence unholy or unclean. Demons are generally referred to as "evil spirits," and not "wicked spirits." This is because "evil" means acting against the will of God, irrespective of whether any given act itself is "wicked" or not

Demons may be "spirits" but they are not *ghosts*. And unlike the Holy Ghost, demons would readily reside within us without our consent, but simply *cannot*.

However *demons* attempt to obtain this consent with *falsehood*. Their main purpose is not the provision of any supernatural power, as after Calvary, they have very little left. Thoughts, ideas and suggestions are what demons generally proffer today. It is the *power of man*; particularly that of man's *free will*; that they both envy and incessantly seek. Demons for the most part can merely act like a thermostat, while man is the furnace—and demons know this quite well.

It must be asked *why* there has been such a diminution or minimization (from *Ghost* to *Spirit*) of the part of the Trinity for which an entire group of religions (Christianity) is actually named? It must also be considered as to whether this current diminution of the Holy Ghost in any way represents commission of the "unforgivable sin" against the Holy Ghost as appears in Matt 12:31-32, Mark 3:28-30, and Luke 12:10? Finally; if so, it must be asked *why* it is that this sin was, and may in fact remain "unforgivable?"

Matthew 12:31-32 (KJV) tells us:

> *"Wherefore I say unto you, All manner of sin and blasphemy shall be forgiven unto men: but the blasphemy against the Holy Ghost shall not be forgiven unto men.*
>
> *And whosoever speaketh a word against the Son of man, it shall be forgiven him: but whosoever speaketh against the Holy Ghost, it shall not be forgiven him, neither in this world, neither in the world to come."*[129]

This and what follows have to do with those enemies of Jesus who claimed it was via *demons*, and not the Holy Ghost by which Jesus performed miracles: "Say whatever you want about Jesus, but don't mess with the Holy Ghost."

Mark 3:28-30 (KJV) tells us:

> *"Verily I say unto you, All sins shall be Forgiven unto the sons of men, and blasphemies wherewith so ever they shall blaspheme:*
>
> *But he that shall blaspheme against the Holy Ghost hath never forgiveness, but is in danger of eternal damnation. Because they said, He hath an unclean spirit.*[130]

And Luke 12:10 (KJV) tells us:

> *"And whosoever shall speak a word against the Son of man, it shall be forgiven him: but unto him that blasphemeth against the Holy Ghost it shall not be forgiven."*[131]

Many believe that those such as the Pharisees and the Sadducees, simply believed that Jesus was a "phony," and it was for this reason that they wished him killed. For some, this may have in fact been true; but many in power knew *precisely* who He was, and it was for this reason they wanted Him killed. A fair read is that they had tried, but were unsuccessful. This was not *knowingly* done in order to "help" fulfill prophesy or facilitate salvation; but rather because of the fear that He would greatly interfere with their socioeconomic status.

"In certain ways, Jesus existed at a time similar to today. Many believe that outside of the practical concerns of those whom He helped, that the main reason for His performing of miracles was the fulfillment of prophesy—so that all would know who He is or was.

"This is an interesting position, and worthy of some analysis:

"If it is believed that the miracles Jesus performed were to uniquely prove Him to be the Messiah; this is simply not true. The truth is that many of the miracles He performed; had already been performed by others, long before His birth. If this were the only criteria for being the Messiah; then Elijah and "double dose" Elisha; as well as others, could also qualify. Heck; a dead man jumped back to life after his body merely touched the bones of a long deceased Elisha.

"The position should not be that of believing that Jesus performed these miracles primarily or simply to fulfill prophesy, even though that did in fact happen. The position should be based upon the answer to a question. The same being: "Why was this or were these prophesied?"

"In other words: Outside of helping some individuals; why was it necessary for Jesus to perform these miracles, many of which had already been performed by others long before his birth?

"The answer is a mere two words: *"They forgot!"*

"The Father *knew beforehand*, that by the time of the birth of Jesus, His chosen people would have forgotten much regarding that which had been written. If it is stipulated that Malachi represents the end of the Old Testament, it is believed that this was written roughly five hundred years prior to Jesus' birth. This represents a substantial period of time for the enemy to "work" His (God's) people; utilizing the old "literal to allegory" trick—a particularly effective tool when dealing with miracles performed a very long time ago.

"Knowing this, and always economizing, He (God) instructed His prophets to include these miracles as parts of those prophesies written prior to Jesus' birth. Thus although Jesus had to perform these miracles to fulfill the prophesy; the true reason for their inclusion in the prophesy was education, or perhaps *re-education*—used here in its original benign meaning."[32] [Excerpt from *"Wisdom Essentials"* Reprinted by Permission]

Thus in a certain sense, the performance of these miracles by Jesus, was to *augment* the awareness of the Holy Ghost with respect to those alive at the time of Jesus, as well as those in the future by the memorializing of these events. And based upon that which is described in the Book of Acts, this was quite successful—at least temporarily.

Today's *diminution* of The Holy Ghost is either accidental or deliberate. It seems difficult to believe that a group of religions could *accidentally* diminish that very entity for which they are as a group named, (Christianity)—whether they realize this quasi-eponymous relationship or not.

The conflation of *structure*; (Jesus); with two related but separate and distinct *functions*; (as Savior, and as The Christ); assists in the erroneous merging of two different aspects into one. The result is the overemphasis of "salvation," (OSAS is a simple matter); at the expense (de-emphasis) of the other; and this "de-emphasis" affects available *dunamis* or supernatural power—or at a minimum, the acquisition of sufficient knowledge regarding the same.

Obtaining salvation is easy by design. And Jesus never said: "Those who believe in me and the salvation I provide shall have even greater salvation because I go to the Father."

Rather, in John 14:12 (KJV) Jesus did in fact say:

> "*Verily, verily, I say unto you, He that believeth on me,
> the works that I do shall he do also;
> and greater works than these shall he do;
> because I go unto my Father.*"[133]

With the exception of in "the minds" of the OSAS (Once Saved Always Saved) deniers, salvation is unrelated to, and thus has nothing to do with works. But this particular passage (John 14:12), has nothing to do with salvation—except as a qualifier for doing *greater* works, ("*He that believeth on me*"). This qualifier in context; seems to be related to the *magnitude* of the works, and not the existence of the capability of performing *any* (miraculous) works, albeit "lesser" works.

Capability is one thing, but the actual *utilization* of dunamis is another matter entirely. This is one reason for the inclusion of the "Talent Man" parable in Matthew.

It must be noted that "shall he do" appears twice in John 14:12 above. So the question then becomes whether these "shall he

"The Force"

do(s)" refer to actual *capability*; or to actual *utilization*; e.g.; "shall be able to do" or "shall do?"
The actual Greek word translated as "shall he do" each time is:

"4160 pŏiĕō; appar. a prol. form of an obsol. prim; to *make* or *do* (in a very wide application, more or less direct): - abide, +agree, appoint, x avenge..."[134]

There seems to be no compulsion in the definition of *pŏiĕō*. Thus it seems that "*shall he do*" is better translated contextually as "shall be *able* to do."
Thus; the more likely explanation is that said diminution of the Holy Ghost was *deliberately* undertaken. The King James Bible is reputed to be the result of a compromise between King James, who wanted the *entire* known Bible released to the public; and the clergy, who did not want to release *any* books of the Bible to the public.
The result is that today it remains unknown which Books *not included* in these 66 are authentic, and which are not. The "Book of Phillip" seems to have been clearly proven to *not* be part of this *Apocrypha* or *hidden things*; (as opposed to *Apocalypsa* or *revealed things*); but "the jury is still out" on many others, such as the "Book of Enoch."
It must be asked what rational argument could have possibly existed for the desire to withhold from the public domain, the "Book of Proverbs;" arguably the Book most pertinent to common every day decisions? The answer is that there is and was none—*if* individual and readily available assistance in making quality everyday decisions is desired.
Despite the fact that Christianity is named after this *Christos* or anointing of the *Third* Part of the Trinity, the same is nevertheless too often minimized—most particularly by those who should, and in fact *claim* to know better.
"*Vicarius Christi*" or Vicar of *Christ*, is often attributed to the leader of one major religion, rather than "Vicar of *Jesus*." Yet it seems that in this same religion, even canonization (sainthood) requires a rather small number; (likely only 2); examples of the

173

utilization of *dunamis* (means); resulting in *miracles* (results). Even assuming these are truthful accounts, and thus are actual stories and not parables (euphemism); these represent a seemingly rather small number for a lifetime of service, compared to say that which is recorded in the aforementioned: "Book of Acts."

The *first* diminution is by *misnomer*. As stated, the name was changed from the specific (Ghost) to the more general (Spirit). As also stated, there are many holy spirits, including God the Father—at least according to many. The only distinctions made seem to be perhaps the use of the capitalized *definite article* of "The;" and the capitalization of both "Holy" and "Spirit." But if it is stipulated that God is also "a spirit," again meaning immaterial (breathlike), and here certainly capable of thought; and it is further stipulated that the Father is also "holy;" then the Father could also qualify as "The Holy Spirit." However, a *definite article* cannot apply to two. Although the Father and the Holy Ghost can both be "a Holy Spirit;" they cannot both be "The Holy Spirit." Thus a distinction would have to be made with regard to which *spirit* it is that is also *holy*, that is the particular one under discussion.

This all may sound a bit odd, but it must again be remembered that in Judaism, the name of God is considered ineffable; or unable to be put into words. Thus the Tetragrammaton (YHWH in all of its variants) is used, and historically was rarely spoken. The name of a thing always influences the *reality* of the thing, even though the *actuality* remains unchanged. To have a *name* for God, would then limit a limitless God to that which the name represents. When God is referred to as "Creator," this limits the reality to that of creation. The reality produced by other uses of "Lord;" often refers to attributes other than creation, and "Lord" is a title not unique to God.

Likewise; changing "Ghost" to "Spirit" changes the *reality*; (but not the *actuality*); from that which is designed to reside in a material vessel, to a much larger set of possibilities. This substantially de-emphasizes a major designed purpose. Again, all ghosts are spirits, but not all spirits are ghosts.

The *second* way the Holy Ghost being diminished is by *omission*. How much is being taught about the Holy Ghost? It may make a nice ending to "The Sign of the Cross," but what is the generally understood function and applicability of the Holy Ghost today? It must be remembered that often the absence of *dunamis* and resultant miraculous acts today is often "explained" by the "Apostolic Era Only" sophistry—a theory for which no Scriptural basis can readily be found.

Unlike the events in the "Book of Acts," it is generally the case that it is only *serendipitously* that dunamis and subsequent miracles are performed today, and perhaps these are some of the reasons why.

As was the case with the King James Bible "compromise;" it seems that mainstream religions simply do not want their petitioners to have substantial information—here substantial information about, or understanding of, the Holy Ghost. This view would then require some type of belief that this type of information is not for "the masses;" but only for religious leaders, or perhaps for no one at all. Withholding information because you believe that God had it written for you only, and it is your "God given" duty to "protect" it from "the masses" (sound familiar?); or perhaps better phrased; protect "the masses" from *it*; is a very dangerous path on which to travel.

And for any group to make the decision that that which is contained in the Bible regarding the Holy Ghost is nonsense, and thus not worthy of mention; is much worse, and clearly meets the "blasphemy against the Holy Ghost" test; and possibly the concomitant "unforgivability."

Precisely what is *a* trinity? What is *The* (Holy) Trinity; and why is there a Trinity? Likely the only thing more difficult to understand than the Trinity; would be the origin of the enemy. Even that which is required to understand "Maxwell's equations," is seriously dwarfed by what is required by either of these. But *trinity* in fact refers to *three*.

The creation of matter; including the creation of the entire material realm; can only be the result of that which is *contained* in God. (It must again be remembered materially, that there is no time in heaven/immaterial realm.) *Creation* in this usage is the bringing forth of something material utilizing nothing material (H. bârâ').

A distinction must be made between an entity containing the *ability* to create matter, and that same entity containing *matter* itself. Even that *essence* (immaterial part or "soul") which is Jesus; although contained *in* matter; did not contain matter. The same is true for humans. It is this *immaterial* portion or *essence* that is the part of "men" that is "created equal."

A + B = C in many ways is a trinity. There is A, there is B, and if and when combined, there is C. "In the beginning" God created. There was *God*; there was the *means* by which he created; and there was *that which He created*. Here A is *God*, B is the *means*, and C is the *result*, or that which was created. This "B" or *means* by which God created and creates, can be considered that which is described in the Bible as the Holy Ghost. But a subtle difference must be noted here. *Dunamis* or supernatural power alone is the means by which miracles are performed. But again, the concept of the *Holy Ghost* also includes the "Ghost" part which will be further addressed.

Here the power of that which is Biblically described as the Holy Ghost, was utilized as the means for *creation*. But it is the entire spectrum of *dunamis* or supernatural power that is in that which is known as the Holy Ghost, and this power is not limited to creation.

In a very real sense, that which is created by God can be considered as a son—irrespective of whatever it may be. The heavens and the earth can be considered as an *inanimate* son or sons of God, depending upon whether taken together or individually. And as stated, any creation can only be the result of that which is contained in the creator, here God. This is often seen when inventors refer to their invention as a "child of my imagination."

"The Force"

This concept of a trinity is seen everywhere. Electricity is where a positive and a negative produce a result different than either of the two components. Chemical reactions of two compounds produce a third—if they react with each other. A man (A) and a woman (B) produce offspring, where C is the offspring.

God also has *animate* (begotten) sons. With respect to H. Sapiens, each is *a* son of God, (as per Genesis 2:7); and one is *The* Son of God. When commonly utilizing "Father, Son and Holy Ghost," each should be preceded by the definite article *the*, when referring to deity: "*The* father, *The* Son, and *The* Holy Ghost."

Assuming there is a "key to the universe," the same would be *free will and balance*.

"But wait, that's two keys."

Not really, as balance is an inextricable part of the exercise of free will. One cannot exercise free will, and avoid the corresponding balancing event(s).

Whenever an action is undertaken by any "I am" in the material, a trinity is created. To be more accurate, this trinity is really a two-part trinity (two trinities) or mechanism. One part is *material* and one part is *immaterial*. Whether these are considered as one with two parts, or two separate but linked parts, is a matter of perspective.

The exercise of free will is not merely *wishing* (desire). The exercise of free will is not merely *hoping* (desire plus expectation). The exercise of free will is *doing* (desire plus expectation plus action); i.e.; "ergs" in some form or another.

Whenever man engages in the exercise of free will, imbalances are created in each of the two (material and immaterial) realms. (see the Monograph: "*Inevitable Balance*")

That in which man engages in the *material* using natural power or *dynamikós* is a trinity. The decision to take action is A. This natural power is B. And the result is C; i.e.; A + B = C. "I am going to throw a ball." A is the decision to do it, B is the force imparted to the ball, and C is the movement of the ball, and where the ball ultimately comes to rest; as the act of throwing the ball generally is merely purposefully changing its location—even if it doesn't go through (or even come close to) the hoop as desired. This of course assumes that it is not mere movement, simply for the sake of movement, that is desired.

At the same time, the *reason*(s) for throwing the ball set up a similar trinity in the *immaterial* realm. Here the the *reason(s)* for throwing the ball, is A; the actual amount of force imparted to the ball is B; and C is what is commonly referred to as *karma*. If one's desire were to cause harm, this "A" would then be entirely different than merely the desire for "shootin hoops." "B" could essentially be the same, but since "A" was entirely different, C or *karma* would likewise necessarily be entirely different, and much worse if the target were actually hit.

But these are, (usually), man's expression of *dynamikós* or natural power, and not *dunamis* or supernatural power of The Holy Ghost.

The same process occurred when God created the heavens and the earth, except it was not *dynamikós* or natural power; but *dunamis* or supernatural power. It could not have been *natural* power, because the "natural" did not exist prior to its creation. The Will of the Father, or A; utilized *dunamis* or supernatural power, or B; and the result was bringing into existence the heavens and the earth, or C. And of course anything created by God, necessarily must ultimately be in His image and likeness in terms of *quality*, even if necessarily much less in terms of *quantity*.

As the previous passage *"Upon whom thou shalt see the Spirit descending, and remaining on him, the same is he which baptizeth with the Holy Ghost"* is re-read, this begins to make much more sense.

But today, baptism is generally considered as a cleansing or ablution, such as the removal of "original sin." This thinking being, that a soul stained by "original sin," cannot return to the Father in that condition. This is entirely different than baptism being utilized as a *symbolic* ablution event demonstrating *repentance*.

There is another word used for baptism, the same being christen(ing); which although today refers largely to a *naming* process, or at best literally means: "to make Christian." Of course no one can ever be "made" Christian by another.

Baptism by *water* is purportedly a cleansing of the effects of sin, so that one's *soul* becomes "just as if one never sinned," and thus capable of living with or "reattaching" to God the Father, (spiritually alive).

But baptism by the *Holy Ghost*, is a cleansing so that part of God (Holy Ghost) can live with, or attach to us. The clear requirement of "*descending, and remaining on him*" given to John the Baptist, cannot be overlooked.

Baptism by *water* is purportedly concerned with the *future*, and the existence in the immaterial realm, *after* the body/soul connection has been severed. But of course if this were actually literally true, and not merely symbolic; one would then have to ask why Jesus had to endure what He endured in order to obtain for us this very same result?

But Baptism by the *Holy Ghost* is concerned with the *here and now*, and our existence in the *material* realm, *while* the body and soul are still connected.

And as stated, the one major purpose of baptism by the Holy Ghost; is the provision of *dunamis* or supernatural power. This is that which was received by Jesus; and it is He who provides a greater level of dunamis to us—just as the passage tells us.

Prior to Jesus becoming "The Anointed One who baptizeth with the Holy Ghost," dunamis or supernatural power was in fact available to man; but this earlier power was *on* man, and not *in* man; and thus of a lesser magnitude.

Is it even possible that the power of *an* anointed one could in any way even come close to, much less ever equal the power of Jesus: *The* Anointed One? And did Jesus ever provide any information about the level of dunamis available to *an* anointed one?

Once again, John 14:12 (KJV) tells us:

"*Verily, verily, I say unto you, He that believeth in me, the works that I do he shall do also; and greater works than these shall he do; because I go unto my father.*"

It is clear and virtually undisputed that these "works" to which Jesus is referring, are not any woodworking projects He may have built as a child. Neither do they refer to any other types of *dynamikós* or *natural* power. Had Jesus said: "My daddy can beat up your daddy," this would have been true; because as previously stated, Mary had no "y chromosome," and thus she did not get it from Joseph, but rather from God via the Holy Ghost. But this is not what Jesus said.

Rather; these "works" refer to *dunamis* or *supernatural* power, and the *miraculous* works He did. No mainstream religion disputes this, and again, the "Book of Acts;" which chronologically follows John; clearly confirms this meaning.

However with respect to other particulars contained in this passage, there are areas of significant dispute, which generally come down to two:

Firstly: as previously addressed, it is often proffered that this passage refers to only the aforementioned "Apostolic Era." Meaning; that what Jesus said, and to which He was clearly referring, had some type of "expiration" or "best if used before" date—e.g.; "Those were different times. Back then people could do those things—but not today." There is no Biblical support whatsoever for this position; thus the same likely merely represents an ineffective excuse for the lack of this (dunamis) capability on the part of the proponents of this position.

The *second* dispute is centered around the word "*greater*." Many proffer that what this actually means, is that since today there are so many more who "believe in Him and what He did;" there of course will be greater *numbers* of works, and that this in no way means works of greater *magnitude*.

However; the actual Greek word translated as "greater" that John used was:

"3187 měizōn; irreg. compar. of *3173*; *larger*..."[135]

It must be remembered that in here John 14:12 *měizōn* or larger, is an adjective describing *works*; and not the *number* of works.

Měizōn refers to *magnitude* of the works and not the *quantity*. The word *number* does not actually appear anywhere in this passage.

And it must be noted that neither of the aforementioned disputes, seem to "dispute" *in-toto* the ability of man to engage in miraculous works. One objects to the applicability today; and the other essentially objects to the idea that man could perform miraculous works that are *měizōn*, or larger than those performed by Jesus—despite the fact that Jesus Himself said so. [It is far beyond the scope of this work to explain the *mechanism* of what Jesus told us in the last phrase: *"because I go unto my father."* This mechanism is explained in exhaustive detail in an upcoming publication, currently in post-production.]

> "A *miracle* is something that occurs in the material realm, but is contrary to natural law. In fact in order to be considered a miracle, it *must* contradict natural law or laws; natural law here meaning the law or laws of the material realm. If it does not contradict natural law via *supernatural* power, (dunamis), it is not a miracle, but merely *natural* power, (dynamikós)—no matter what it may otherwise seem to be.
>
> "A "miracle" is the transformation of immaterial potential energy, into immaterial kinetic energy, which then produces an *effect* in the material realm which defies natural law. This is precisely what is happening in the early Genesis passages. It *is* the case, that all miracles are caused by immaterial kinetic energy; but it is *not* necessarily the case that all immaterial kinetic energy manifests as miracles in any absolute sense. As it is so that *material* kinetic energy has many manifestations, the same can be said about the manifestation of *immaterial* kinetic energy.
>
> *"When immaterial kinetic energy*
> *is imparted to the material realm,*

> *it is generally balanced by some type of motion in the material realm.*
> —Emma B. Quadrakoff

"In the case of bârâ or *creation*, this resultant motion exists at almost all levels, including the atomic and subatomic. All is in motion, with temperature being one way to indicate the amount of motion at the atomic or molecular level. *Absolute Zero* is considered to be the temperature at which all such atomic and molecular motion ceases. It is not known if absolute zero exists or can exist anywhere in the material realm.

"In other material manifestations of *immaterial* kinetic energy, generally there is also some type of movement in the material realm."[136] [Excerpt from *"Wisdom Essentials - Inevitable Balance"* Reprinted by Permission]

How does one obtain this dunamis, or supernatural power?

One way is as previously stated—*serendipitously*. Like the person with chronic back pain who falls, and when he/she gets up, the back pain is gone. Bartlett Joshua Palmer, the "developer" of chiropractic, is reputed to have once jokingly said: "If all of my patients fell down the stairs, half of them would get well." But although serendipitous *dunamis* does in fact happen; it is unpredictable, and generally non-repeatable.

Another way is to do it the way Jesus told us to do it, but it seems that few understand this today, likely because of centuries of misinterpretation—accidental or otherwise. The same of course being the "Talent Man Story," referenced in Chapter 3, where talanton, dunamis and massa were introduced. [see Matthew 25:14-30, or *"Donald Trump Candidacy According to Matthew?"* included in the pentalogy: *"Wisdom Essentials."*]

The "Talent Man Story" is actually a parable and not a story, and is about three (arguably four) men, so actually the plural; (Talent

Men); should be utilized. A *story* is about actual events using actual names; but *parables* are not actual recollections, and are used as teaching tools.

A talent is usually considered as a Hebrew unit of measure, ranging between eighty and one hundred twenty pounds, depending upon the source, and whether it is a *common* talent or a *royal* talent being referenced. But this is all nonsense, as there is not and never has been any such Hebrew unit of measure—statements to the contrary notwithstanding.

The word "talent" seems to be an altered and truncated form of the Greek word *talantŏn*. Talantŏn is not a measure of *objective* weight such as pound or kilogram; but rather a *subjective* balancing weight or weight to be *borne* or *carried*.

What is it that this *talantŏn* is balancing? According to the "Talent Man Story," what is being balanced by this talantŏn, is *dunamis*. The word "ability" in this story is actually not *dynamikós*, or natural power; but *dunamis* or supernatural power.

Again, in Hebrew there is "that word" that is sometimes translated as *oracle*, and sometimes translated as *burden*; and thus includes both (*dunamis* and *talantŏn*) meanings (see Proverbs 30:1; and Malachi 1:1, comparing KJV with NAS)

This actual Hebrew word again is:

"4853 massâ'; from 5375; a *burden*; spec. *tribute*, or (abstr.) *porterage*; fig. an *utterance*,..." chiefly a *doom*, espec. *singing*; mental, *desire*: - burden, carry away, prophesy..."

"Porterage" generally refers to carrying a weight or burden; e.g.; a porter.

Thus there are several seemingly unrelated meanings to massâ' et. seq. They can be translated as an utterance, prophetic or "retrophetic," (prophesy about past events) in nature—hence the translations as *oracle*; as well as a *burden* or lifting; as well as desire and ability.

As previously addressed, it seems clear that massâ' represents the understanding or comprehension of a given actuality in Hebrew; for which the use of both *dunamis* as well as *talantŏn*, and comprehending their relationship; is required for understanding or comprehending of the very same actuality in Greek. The Hebrew massâ' = (Greek) dunamis + (Greek) talantŏn.

Dunamis may *appear* to exist alone; but again it cannot exist without the corresponding talantŏn. However; the mere *existence* of the talantŏn, does not necessarily mean it will be "carried." This is what happened with the "one talent man."

This of course leads to the common "understanding" (doxa), of terms such as *talented*, or the aforementioned *gifted*.

The common use of *talented*, generally refers to some type of extraordinary skill in some particular area, which is either extreme *dynamikós* or *dunamis*. And often times that which is considered as extreme *dynamikós*, is in fact unrecognized *dunamis*. But the word *talented* actually literally refers to the *burden* part, and not the corresponding *skill*.

And the use of *gifted* implies that there is only the skill, without the corresponding burden. Hence it is considered a gift, meaning an unbalanced condition; which simply cannot exist. "Free—just pay separate fee," is not free.

A talantŏn can sometimes be referred to as passion, drive, etc.; the nature of which can often seem to be "downright nuts," and may even be mistaken for a problem by others. "Junior; you're not at that piano again are you?" "He drives me nuts. Since he was able to walk, I can't get him away from that #$%* piano. I think there may be problem."

"Hello! . . . There is a problem, and that problem is *you*." Mozart is reputed to have been "piano proficient" and a composer at age five.

When a talantŏn seems to be present, the same should be examined in order to determine if it is in fact a talantŏn. This is much simpler than it may seem, as it merely has to be determined if "working" it will result in any type if sinful behavior. God will not provide a sinful talantŏn, as there is another who will most certainly, (absolute superlative noted), try. [That "talantŏn" which the enemy will attempt to provide, is actually an "a-talantŏn."]

This determination has nothing to do with what others may think, or if it seems bizarre; as the talantŏn is only one half of the potential actuality. If one could develop the *dunamis* to walk on water, or even fly through the air; it must be asked precisely what one might reasonably expect the corresponding *talantŏn* to *appear* to be?

Sometimes when someone says: "What are you waiting for—the spirit to move you?"; the correct answer is: "As a matter of fact—yes."

There are many "forces" in the universe, each of which can correctly be termed "a force." But if it is the power of the Holy Ghost, it must be described similarly with the *definite* article, and *capital* letters as "The Force."

It was not the power of Gabriel that was responsible for the "Immaculate Conception." As it reads, Gabe's purpose was to obtain Mary's "informed consent." It was the Holy Ghost that provided what was necessary, including the aforementioned "y chromosome." Women essentially by definition do not contain this "y chromosome," and said chromosome is necessary in order to be male—any current attempted *subjective* determinations of gender notwithstanding.

It is known that the individual soul exists after physical death. The Bible tells us of the souls under the altar who had consciousness and communicated with God. The Bible also tells us about those souls contacted by necromancy. These were also conscious and able to communicate with man. So there is no question of the continued existence of that immaterial quantity (soul) that departed the body at physical death. And there is no question of the individuality of these entities—at least those who were "under the altar," and those who are or were contacted via necromancy.

There is no question that the Holy Ghost has the *means* to *reintroduce* into a physical body, that which once had resided in a physical body. This very thing happened with the aforementioned dead man who came back to life after merely touching Elsiha's bones, Lazarus, and others. It must also be asked how, (by what means), that *that* which Jesus had commanded to the Father, later returned to His physical body?

The only notable difference between the events of resurrection, and reincarnation; is that these reintroductions via *resurrection* were into the *same* bodies. So it seems that the *means* is readily available. In fact it could be argued that resurrection requires a greater quantity of dunamis than would reincarnation. This is because in resurrection, the physical body has had time to degrade via "biological death," (which begins minutes after "clinical death"), and according to *natural* law. However a healthy newborn taking its first breath is "ready to go."

With regard to the *opportunity*, babies are born all of the time. It is God who decides which soul enters or is "breathed into his nostrils." Thus God has an essentially constant opportunity to introduce any soul; either "new" or "used;" into a physical vessel capable of containing the same.

The only thing left would be *motive*. Are those who incessantly claim that "no one knows the mind of God," correct in their position that despite numerous *resurrections*, under no circumstances and at no time, would God have any *motive* to participate in *reincarnation*? Or does a reasonable read of His Word; particularly with respect to Elijah; prove that these aforementioned claimants are factually incorrect?

CHAPTER 9

Internals—Externals

Internals

Thus far, much has been discussed about what the Bible does, and does not have to say about reincarnation. This of course is an entirely different matter than the matter of what it is that the Bible actually *says*, actually *means*. One cannot easily control or change the actual original verbiage. *Easily* must be included here, as some have tried and were "caught" by Strong—but there is no reason to believe that Strong "caught" them all.

For example: in the case of Matthew 17:21 regarding the "fasting and prayer" to cast out demons, some Bible "versions" include it; some include it, but dispute its authenticity; and some do not include it at all. In the case of the latter, there simply is no verse 21 present at all. Like omitting the thirteenth floor on some buildings, Matthew 17:20 is immediately followed by Matthew 17:22. However a similar passage contained in Mark 9:29, as of yet appears to remain "officially" undisputed.

But with regard to reincarnation, most Western religions will simply not entertain even the possibility that what the Bible states, could in any way mean that which appears to be the most likely meaning. Thus they are forced to engage in philosophunculistic and fanciful interpretations—incessantly proffering dubious and unlikely meanings for that which is reasonably clear, and thus most likely represents the truth. They not only assiduously look for; but staunchly and consistently *claim* that there are zebras; where it is reasonably clear that only horses exist—*that's the surprise*. And the unfortunate reasons for this have been discussed.

If it is assumed that any living individual represents a set, then what are the members of this set? Why body (soma), and soul of course. But of course *nothing* is ever that easy. With regard to reincarnation, clearly it is the *soul* that would be the most important member of this set, and thus generally the main concern—same soul, different body. But even the soul is often considered by many to have subsets such as: "will, intellect, and emotions;" as this is in fact how "soul" is defined by most.

But almost without exception, *memory* or *recollection* is never included in this "will, intellect and emotions" definition; and neither is *imagination*.

In certain senses, *recollection* (past), *imagination* (future), and *perception* (present), form another type of trinity; with *time* as the differentiator. Recollection and imagination are very similar. *Recollection* refers to "a thing" that may have existed in the past; *imagination* refers to something that may exist in the future; and *perception* is considered to be "real time"—only for that particular instant.

But imagination alone is insufficient. In order to "actualize" or bring "the thing" into actuality or existence, a force is required, which leads to another trinity. The *will* to bring it into existence; the *force*, either dunamis or dynamikós ; and the resultant "*thing*."

This is precisely what God did "In the Beginning." Although there is no recorded: "Let there be" in Genesis 1:1, the process remains the same. And it must be asked precisely who or what is the "us" later in: "Let us make?" Perhaps the third part of the Trinity; AKA; The Holy Ghost, provides one possible answer.

If the "body and soul" are considered what in a "living" individual represents a "set;" then these two members of this set; "body and soul" each also have subsets.

Clearly the *body* as a member of the "living individual" set; also has subsets; such as cellular, histological, visceral, etc. These often form the basis for the various "systems" in Anatomy, Physiology; and virtually all the human biological sciences.

The soul likewise has subsets, including the aforementioned *will*, *intellect*, and *emotions*. But any living entity capable of conscious thought, likewise has memory or recollection capabilities abilities in some fashion. Are these memories or recollections part of the body, or part of the soul? Clearly they are part of the soul. Whether they are also part of the *physical* body; as opposed to say being contained solely in the immaterial *Akashic Records*; remains essentially unknown at this time.

In the case of damage to the physical body resulting in memory loss, is it a *physical* recollection "storage area" that is damaged? Or is it the *physical* area that allows *access* to that information stored in the *immaterial* realm that is damaged?

The "set" known as a living human being has many members. Some are material or physical; and some are immaterial or non-physical. But *all* that exists in said human being; ultimately is *caused* by that which is *immaterial*; as can also be said about the entire *material* realm.

"Not so," many would say. "That which is the physical body is not caused by immaterial, but by genes; and genes are quite material." But the truth is that it is not actually the genes, but the *information* (code) contained in these genes that produces and assist in maintaining the physical body. No reasonable person would claim that it is the physical storage device containing software that is the software itself; and therefore the very software itself is physical.

If there is reincarnation, then at least some of the *immaterial* attributes of a previously living (physically alive) human being, are again "breathed into the nostrils;" i.e.; re-breathed; but here utilizing the "nostrils" of *another* and *different* physical body. If it can be stipulated that the *cause* of said previously living human being is ultimately *immaterial*, it should be asked which of these immaterial entities it is that is or are again "breathed?"

"The soul" would most likely be the first answer. But as previously stated, the soul is often described as "will, intellect, and emotions." Obviously this definition is inadequate, as it does not reasonably address the "I am," or consciousness; i.e.; self-awareness—the same being the only thing true solipsists truly believe.

One cannot easily have *will* without consciousness. Rocks do not generally fall as the result of the will of the rock. Likewise *intellect* seems to require some level of consciousness. And even though *emotions* can be present while sleeping, it seems *some* level of consciousness is required for any emotional perception, or subsequent recollection.

This *consciousness* or *self-awareness* represents the most fundamental requirement for the purposes of reincarnation. This self-awareness was seen previously with the souls under the altar who: "*...cried with a loud voice, saying, How long, O Lord, holy and true, dost thou not judge and avenge our blood on them that dwell on the earth?*" This self-awareness was also seen with the necromancy: "*And Samuel said to Saul, Why hast thou disquieted me, to bring me up?*" It must be remembered that these are direct Bible passages, and there are more.

In each case, these were "disembodied souls," who maintained their individual self-awareness. And it seems that in addition to self-awareness, each had will, intellect, and emotions. These souls were not at that time incarnate, although each had once been.

Again, it seems that the reintroduction of this self-awareness (I am) into a *different* physical body; (as opposed to the reintroduction into the *same* body as is the case with resurrection); is the key to reincarnation. Thus those who object to even seriously discussing reincarnation; are therefore necessarily objecting to discussing just that one difference.

Most or all Western religions agree that this reintroduction into the *same* physical body—even days later (resurrection); is truth, and in fact that this happened more than once.

Internals—Externals

But to even so much as suggest that if a *different* physical body were involved, that this could even be *possible*; (even with a God "With Whom all things are possible"); is an entirely different matter, and to many represents "absolute heresy."

Of course when a patient "dies" and then "comes back," this event is accepted as a fact, and could be considered as a type of "resurrection." But here "clinical death" is generally based upon when the heart stops beating, as this is clinically demonstrable. It is not based upon the exit of the soul.

Many in the health care delivery system maintain that ultimately everyone dies from cardiac arrest, as that is how "clinical death" is defined. [This is to be distinguished from the aforementioned subsequent "biological death," which is when significant catabolic physical changes begin.]

There currently is no reliable or objective way to directly ascertain if and/or when the soul actually exited the body in the "short term."

These "near death" experiences require some level of consciousness, as well as "recollective" capability—at least if the story is ever to be told. That seemingly ubiquitous moving "toward the light" may in fact be the imminent exiting of the soul (a process); which is then countermanded by free will; or perhaps a firm "no" from "above," in those "near death" experiences.

Distinctions must be made here between "I am;" "I know I am;" and "I know who I am."

The first is the minimal form of self-awareness. The second is a bit more introspective; and the third likely represents the antithesis of the condition of John the Baptist when asked if he was Elijah—assuming he was not lying.

"Who I am" can represent a myriad of factors, including unwarranted opinions and falsehoods; e. g.; "Just who does he think he is...?" A better way to consider this is "I know *what* I am." The same of course is being a child of God; made in His image and likeness; and brought into existence as a "dual being," for the purpose of conducting warfare. The objective of this warfare is the redemption of the earth just as we are told in Genesis 1:28. And no matter what else may happen, this *purpose* will never change until this redemptive process is complete.

It must once again be remembered that God Himself called us tsâbâ'; translated as "hosts," which again is:

> "6635 tsâbâ' or tsᵉba'ah from 6633; a *mass* of persons (or fig. things), espec. reg. organized for war (an *army*); by impl. a *campaign*,... 6633 tsâbâ' a prim. root; to *mass* (an army or servants): - assemble, fight, perform, muster, wait upon, war."

He instructed us to kabâsh (H), or in more present day vernacular "put the *kibosh* [again kybosh spelling duly noted]," on the earth. Thus when the Bible is said to be a "book about redemption" this represents truth. The problem is that this is generally understood to refer exclusively to the redemption of *man*; and it is not generally understood to mean the redemption of the *earth*—even though God's instructions are clear in this regard.

Christians with this misunderstanding; since this redemption of man has already happened, (It is Finished.); are then left with the fair question of: "Other than spreading the gospel (good news) of "Christianity" (which is generally considered *salvation* via *Jesus*, as the Second Part; and not the actual *Christos* or *dunamis* via The Holy Ghost, as the Third Part); what is it that remains for Christians to do?" Realizing this, it seems that many religious leaders have elected to engage in quasi-political matters, without ever being "elected" to anything

If it is stipulated that at a minimum it must be this same self-awareness (I am) that is reintroduced into a physical body for either resurrection or reincarnation, it must be asked what else may "go along" with it?

Barring unusual circumstances, it seems that the same will, intellect, and emotions are or were contained in those who were *resurrected*. And it also seems that memories or recollections, or at least access to these; are also included in those *resurrected*.

But what else besides this self-awareness is included in the case of *reincarnation*?

Internals—Externals

The answer is whatever it is that God determines should go along. This is not meant to be flippant, but rather as a truth that appears much simpler than it actually is. If God chooses reincarnation; as is the most likely explanation for John the Baptist; then there are or were reasons for this. After all, the "spirit and power of Elijah," sounds remarkably similar to the "spirit and power of Elijah"—and for good reason. Consequently, if someone states: "spirit and power of Elijah," they probable mean "spirit and power of Elijah;" rather than merely providing a starting point for someone else to many centuries later conclude that what this statement actually means is anything but: "spirit and power of Elijah."

But John the Baptist either did not know "who he was," or he lied about it. Assuming JTB was actually *unaware* of his former status, (as Elijah); then; unlike as is generally the case with memory and *resurrection*; either God did not desire this knowledge to "go along" with JTB's self-awareness; or God somehow made a mistake.

There are those who claim to be able to assist in extracting information about "previous lives," or *regression*, and here defined as such in this particular usage. If it is stipulated that this is possible; it must be asked wherein this information exists prior to said extraction? To the extent that regression is an actuality, this extracted information either exists in the physical vessel of the person from whom it is being extracted; or is accessed via the immaterial; e.g.; said "Akashic Records," or something else, (x factor).

It seems that a *new* physical vessel could not contain this information unless acted upon by an immaterial force. So either way, this information likely resides in the immaterial. It was dunamis that brought a dead man back to physical life just from contact with the bones of a long deceased Elisha. There is no record of any aspect of Elisha's personality being involved.

Since even so much as the very existence of any actual photographs and or videos of Elijah and John the Baptist remains highly classified, and are likely stored under heavy guard in Area 51; it is not known if John the Baptist physically resembled Elijah. The truth is that he may or may not have. Why would he have? He would have if God had determined that the purposes for which JTB was brought into existence were best served by this resemblance. If not, then JTB's physical appearance would likely have been that which would best serve both his and His purposes *at that time*.

If God desires a particular type of *physical vessel*, it seems that there are two ways that He can accomplish this:

One would be to reintroduce (breathe) a particular "I am" into the new vessel (newborn) that most closely resembles that vessel which God desires. But since man's free will is involved, this can present problems with respect to both *timing* and *location*. This new vessel may be "ready" too late to fulfill God's purpose at a particular material or earthly *time*.

Or it could be the case that the *timing* may be perfect, but the physical *location* would present a problem. What if Zacharias had lived in a different part of the world at that time? Or what if he had "shot his mouth off?" Surely God has the power to cause a thing to be in a particular place at a particular time, but this introduces more "man variables."

Or God can directly intervene in the *formation* of the vessel; just as he did alone with Adam, or later with God's "partner" in this who was named Mary.

All material existence ultimately originates from the immaterial realm, as does the *vital life force*; which *maintains* the physical vessel when that dual condition of physical life is present. There is that which is; and there is that which is not. This seemingly sophomoric statement is often forgotten by many; and represents the very *antithesis* of the statist's "creed." [For further information about this "creed," see: "*Statists Saving One*"]

Again, for the purposes of analysis, *actuality* is what currently exists or what is. *Reality* is that which is believed to exist based upon perception and other factors.

The process of an *actuality* becoming a *reality* is called *realization*. The *reality* of a true mirage includes water; but the *actuality* of a mirage includes no water. No actuality can ever be 100% accurately perceived, thus reality always falls short.

Under *normal* circumstances, one perceives only some portion of that which exists. The *reality* of a thing is *caused* by, or can be considered the *effect* of, some degree of perception of the *actuality*. It is true that there can be false perceptions such as the aforementioned mirage; or a movie (which all involved usually know the true actuality); but the reality is the *result* of some type of actuality. Something exists and is perceived, and even if perceived incompletely, or erroneously; (e.g.; the mirage); the actuality *produces* a reality through perception. *Realization* is largely a *passive* event.

Thus this is as opposed to *actualization*. To *actualize* something, is to bring something from the thought process; (quasi-reality); to a current actuality. As stated; one can ultimately produce an actuality through a reality (actualization), but not just by the existence of the reality alone—at least when confined to the material realm. *Actualization* is largely an *active* event.

Imagination is similar to a reality, but with the subjective knowledge or belief that "the thing" does not yet exist. *Recollection* is also similar to a reality, but with the subjective knowledge or belief that "the thing" may no longer exist.

Unless the immaterial realm is involved, the existence of a reality alone will not bring into existence an actuality; neither will reality alone cause any changes in an existing actuality. Although a reality can change based upon actuality; an actuality will in no way exist or change, simply and solely because of the existence of a reality—again at least when confined to the material realm. An actuality; even an immaterial actuality; always represents only *that which is*.

Externals

When considering reincarnation, it is the *immaterial* portion of man that normally is under discussion. The "subject" is that which enters the material portion of man, as per the *general* process as described in Genesis 2:7. (First the material vessel is formed, and then the soul enters.) It was not so much the *body* of John the Baptist that was the issue; but rather the particular *"spirit and power"* that was contained therein.

Thus reincarnation is *immaterial* focused in this sense, and not *material* focused; although it is the presence of the physical body containing this *"spirit and power"* that is the "evidence." It is primarily concerned with the active *transmission* of the immaterial "used" or "pre-owned" soul; and not the passive *reception* of the soul by the *material* body that is generally the focus of any discussion of reincarnation.

To phrase this a bit differently, the question of reincarnation is primarily one of whether God re-sends a soul into another and *different* body or soma; and not so much whether a given body or soma is capable of receiving a reincarnated "soul," or must receive only a "new soul." Identification of "past personalities" is generally based upon the person, (immaterial), *contained* in the vessel; and not the vessel (material).

If it can be stipulated; even if only for the purpose of discussion, that reincarnation exists; then *structurally*, (whatever this may mean with respect to the immaterial realm); this immaterial portion or soul remains structurally a "relative constant," and the physical vessel structurally is a "relative variable" while the "physically alive" state is in process, and afterward.

It would be fair to state that the physical body is a "more constant" variable during the "physically alive" state than afterward—because of the presence of the vital life force. Meaning: that this immaterial portion or soul continues to exist, and maintains its immaterial "structure," after the physical vessel becomes incapable of containing it. But then the physical or material vessel; no longer maintained by the "vital life force;" becomes "less structured" as entropy proceeds.

If reincarnation is a fact, then the same immaterial entity is contained in different physical vessels, at different times; and all and always in furtherance of God's will. It must be remembered that although man has some say in the choices with respect to the

Internals—Externals

attributes of the *vessel*; what it is that is "breathed" into that vessel belongs largely; although not necessarily exclusively; to God.

The use of "largely" is deliberate. As will be seen shortly, in certain senses man can exert some influence with respect to what it is that is "breathed in"—whether man is aware he is doing this or not.

And the term "not necessarily exclusively" was also chosen with great care, as depending upon man's actions and inactions; things can be "breathed into" man; that are not of God;"—whether man is aware this is happening or not.

The concept of any "constant structure" in the *immaterial* realm in terms of an actual "structure," is as difficult; or perhaps even more difficult to grasp than $\sqrt{-1}$. And in a realm with no time and thus no duration, a "changing structure," in terms of "changing" is likewise difficult to comprehend.

The square root of a given number (e.g.; $\sqrt{X}$), is the number, that when multiplied by itself, will produce that given number (X). A negative number multiplied by a negative number (here itself) will always produce a positive number. Thus $\sqrt{-1}$ only exists in the imagination; and is considered an "imaginary number," quasi-eponymously symbolized by "*i*." These "imaginary numbers" have a *reality*, and are used in calculations; even though mathematicians agree there is no corresponding *actuality* for the mathematician's *reality* of "*i*."

But that person you knew and liked so much was an *actuality*. In fact the "true person," that "animating" or immaterial portion once contained in a vessel *still exists*—even if interactions with it are difficult. This "immaterial structure" remains as a "relative constant," even if the physical "remains" do not.

With regard to understanding "immaterial structure," simply because a rational *reality* is difficult or impossible, this in no way changes the *actuality* for which this reality is being sought—assuming of course that unlike imaginary numbers, said given *actuality* in fact exists.

And what about function? *Structure* is generally what it is, in furtherance of *function*. When God brings into existence a particular "living soul," (physical life), for the first time; or resurrects, or reincarnates a soul; it must be asked if there are functional reasons for this action, or if this is done for no particular functional reason.

Does God bring into existence souls that will never be incarnated? The truth is that the answer to this question is unknown. It is also true that the subject under discussion is reincarnation, and thus any "never to be incarnated" souls; as important as they may otherwise be; would not seem to be particularly germane to this subject.

It must once again be remembered here that man was created in God's own words as tsâbâ': "to mass (an army or servants): - assemble, fight, perform, muster, wait upon, war;" and was instructed by God to "put the kibosh" on the earth.

It must also be remembered that the overall general physical structure of the material part of man was originally chosen by God when He *created* man—presumably in furtherance of this same function. This physical structure was maintained when the original created hosts had offspring; and when God much later *formed* Adam.

Thus we have the general physical structure of man originally chosen by God; as well as that particular "soul" which animates this physical structure also being chosen by God. As previously stated, man has some control over the attributes of the physical vessel, but these characteristics are relatively minor. If it is stipulated that a height of 5'5" is relatively "short" for a man; and a height of 6'5" is relatively tall for a man; the man who is 6'5" and considered as "tall," is a mere 18.2% taller than the man who is 5'5" and is considered "short," or perhaps "substantially vertically challenged." And it must be asked how much other traits such as gender, hair color, eye color, etc., are relevant to man's function according to God.

It seems reasonable that an omniscient and omnipotent God would choose a *particular* physical vessel *structure*, (within His original previously chosen *general* parameters); that would best conform with His plan for that particular "soul," (either "new" or "used"), which He plans to introduce into that very same vessel. This may be one reason why the physical vessels of suspected

Internals—Externals

"reincarnationees" of those who physically died at a relatively young age, can resemble their prior physical vessels. Their original vessel was designed for a function that was prematurely terminated. Thus since their *original* function remains, the chosen vessel structure is similar.

This is done in order to optimize *functional* success as tsâbâ' in furtherance of kiboshing the earth. One might ask: "For what possible reason would God need a basketball player and an entertainer to put the kibosh on and redeem the earth?" The mere asking of such a question proves that one claims to know the mind of God; and to them this "knowledge" includes no subset of basketball and entertainment—at least with respect to man's God stated role as tsâbâ'.

God could have introduced a "soul" designed to play basketball into newborn Mickey Rooney, who became 5'2"; and introduced a "soul" designed to be an entertainer into newborn Wilt Chamberlain, who became 7'1"; but He did not.

If God wished to reincarnate either of these "souls," it would make little sense to reverse His original choice of vessels—*assuming their new functions were to be the same as before.*

As previously addressed, in a real sense when man chooses the physical attributes of offspring to the extent that he is able, man is likewise placing restrictions upon the souls that God will choose to "breath into" these vessels; whether a "new soul" or a reincarnated one.

Two relatively "vertically challenged" individuals, should not expect that God would want their offspring to be a star basketball player. This is not to say that it could not be done, but only that the road is much more difficult.

Again stipulating that reincarnation is an actuality, and thus the Bible is stating the truth; why was it that John the Baptist did not physically resemble Elijah—assuming of course that he did not? It seems clear that God wanted us to *know* that JTB was Elijah, as His Word is reasonably clear; and again, JTB's mother's name Elizabeth *means* "house of Elijah." The most likely answer is that each had different *functions*. Meaning; that since Elijah and JTB had different *functions*, the vessels God chose to contain the soul of

Elijah/JTB were the best available that were most consistent with these different functions.

It must be remembered what God was required to do to get Zachariah and Elizabeth "in a family way"—including rendering Zachariah effectively dumbstruck. And it must also be remembered that in order for God to get the vessel he wanted for Jesus, He had to do half of it himself via "The Force."

Was the vessel of JTB the perfect vessel for the "soul" of JTB? This is not known. Was the vessel for the "soul" of God Himself via Mary the perfect vessel? This is not known either. But the answer to each is likely no; as once God gets *man* involved, the devil gets involved. And of course the more danger any given action represents to the devil, the more involved the devil becomes—at least up to a point.

If it is stipulated that God will "re-send" a previously physically "alive" soul back for TDY (temporary duty), His choices for the vessel are based upon at least two important criteria:

The first is the nature of the "mission;" i.e.; what is the primary function for which the vessel is required? "Kiboshing" the earth is very broad, and thus is more like a *goal* than an *objective*. Thus the "primary function" of any given tsâbâ', needs to be much more specific.

And the second: Which individuals currently exist that are capable of providing this vessel in the form that most closely matches the desired functions, via the "normal" reproductive mechanism? In the case of the "first Adam," the answer was none.

"That aint so, God is all powerful and can do whatever He wants to." A statement like this shows substantial lack of understanding of process, unintended consequences; and most particularly: *balance*.

God formed the "First Adam" to begin the process for the bloodline for the "Last Adam." This process took place many millennia ago, and yet later God *still* had to intervene with Mary to provide the "y chromosome;" and no one has suggested that "Joe" was a "bad guy." God follows His own rules—including that any "violations" are "paid for." Thus God cannot make two plus two equal four in some instances, (say when a check is written); and

Internals—Externals

then make it equal to eight in other instances, (say when that same check is deposited)—lest the entire universe collapse. Certainly God can obtain the same *effect*, but it must be balanced.

So except as noted, God is and has always been forced to utilize that which is available to Him,

Thus if the "return TDY" (temporary duty) is to perform the same or similar functions, it seems logical that God would choose the best available vessel for whatever these functions are to be.

Does a "soul's" "return" for the *same* function necessarily prove failure the first time? Probably not for a variety of reasons including:

1. The deceptive actions of the enemy shortening the period of "physical life."
2. The nature of the function being so complex, as to require additional efforts. Here it may actually have been *success* and not failure that prompted the "resending." "He is good at it, it is just that it is a really big job."
3. The deceptive actions of the enemy "undoing" previous progress. This is one reason why Jesus performed some miracles that had already been performed by others before Him: "They forgot."
4. The "X" factor or factors.

It must also be asked how an omniscient God could *not* know that a given host would fail; and also given a given host's previous failure or failures, why would He ever send him back again? It must be remembered that it is functioning as tsâbâ', and not acceptance of salvation that is under discussion here.

It seems reasonable that "success" in "kiboshing," means any movement *forward* in the redemption process; with the *degree* of success determined by the *amount* of movement forward. "Failure" would then be considered as either *backward* movement, (perhaps here yet another use of the term *regression*); or *no* movement forward.

And it must likewise be asked that if in fact reincarnation is an actuality, does this represent a *punishment* or a *reward* to *that* particular "soul?" It seems that both religiously and Biblically, (these are often at odds), the afterlife is much more pleasant than is "physical life"—assuming of course that salvation was available and accepted.

This is a bit more complex than it sounds. With the "Transmigration of Soul's" belief, man is returned in a "lesser state" for a "sinful" physical life. But that is not what is under discussion here. It is not the level of sophistication of a reincarnated host representing "punishment or reward." It is whether returning a "soul" to physical life—period—represents a *punishment* or a *reward*.

As stated, the "afterlife" is both religiously and Biblically considered as far superior to physical life for a "saved soul." "Streets paved with gold," no devil to deal with, no sin, and perhaps maybe even being reunited with loved ones. Here it seems that reincarnating a "soul" from this more desirable existence to a less desirable existence would be *punishment*. [Reportedly, Katharine Hepburn was once asked if reincarnation is real. She is reputed to have replied: "God I hope not."]

But if "quality in kiboshing" is stipulated as that which is desired, and is the true criterion for reincarnating a "soul;" then it seems reasonable that God would tend to want to reincarnate those who qualify for the "A team." Thus with this stipulation, the "best players" are the most likely to be "punished" by going from the more desirable existence to the less—again.

But there also is the *reward* of "moving the ball" in God's direction of "therapeutic intent." This of course assumes that a particular "soul" knows what he is doing (kiboshing); *and* finds pleasing God rewarding.

It seems most likely that John the Baptist earned the "trifecta." First appearing as Elijah; then appearing as JTB; and then possibly appearing once again as Elijah in original "corpus," as one of the two "witnesses" during "end times."

In addition, if JTB was in fact Elijah reincarnated; this likely somehow happened while Elijah was still physically alive; either somewhere in heaven; or more likely by some means from the *kŏlpŏs*, or by some "X" factor." It must be remembered that there is no evidence to suggest that Elijah physically died at any time after Elisha saw Elijah "go." This represents another rather complex immaterial/material dilemma.

Numbers 14:18 (KJV) tells us:

> "*The LORD is longsuffering, and of great mercy,*
> *forgiving iniquity and transgression,*
> *and by no means clearing the guilty,*
> *visiting the iniquity of the fathers upon*
> *the children unto the third and*
> *fourth generation.*"[137]

And Deuteronomy 5:9-10 (KJV) tells us:

> "*Thou shalt not bow down thyself unto them,*
> *nor serve them: for I the LORD thy God*
> *am a jealous God, visiting the iniquity*
> *of the fathers upon the children unto the third and*
> *fourth generation of them that hate me,*
>
> *And shewing mercy unto thousands of them*
> *that love me and keep my commandments.*"[138]

So at first blush, it seems that in Numbers 14:18, we have a pretty nasty God here. He will not only punish sinners, but He will extract His "pound of flesh" from the offspring as far out as the great grandchildren. No wonder the disciples wanted to know if the man who was born blind was being punished for the sins of his parents.

It also appears that we may also have either a *lying* God, or possibly a *schizophrenic* God here as well; as we are first told here in Numbers 14:18: "*The LORD is longsuffering, and of great mercy, forgiving iniquity and transgression.*" Thus we are first told that God is a forgiving and merciful God. But then we are immediately told that *"and by no means clearing the guilty, visiting the iniquity of the fathers upon the children unto the third and fourth generation."*

It must be asked what is meant here by "clearing" and "guilty?" It contextually appears that *"by no means clearing the guilty"* may mean to simply transfer the penalty from the "guilty" to his or her offspring—assuming of course that "guilty" refers to the one who committed the *"iniquity and transgression"* for which *"forgiving"* was promised in the first part of the passage.

If this were so, then the passage would better read: "The LORD is longsuffering, and of great mercy, forgiving iniquity and transgression (for the one who committed it), (but) by no means clearing the guilty, (but instead) visiting the iniquity of the fathers upon the children unto the third and fourth generation, (who may commit iniquities and transgressions of their own, but did not commit the particular iniquities and transgressions for which they are now being punished.") Here being *"of great mercy, forgiving iniquity and transgression,"* would not be *removing* the penalty; but simply *transferring* the penalty.

This sounds neither like justice, nor a "just God." In fact, what this does sound like, is support for the "Transmigration of Souls" view on reincarnation. "Sin now, and I will reincarnate you at a lower level."

The actual Hebrew word translated as "clearing" is:

"5352 nâqâh; a prim. root; to *be* (or *make*) *clean* (lit. or fig.) by impl. (in an adverse sense) to *be bare*, i.e. *extirpated*: - acquit..."[39]

Following is the actual Hebrew word translated as "guilty;" followed by two words derived from the same:

"816 'âsham; or 'âshêm; a prim. root; to *be guilty*; by impl. to *be punished* or *perish*..."[40]

"818 'âshêm; from 816; *guilty*; hence *presenting a sin – offering*: - one which is faulty, guilty."[41]

"817 'âshâm; from 816 *guilt*; by impl. a *fault*; also a *sin offering*. – guiltiness (offering for) sin, trespass (offering)."[142]

Two of these three Hebrew "âsh" words have to do with "sin offerings," that God will not make *nâqâh*, or "clean." So even if sin offerings are made, it seems they will not work according to these passages.

Perhaps the *second* of the above verses in Deuteronomy 5:9-10 (KJV); which contains essentially some of the very same verbiage, can provide some clarity.

The first part of Deuteronomy 5:9 states: *"Thou shalt not bow down thyself unto them, nor serve them: for I the LORD thy God am a jealous God..."*

In Numbers 14:18 (KJV), there were only three entities or "players" involved. There was the Lord, the sinner/father, and the "children."

But here in Deuteronomy 5:9, a "them" appears twice, and refers to none of these three; but rather seems to refer to something else entirely: *"Thou shalt not bow down thyself unto them, nor serve them: for I the LORD thy God am a jealous God."*

And the *context* reasonably infers that this "them," refers to some purported other "gods" to which *"I the LORD thy God"* is referring. And jealousy, often confused with envy; means distrust of someone—usually a spouse, but here the jealousy must either refer to these "them," (other "gods"), or refers to God's children.

As stated, the second part of Deuteronomy 5:9 contains the same verbiage in Numbers 14:18, but adds the "prepositional phrase:" *"of them that hate me;"* here in its entirety: *"visiting the iniquity of the fathers upon the children unto the third and fourth generation of them that hate me."*

So here in Deuteronomy 5:9, the concept of *emotion* vs. *action* (or *inaction*) is introduced. Unlike in Numbers 14:18, this *"visiting the iniquity"* in Deuteronomy, is because of *hatred* of the "Lord," and not *sin* due to action or inaction.

And this is confirmed by that which immediately follows Deuteronomy 5:9, and is contained in Deuteronomy 5:10: *"And shewing mercy unto thousands of them that love me and keep my commandments."*

This is hate vs. love: *"Them that hate me"* v. *"Them that love me."* But there is also a second part to the requirement for God's "mercy." The same is the *"keep my commandments"* part. It does not state "obey" in the translation.

But wait a minute. Doesn't it amount to the same thing? Isn't keeping the commandments and obeying the commandments the same thing? God didn't say if you just *"love me."* What He said represents a "two pronged" test. He said: if you: *"love me and keep my commandments."* So aren't we back to the same thing. If you disobey my commandments, this is sin; and I will show you my "mercy" by punishing your offspring for your sins, instead of punishing you. [One might argue that the federal debt amounts to the same thing, but any "political discussion" is deliberately avoided here.]

"The Commandments appear for the first time in Exodus 20.

"And in Exodus 20:6 we are told:

> "And shewing mercy unto thousands
> of them that love me,
> and keep my commandments."[SH1]

"One might reasonably first ask what need there would be for mercy to be shown (shewn) to those who both love God and also keep, (i.e.; obey), (His) commandments? *Mercy* generally refers to not getting what one deserves (usually in the negative); as opposed to *grace*, which is getting what one does not deserve, and is usually in the positive. So then it must be asked that if "keep" means obey, then why would there be any need for any type of mercy to be shown to those "thousands" who are obeying said Commandments. The answer of course: is that by definition there would be no need whatsoever for any such mercy.

"The actual Hebrew word translated here as "mercy" is:

> "2617 checed; from 2616; *kindness*;..."[SH2]

> "2616 châcad; a prim. root; prop. perh. to *bow* (the neck only [comp. 2603] courtesy to an equal), i.e. to *be kind*;..."[SH3] as opposed to

> "2603 chânan; a prim. root [comp. 2583]; prop. to *bend* or stoop in kindness to an inferior; to *favor bestow*..."[SH4]

"A distinction is made here with regard to the roots of the Hebrew word originally contained in Exodus 20:6, which is translated as "mercy" (checed from châcad). It seems that the actual definition of *checed* is concerned with showing or providing kindness or courtesy to an *equal*; versus the similar word *chânan*, which is concerned with providing kindness to an *inferior*.

"Thus it remains unclear as to why the translators chose "mercy" as the English translation of checed; as this seems antithetical to its actual meaning. More precisely; in order to show "mercy" one must necessarily be in a position of superiority with regard to the potential recipient of any "mercy," at least with respect to that particular situation. Here with the use of *checed*, a position of equality is required.

"In Exodus 20:6, it is God who is or was communicating, so it seems likely He would have known which Hebrew word to choose to convey His precise meaning. And He chose the word checed and not chânan. Thus what is clear, at least in this regard; is that from this standpoint; with regard to showing kindness in *this* context; He, (God), considers or considered us to be equals—else He would have used chânan—which He did not.

"This may be disturbing to those who attempt to reconcile that which is originally and by design brought into existence in the "image and likeness of God (H. Sapiens);" with their view of the actual (real time) *current* state of H. Sapiens. This is the inevitable result of conflating the original pure and perfect product, with the current polluted result.

"But it seems there is an additional requirement in order to obtain said kindness from the standpoint of being shown kindness as an equal and not as an inferior; as it must be remembered we were told: *"And shewing mercy unto thousands of them that love me, and keep my commandments."*

"This can be rephrased as a reversed "if then" declaration: "

> "I (God) will show you kindness from the standpoint of an equal, if you both love me *and* also keep my commandments."

"The actual word translated as "love" is:

> "157 'âhab or 'âhêb; a prim. root: to *have affection* for (sexually or otherwise): - (be-) love (-ed, -ly, -r), like, friend."[SH5]

"Thus the translation as "love," seems reasonably straightforward.

"The answer to this "obedience" matter lies in the actual word which is translated here as "keep."

"The actual Hebrew word translated here as keep is:

> "8104: shâmar; A prim. root; prop. to *hedge* about (as with thorns), i.e. *guard*; gen. to *protect, attend to,* etc.: - beware, be

circumspect, take heed (to self), keep (-er, self), mark, look narrowly, observe, preserve, regard, reserve, save (self), sure, (that lay) wait (for), watch (-man)."[SH6]

"As can easily be seen, the Hebrew word shâmar does not in any way mean obey; but rather to *protect* as though surrounded by a hedge of thorns. According to Strong, shâmar is in fact not translated as "obey" anywhere in the entire Bible.

"Perhaps God made an error, in that He actually meant to use a word that meant "obey," but was just preoccupied with the ongoing follies of His Chosen Ones at the time. Or perhaps in fact He actually did use a word that meant "obey," and somehow an error just cropped up in the translation. Or perhaps Moses actually spoke Hebrew with a serious "Brooklynese" accent, and thus just misunderstood God.

"The first of course is impossible. The second is possible; but the problem with this as well as the latter, is the pesky matter of the "written in stone" part for the content. If God was that serious about not being misunderstood about the rules, He would likely be just as clear about what to do with them.

"Much later, Jesus addressed this same issue of love and "obeying" the Commandments in John 14:15 where Jesus tells us:

"If ye love me, keep my commandments."[SH7]

"So it seems clear that Jesus is merely saying: "If you love Me, then show it by obeying My commandments."
"Or is He?
"Here the actual Greek word translated as "keep" is:

"5083 tērĕō; from tĕrŏs (a *watch*; perh. akin to 2334); to *guard* (from *loss* or *injury*, prop. by keeping *the eye* upon..."[SH8]

"Thus the Greek word *tērĕō* is very synonymic to the aforementioned Hebrew word *shâmar*. And neither *shâmar* nor *tērĕō* is even remotely concerned with obeying the Commandments, or showing obedience to anything else.

"It is clear that Jesus was not asking for, or even addressing obedience either. In Exodus 20:6, when the Father addressed the matter, He said to shâmar His Commandments—meaning that we should *protect* His Commandments as though to "surround them with a hedge of thorns." Then when Jesus addressed this same matter in John 14:15, the best Greek word for whatever Aramaic word it was that Jesus actually spoke, was the Greek word tērĕō—meaning to watch or guard from loss or injury by keeping the eye upon His (My) Commandments. In neither case was any type of *obedience* to the Commandments sought.

"So when God referenced *keeping* his commandments: ("And shewing mercy unto thousands of them that love me, and keep my commandments."); what is under discussion with regard to His Commandments is to *protect* (them) as though surrounded by a hedge of thorns. And much later Jesus essentially stated the very same thing.

"What good are the Commandments if H. Sapiens are not required to obey them, but only asked to guard them? The truth; at least in this passage; is that He did not even *require* us to guard them; but rather advised us as to what would happen if we loved Him and if and when we did shâmar or guard or protect said Commandments. And why is it that God will show us kindness *as though an (His) equal*, if we merely shâmar

His commandments; irrespective of whether or not we actually obey them?

"Can it be stated that God does not care if we obey His Commandments? Of course not; as He cares very much whether or not we obey His Commandments—else why would He have provided them. If for no other reason; He cares because of the matter of what is often referred to as *karma*. This subject is addressed in great detail in the "Second Intermission" of *"MeekRaker Beginnings..."* This mechanism is therein analyzed and explained on a strictly scientific basis; with the application of the Newtonian laws of F=MA, inertia, and equal and opposite reactions."[43] [Excerpt from *"Wisdom Essentials – Shâmar to Sharia"* Reprinted by Permission]

Thus it can be reasonably argued that to have *knowledge* of and *guard* that which we are told in these commandments, is what we are supposed to do if we love God. Their purpose is to *guide*, but not *compel* our thinking and behavior.

Acting *with* (con), this *knowledge* (science, or "to know"), here in the specific (the commandments); forms the basis of that which we in the general call *conscience*. These are deep seated and well guarded "principles" which we utilize in the decision making process. Of course the commandments do not represent all that should be part of *conscience*, but these are some of the "biggies."

Obviously the enemy does not like any of these "principles," and is incessantly trying to supplant these with his own version—hence the need for the constant *guarding* of the same.

If one loves another, then one normally wishes to please that person. If one loves God, then the same rule applies. When one loves God, and *guards* his commandments, then behaviors *consistent* with these commandments are the desired result; and behaviors inconsistent with them are an error. These are the "*saints*," in that they try to act upright, and *fail* when they do not.

However when one hates God, (*"them that hate me"*) in a binary system, (either God or not God); the only alternative to "*I the LORD thy God*" is the "them" in: *"Thou shalt not bow down thyself unto them.*" This is providing that which should be directed toward God, instead to these "them;" i.e.; the enemy and his minions.

Thus *"them that hate me"* have their own set of principles contrary to those contained in the commandments. Here behaviors *inconsistent* with these (God's) commandments are the desired result; and any behaviors *consistent* with them are an *error*. These are the *"sinners,"* in that they try to act non-upright and *fail* when they serendipitously do.

Earlier it was asked that if reincarnation; assuming it is an actuality; represents a punishment or a reward? To go from a more pleasant environment to a less pleasant environment; simply because one is or was good at some particular function; seems unjust; i.e.; delivering punishment for success.

But if one truly is more concerned with pleasing God than the comfort of their environment, this is a different matter. For those who desire to please God, to then again be afforded the opportunity to continue their role as a physically alive tsâbâ', in "kiboshing" the material realm, to facilitate redemption of the same; then this represents a *reward*. It all depends upon precisely what it is that one *believes* one is trying to do.

Although that which we are told in Genesis regarding man's purpose with regard to "putting the kibosh" on the earth is not a represented as a "commandment," it is nevertheless clearly God's will. In fact, if the Bible is the source; it seems that this represents the very purpose for which man was created. There are many views regarding "man's purpose in the universe," but the Biblical answer is quite clear.

One is not required to believe that that which the Bible clearly states is in fact true. But one cannot maintain intellectual honesty, and yet "not believe" that the Bible literally states what it literally states—assuming the literal meanings are maintained.

That which was addressed earlier with regard to *religion*, likewise applies here. Correctly analyzing what it is that the Bible actually states, results in *epistémē* in regard to these Biblical *statements*. But whether or not that which is Biblically *stated* is in fact true, (*epistémē*), is something each individual must decide.

Internals—Externals

The commandments are tactical. They are designed to minimize: "No battle plan remains intact after first contact with enemy." God does not ask that we *obey* them. He only asks that we *guard* them, and utilize them in the decision making process.

There is "that one" about minds being like parachutes—they have to be *open* to function properly. And there is that other one about there being a stark difference between an open mind and a "hole in the head."
Here again is Max Planck's quote:

"Science changes one funeral at a time."

The willingness to "go where the evidence leads," is likely the best example of an "open mind." Common to both science and criminal investigations, this represents a "common sense" approach. Deviating from this in either direction; whether believing that which is unsupported by facts; or not believing that which is supported by facts; can be by definition—*delusional*.
Delusion is generally defined as the maintaining of a belief or position, despite of overwhelming evidence to the contrary. Here the more deviation from the "go where the evidence leads," the greater the level of delusion—whether one is *believing* or *not believing*.
Ian Stevenson (1918-2007), was a psychiatrist who studied reincarnation. He was extremely interested in things such as recurrence of birthmarks, scars from fatal injuries in previous lives, and *xenoglossia*.
Xenoglossia is considered the ability to speak in a language, the knowledge of which or for which, there is no *natural* explanation. Here the speaker is speaking a language that he could *not* possibly be capable of speaking via any "natural" means. The word is derived

from *xeno*, generally meaning *foreign*; and *glossia*, meaning *tongue*. [*Glossitis* is inflammation of the tongue. Thus xenoglossia is literally "foreign tongue"]

It must be asked precisely what "foreign" actually means in this usage. Is this term "foreign" *listener* dependent? Meaning; does "foreign" mean that this language needs to be "foreign" to those listeners who may be present? What if the person purportedly engaging in *xenoglossia* were a true foreigner who spoke a different language than the listeners, but nevertheless spoke to these same listeners in *their own* language; and yet had no "natural" way of knowing their language?

Does "foreign" require a different language be spoken; or could this speaking be considered *xenoglossia*, if the language were the same; but the *content* would be such that the speaker would have no "natural" way of knowing it?

Or is it that "foreign" here means that the *source* of the information is foreign to the speaker? Meaning; that there are no possible subsets to the "set" known as that individual engaging in *xenoglossia*, that could possibly include this knowledge.

Or could foreign mean something else?

Xenophobia is generally considered as fear of those from other countries. In terms of "nationalism," this means fear of those that are not the same as the person who is xenophobic. But xenophobia is more than mere ethnicity, as generally those "feared" have a different *immediate* source than the xenophobe; i.e.; "those newcomers."

Accurately distinguishing *xenoglossia* from the similar word *xenolalia*, is not an easy undertaking; and although there is much "opinion;" no reliable source in furtherance of this could readily be found. There is the commonality of the prefix or *xeno*, again roughly meaning foreign, but here with different suffixes.

Perhaps *xenoglossia* refers to speaking in a recognized foreign language; with "recognized" here meaning the ability for a listener to determine precisely *what* language it is that is being spoken, even if not understood by them. If so, then *xenolalia* would require that the language be foreign, but not necessarily identifiable. If today one heard a "recording" of Jesus speaking without knowing

He spoke Aramaic, one might believe He was speaking a foreign language, but not know which one.

Or perhaps the suffix *glossia* or "tongue" refers strictly to the fact that a foreign *language* or "tongue" actually spoken; and the *"lalia"* refers to the actual type or *purpose* or *content* of the "speaking;" e.g.; telling a story or parable, bloviating, a "harangue."

Although Strong's does not appear to contain either *xenoglossia* or *xenolalia*, Strong has the suffix "lalia" as:

"2981 lalia; from 2980; *talk*: - saying, speech."[144]

"2980 lalĕō; a prol. form of an otherwise obsol. verb; to *talk*, i.e. *utter* words; - preach, say, speak (after), talk, tell, utter. Comp. 3004."[145]

"3004 lĕgō... [... while 4483 is prop. to break silence merely, and 2980 means an extended or random harangue];..."[146]

Here is seen some distinction between lalia and its root lalĕō. Although lalia is defined as *"talk:* - saying, speech," its root lalĕō seems to have the sense of long winded "nonsensical" or ranting speech.

With regard to those who consider any serious discussion of reincarnation "profane" or obscene; but as of yet have not attempted to rewrite the entire Bible; *xenoglossia* and *xenolalia* would likely cursorily and immediately be explained as "speaking in tongues."

Thus to them, neither would have anything whatsoever to do with any type of "profanities" or "obscenities"—including reincarnation. Here many who previously professed that the "gifts of the Spirit" were only for the "Apostolic Era," and not for today; will embrace even this "stone the builders rejected"—if the alternative would in any way "move the needle" toward proving reincarnation. [It must again be noted that no Biblical evidence can be found that in any way supports this "Apostolic era" position. It is likely merely proffered as an excuse for "Spiritual impotence."]

Acts 19:6 (KJV) tells us:

"*And when Paul had laid his hands upon them,
the Holy Ghost came on them;
and they spake with tongues, and prophesied.*"[147]

"Spake" is the same as the above:[148]

"*2980 laleō; a prol. form of an otherwise obsol. verb; to talk*, i.e. *utter* words; - preach, say, speak (after), talk, tell, utter...." "...2980 means an extended or random harangue."

"Tongues" is:

"*1100 glōssa; of uncert. affin.; the tongue;* by impl. a language (spec. one naturally unacquired): - tongue."[149]

"Prophesied" is:

"*4395* prŏphētĕuō; from *4396;* to *foretell* events, *divine speak* under *inspiration, exercise* be prophetic *office:* - prophesy"[150]

Firstly, it must be asked precisely how one could possibly have either a literal structural tongue, or by implication a language; be "*spec. one naturally unacquired*"? Unlike apples falling from a tree, it does not seem likely that one's literal tongue could be "*naturally unacquired.*" Neither does it seem likely that any previously known language could be "*naturally unacquired.*"

Literal tongues and language can in fact be "*unacquired*" by disease or trauma, but if disease or trauma is to be considered as "natural;" then a fair argument exists that the absence of disease or trauma represents the "unnatural" state.

Internals—Externals

What is likely; is that "spec. one naturally unacquired," is a typographical error; and should read: "spec. one unnaturally acquired." This would be perfectly consistent with the context.

If two of the above referenced words: glōssa and the lalĕō are combined, the word *glossolalia* would be the "English-ized" result. Dictionary.com defines glossolalia as:

> "incomprehensible speech in an imaginary language, sometimes occurring in a trance state, an episode of religious ecstasy, or schizophrenia."[151]

Here we have the correct and accepted English word for the aforementioned "speaking in tongues;" *glossolalia*; which is based upon the Greek *glōssa*, and either the Greek *lalĕō*, or its derivative *lalia*—literally: "tongue-speak."

Thus unless the position is taken that these three words: *xenoglossia, xenolalia*, and *glossolalia* refer to the very same "speaking in tongues" phenomenon; then they each necessarily must refer to something different.

Does this matter? The answer is yes. Lumping a number of words together to mean the same thing is at best Orwellian, and limits; whether inadvertently or by design; the ability to make the distinctions necessary for proper analysis, and subsequent understanding.

If it is stipulated that *glossolalia* is the correct word for the Biblical "speaking in tongues," it cannot be overlooked that *glossolalia* does not include the prefix *xeno*, as do *xenoglossia and xenolalia*. Thus *glossolalia*; unlike *xenoglossia and xenolalia*; does not include the requirement of "foreign."

Why does *glossolalia* not include *xeno* or "foreign?" There are at least two evident reasons:

Firstly, the *source* of *glossolalia*; whether "believed in" or considered as "nonsense;" (*glossolalia* either exists as an actuality or it does not); is nevertheless known. As Jesus told us, it is the Holy Ghost.

Secondly, the Holy Ghost should normally be in every Christian—else given that the capitalized "Christos" literally means

217

the anointing of the Holy Ghost, why then call one's self a Christian, rather than "Jesusite." Once a "physically alive" person has the Holy Ghost within them (hence the term Ghost); the source of "speaking in tongues" and any other similar phenomena is *within* them, *part* of them, and thus not in any way foreign.

But with the use of prefix *xeno* or "foreign," it is being stated that whatever the suffices *glossia* or *lalia* manifestation(s) may represent, the *source* of the same is *not* contained within that particular "physically alive" person—hence "unnatural" or "spec. one unnaturally acquired (corrected)."

This is an important consideration, because whatever the actual source of that which is "xeno" may be, it is by definition is *not within* them. However the ability to to "speak in tongues" requires that the source (The Holy Ghost) *be within* them, and in fact is generally considered as the indisputable proof that said source is in fact *not* foreign to them, but is in fact *within* them. The inability to "speak in tongues" does not necessarily prove the absence of the Holy Ghost, as there may be different "gifts" involved. But the ability to speak in "tongues" is generally recognized as the "classic confirmation."

Ergo this "foreign" source in *xenoglossia* and *xenolalia* is separate and distinct from that "within" source that provides the ability to "speak in tongues, (glossolalia);" as well as the ability to perform many other miraculous (violate natural law) actions.

Here the use of the term "foreign," means *not* part of that person's current abilities. They are speaking a foreign language; that cannot be explained by the sum total of their (current) lifetime experiences.

Those who consider reincarnation as profane, would take the position that simply because someone *has* "unnatural" knowledge of a foreign tongue or content, this in no way proves reincarnation is an actuality. They would much rather credit the internal Holy Ghost for this—at least until their current "reincarnation crisis" subsides.

And these very same individuals, will, at the very same time maintain that because John the Baptist *did not know* that he was

Elijah, this likewise also proves that reincarnation is not an actuality.

So according to these positions, *having* the "unnatural" knowledge of a "tongue" or content *does not prove* reincarnation is an actuality; while *not having* the knowledge regarding a "former life" or "previous personality" *disproves* that reincarnation is an actuality.

Proponents of the "wave theory," (reincarnation exists); love Dr. Stevenson and his work, because of the immensity, impeccability, thoroughness, and undeniability of his work.

Proponents of the "curve theory," (reincarnation does not exist); hate him in at least equal measure, and for precisely the same reasons.

It would be fair to suggest that Dr. Stevenson was more concerned with *studying* reincarnation, than he was with litigating the case for reincarnation being an actuality. Thus the existence of reincarnation was essentially presumed to be a fact, with the bulk of his work arising from that point onward.

It seems that the common sense approach to the best way to make a decision regarding the truth or falsity of the existence of reincarnation based upon *externals*; i.e.; current or recent *material* evidence; would be to have a *reasonable* person; preferably one who *reasonably* does or did not believe reincarnation is an actuality; evaluate the same with a healthy degree of skepticism. Does any person exist who is capable of this?

In 1999, Tom Shroder, journalist, editor, and author, published a book entitled "*Old Souls—the Scientific Evidence for Past Lives.*" After much effort, Shroder had finally convinced Stevenson to allow him to accompany Stevenson on his research trips; and this book was the result of Shroder's findings. For those interested in the "material evidence," Shroder's book is a must.

Shroder makes his initial skepticism quite clear. He also describes the importance and efforts made by Stevenson to avoid "contamination" of any potential cases. And Shroder quotes Stevenson's recurring question: "Why do mainstream scientists refuse to accept the evidence we have for reincarnation?"[52]

It is ironic that there nevertheless exists a commonality between mainstream science—at least according to Max Planck; and reincarnation, in this one sense: Each is concerned with what changes occur after a funeral.

To cite all of the evidence that prompted Shroder to change from "skeptic" to "believer" is beyond the scope of this book. And to only partially cite the evidence would not only be disrespectful to both Stevenson and Shroder; but counterproductive. "Best evidence" requires that what Shroder personally witnessed, be recounted by the very witness himself.

It seems that there is no actuality that includes what Shroder personally experienced, *and* reincarnation not being a fact. There simply seems to be no other possible reasonable explanations for these phenomena. To maintain staunch denial of the existence of reincarnation given the level of evidence presented, would be to "go anywhere *except* where the evidence leads." But of course ultimately this would say nothing about reincarnation; but instead says much about one's version of "scientific method."

There seem to be three categories of tactics with regard to "dealing with" the subject of reincarnation:

It is unclear if the term "new age" is still in vogue. Many of these "adherents" are often purely emotionally driven, with little regard for any factual basis supporting their beliefs. Pick the facts that support what you *feel* you want to believe, and if you *feel* you should change your mind—simply just ignore the ones previously picked, and pick some of the ones previously ignored. Wisdom can sometimes be found here, but its acquisition is often serendipitous.

The *second*, is the aforementioned "go anywhere *except* where the evidence leads" group. Their "views" on reincarnation represent merely a tool in furtherance of things that have nothing whatsoever to do with reincarnation. Much of this has been addressed. Here reincarnation represents an obstacle—which is precisely why Shakespeare's (via Hamlet): "The lady doth protest too much, methinks," applies to their "views." After all, why would the mere prospect of additional opportunities to be physically alive as a "cause," produce such a disproportional "effect?"

And the *third*, are those who "go where the facts lead." This is the intelligent way to approach the study of any phenomenon or phenomena.

If it is stipulated that *xenoglossia* is the ability to speak a language one has had no way of learning; and *xenolalia*, is at least somewhat similar; precisely how does one explain either of these when truly encountered—most particularly when the suspected "past personality" is known to have had this knowledge when previously physically alive?

When the *explanations* for an otherwise inexplicable phenomenon require a more bizarre list of suppositions and stipulations than the very phenomenon itself requires; whatever "road" this represents, truth cannot be a possible destination.

Much has been presented here. And much effort has been taken to *not* advocate for any position regarding the truth or falsity of the existence of that phenomenon referred to as reincarnation. This evidence should be evaluated, and we each must decide precisely what it is we choose to believe.

ABOUT THE MEEKRAKER SERIES

What on earth is a MeekRaker? This word can be broken down into two parts "Meek" and "Raker." Capital letters were used in order to minimize any mispronunciations such as Mee-kraker; but the "etymology" is actually the fusion of these two words.

What is meek? And who in their right mind would ever want to be meek? Courage, strength, and bravery are characteristics that are generally considered desirable; but meek? No thanks. Unfortunately, the meaning of this word has been distorted over time to include things such as timidity, or shyness; weakness, or cowardice, but this is not; or rather should not be so.

Chambers states:

> "meek adj. Probably before 1200 meok gentle, humble, in Ancrene Riwle; later mec (probably about 1200, in the *The Ormlum*); borrowed from a Scandanavian source (Compare Old Icelandic mjukr soft pliant gentle...."[AT-1]

These origins seem to be adjectival in nature, and describe a condition of humility or softness. Thus a meek person, by these definitions would indicate a humble or soft person. The opposite of this would then be a person who is prideful or hard.

Humble vs. prideful is an easy one. Who would want to be prideful? The Bible is replete with warnings about pride; and it was pride that started all of the messes to begin with. Pride may make one "feel good" for a short period of time, but as previously referenced; the Bible is quite clear that on that path there lies destruction.

But what does the Bible actually have to say about being a meek person?

- It tells us that the meek shall (*not will or might*) inherit the earth.[AT-2]
- It further tells us that the meek will be guided in judgment will be taught His way.[AT-3]
- The meek will be lifted up by the Lord, and He will cast the wicked down to the ground.[AT-4]
- He will save all the meek of the earth.[AT-5]

And what about the Bible's statements regarding being "hard?"

- "For their heart was hardened."[AT-6] "Have ye your heart yet hardened?"[AT-7]
- "... their eyes and hardened their heart."[AT-8]
- "But they and our fathers dealt proudly, and hardened their necks, and hearkened not to thy commandments, and refused to obey, neither were mindful of thy wonders that thou didst among them; but hardened their necks, and in their rebellion..."[AT-9]
- "Happy is the man that feareth always: But he that hardeneth his heart shall fall into mischief."[AT-10]
- "He that being often reproved hardeneth his neck, shall suddenly be destroyed, and that without remedy."[AT-11]

The actual word in all of these citations which is translated as hard is:

About the MeekRaker Series

"4456 poroo (a kind of stone); to *petrify*, i.e. (fig.) to indurate (*render stupid* or *callous*): - blind, harden."[AT-12]

With respect to hard, there is a clear Scriptural relationship between the same and disobedience; not being "mindful" of God performing wonders in one's life, rebellious, falling into "mischief," and being "destroyed," "without remedy."

In addition, by the very definition of the original word, one who is "hard" is also stupid callous and blind. (If a physical heart were actually to turn into stone, you are just dead; so surely that definition does not apply in this context or usage.)

Thus, meek or soft; that being the opposite of hard; would tend to be obedient, be mindful of God performing wonders, not rebellious, not falling into mischief, and not destroyed. Furthermore, one would not be "stupid," "callous" or "blind."

The use of the term meek as "soft," also implies *teachable*.

Hardhead: will not change mind. Hardhearted: will not change heart. Hard necked: junction between head and heart is hard, and will not permit mental change to be transmitted to change the heart.

If it is firmly established that the term "revelation" has the prerequisite of being *the* truth; when confronted with potential revelation; it has been the authors' experiences that hard persons; specifically those of the head, neck, and heart variety; will generally behave according to the "Three A's:"

> A_1 is *anger*. This is the first response. This anger is not so much because there is a remote chance that they may be wrong, but rather when it is somewhat clear that they *are* wrong. This would be best illustrated as a line on a graph rising from left to right; with the level of anger represented by the vertical axis, and time represented by the horizontal axis.
>
> A_2 is *argument*. This generally begins with emotionally (anger) driven arguments. As the arguments begin to fail, the level and usually the slope of A_1 will increase.

When all possible arguments, logical, relevant or otherwise have been proffered, the original arguments will then return. This would be best illustrated as a circle under the rising anger line referenced above. Often, what is just under the skin, (which is generally the reason for the pride and subsequent anger) will pop its "head" out; revealing things previously unknown about this individual.

A_3 is *absconding*. When all of the arguments and the repetition thereof have unquestionably failed, the hard person will generally abscond; or run away. This may be represented by actual physical separation, changing the subject or in some other manner. This could be perceived as the disappearance of the anger line, but is only subjective; as the true level of anger then becomes somewhat hidden.

Contrarily, the *meek* will weigh the value of any purported revelation; and then decide precisely what it is that merits their belief. Sincere questioning and even some arguments will be presented; but here not with the primary purpose of proving that they, the inquirer, is correct; but rather to understand precisely what it is that this revelation represents; knowing that if it in fact does represent revelation, then this will be to their benefit. A logical decision will then be made with respect to what constitutes the truth.

The primary basis for the actions of a "hard-head," is *emotional*. The primary basis for the actions of the meek; although perhaps including some emotional factors; (i.e. passion); is largely *intellectual*.

In a sense, the purpose of a rake is to separate the soft from the hard. The Bible refers to separating the wheat from the chaff, the silver from the dross; hence the origin of *"MeekRaker"*. Meek or hard is not so much determined by what one believes; but rather by the *process* involved in making these determinations.

GLOSSARY

Abraham's Bosom: see *kŏlpŏs*

actuality: "*actuality*" is what currently exists or what "is;" what a thing objectively is, as opposed to a *reality* based upon *perception*. An "un-acted upon" actuality, remains an actuality; and that which is not an actuality remains not an actuality—irrespective of any *reality* of the same. The *reality* of a mirage is water, but the *actuality* of a mirage can be anything *except* water—if it is a mirage. No actuality can ever be 100% accurately perceived, thus reality always falls short.

actualization: to bring something from the thought process; (via imagination, quasi-reality); to a current actuality. One can ultimately produce an actuality through a reality (actualization), but not just by the existence of the reality alone—at least when confined to the material realm. Some level of energy or effort (ĕrgŏn) must be also utilized in the actualization process.

afterlife: That "state" of the immaterial part of man (soul), *after* leaving the previously alive or connected (incarnated) body or soma.

'*âhab*: (H) "157 'âhab or 'âhêb; a prim. root: to *have affection* for (sexually or otherwise): - (be-) love (-ed, -ly, -r), like, friend."^SH5

alive: in the *general* sense, refers to a *connection*, or connected

amphigory: "a nonsense verse or composition: a rigmarole with apparent meaning which proves to be meaningless."^G1
https://www.merriam-webster.com/dictionary/amphigory

anastasis: (G) "386 anastasis; from 450; a *standing up* again, i.e. (lit.) a *resurrection* from death..."^100

'*âphâr*: (H) "6083 'âphâr from 6080; dust (as powdered or gray); hence clay, earth, mud: - ashes, dust, earth, ground, morter, powder, rubbish." "6080 'âphâr a prim. root; mean. either to be gray or perh. rather to pulverize; used only as denom. from 6083, to be dust: - cast [dust)]."^G2

apocalypsa (apŏkalupsis, apocalypse): (G) "from Greek *apokálypsis*, literally meaning "uncovering," from *apokalyptein* uncover (*apo-* off, un- + *kalyptein* to cover, veil; (Chambers)"^G3 42 "602 apŏkalupsis; from 601; disclosure: - appearing, coming, lighten, manifestation, be revealed, revelation (Strong)."^G4

apocrypha: "from Greek *apókryphos* hidden, as of hidden or unknown authorship (*apo-* away + *kryptein* to hide; see CRYPT)." ^G5

apokeimai: "606 apokeimai, from 575 and 2749; to *be reserved*; fig. to *await*: - be appointed, (be) laid up."^12.16

'*âsham*: "816 'âsham; or 'âshêm; a prim. root; to *be guilty*; by impl. to *be punished* or *perish*..." ^140

'*âshâm*: And "817 'âshâm; from 816 *guilt*; by impl. a *fault*; also a *sin offering*. - guiltiness (offering for) sin, trespass (offering)."^142

Glossary

'âshêm: "'âshêm 818 from 816; *guilty*; hence *presenting a sin – offering*: - one which is faulty, guilty."[141]

bârâ' "1254 bârâ', a prim. root; (absol.) to create; (qualified) to cut down (a wood), select, feed (as formative processes): - choose, create (creator), cut down, dispatch, do, make (fat)."[G6]
"The verb expresses creation out of nothing..."

beforelife: That "state" of the immaterial part of man (soul), *before* entering into that alive or connected (incarnated) condition with a body or soma. Whether souls are always "new," or sometimes "recycled," is irrelevant to this definition.

bibliomancy: using a "book" to obtain unknown information, often "randomly" opening a book, and often it is the Bible

body or *soma*: in these usages refers to that *material* or *physical* part of man; i.e.; the physical structure which is designed to contain the immaterial part of man.

châcad: "2616 châcad; a prim. root; prop. perh. to *bow* (the neck only [comp. 2603] courtesy to an equal), i.e. to *be kind*;..."[SH3]

châlâq: "2509 châlâq; from 2505; smooth (espec. of tongue): - flattering"[35]

chânan: "2603 chânan; a prim. root [comp. 2583]; prop. to *bend* or stoop in kindness to an inferior; to *favor bestow*..."[SH4]

charis: "5485 charis; from 5463; *graciousness* (as *gratifying*), of manner or act..."[10.2]

checed: "2617 checed; from 2616; *kindness*;..."[SH2]

chiromancy: palm reading, sometimes called palmistry ("chiro" means hand)

233

chrŏnŏs: "5550 chrŏnŏs; of uncert. der.; a space of *time* (in gen. and thus prop. distinguished from 2540, which designates *fixed* or special occasion; and from 165, which denotes a particular *period*) or *interval* by extens. an individ. *opportunity*; by impl. *delay*"[8]

cleromancy: the casting of lots, believing that the outcome will be influenced by God and reveal unknown truths.

curve: "borrowed from Latin *curvus* curved, crooked, or bent."[G7]

çûwr: "5493 çûwr, or sûwr; a prim. root; to turn off (lit. or fig.)..."[45]

dead: in the *general* sense refers to a *disconnection*, or disconnected

death: is roughly synonymous with "dead," but refers to the *event* of disconnection, rather than that *general state* where there is no connection. "Death" is when this disconnection occurs; and "dead" is the state after this occurrence.

dia: "1223 dia; a prim. prep. denoting a *channel* of an act; *through* (in very wide applications..."[10.3]

diamarturŏmai: "1263 diamarturŏmai; from 1223 and 3140; to *attest* or *protest earnestly*, or (by impl.) *hortatively*: - charge, testify (unto), witness."[98]

diapŏnĕō: "1278 diapŏnĕō; from 1223 and a der. of 4192; to toil through, i.e. (pass.) be worried..."[41]

divination: "*n.* before 1384 *dyvynacioun* foretelling, in the Wycliffe Bible; borrowed from Old French *divination*, learned borrowing from Latin *dīvīnātiōnem* (nominative *divinātiō*), from *divināre* foretell, predict; for suffix see – ATION."[18]

divine: "*adj.* about 1380 *devyne* of God or a god; godlike,..."[17]

Glossary

doxa: commonly *believed*, *possible* or *probable* knowledge; (as opposed to *eptisteme*, or certain knowledge); "from (Greek) *dokeín* to seem good, seem, think." [G8]

dunamis: supernatural power "*1411* dunamis; from *1410*; *force* (lit. or fig.); spec. miraculous *power* (usually by impl. a *miracle* itself)..."[25]

dynamikós : (G) natural power, "from Greek *dynamikós* powerful, from *dynamis* power, from *dynasthai* be able, have power;"[G9]

ĕlĕŏs: "1656 ĕlĕŏs; of uncert. affin.; compassion (human or divine espec. active)"[10.10]

'ĕlôhîym: "430 'ĕlôhîym; plur. of 433: *gods* in the ordinary sense but spec. used (in the plur. thus, esp. with the art.) of the supreme *God*; occasionally applied by way of *deference* to *magistrates*; and sometimes as a superlative..."[53]

epistémē: "knowledge (Iconic Greek *epístasthai* understand, know how to do, from *epi-* over, near + *hístasthai* to STAND)" [G10]

ĕrgŏn: "2041 ĕrgŏn; from a prim. (but obsol.) ĕrgō (to *work*); to *toil* (as an effort or occupation) by impl. an act."[10.4]

fanum: (L) root of profane, "... from the phrase *prō fānō* not admitted into the temple (with the initiates); literally, out in front of the temple (*prō* before, see FOR; and *fānō* ablative case of *fānum* temple;...)" [G11]

fanumites: religious folk," in the sense of their temple or *fanum* being the only true and correct one, with all others being "profane." See philosophunculist

First Adam: Adam, or the man *formed* by God from *something*; as opposed to the original hosts who were *created* from *nothing*. The First Adam was the beginning of the redemptive process for *man*

235

undertaken by God, and was completed "It is finished;" by the Last Adam, who was Jesus.

ghost: an immaterial breath-like (spiritus) entity specifically designed to "live in" or be connected with a physical vessel.

glōssa: "*1100* glōssa; of uncert. affin.; the *tongue*; by impl. a language (spec. one naturally unacquired): - tongue."[149]

glossolalia: "Speaking in Tongues," via the *internalization* of the Holy Ghost. "glōssa; of uncert. affin.; the *tongue*," and "lalia; from 2980; *talk*: - saying, speech." This is to be distinguished from *xenoglossia* and *xenolalia*, each which have the requirement of *external* or *foreign* (xeno) sources.

hamartano: "264 hamartano, perh. from 1 (as a neg. particle) and the base of 3313; prop. to miss the mark (and so not share in the prize), i.e. (fig.) to err, esp. (mor.) to sin; - for your faults, offend, sin, trespass."[12.11]

heaven (singular): "in the *singular*; generally refers to the *immaterial* realm where God resides; e.g.; the "heaven" in "Who art in heaven," refers to the *immaterial* realm."

heavens (plural): the *plural* of heaven: "heavens," generally refers to the space between the celestial bodies, and thus is contained (as "space") in the *material* realm.

imagination: *Imagination* is similar to a reality, but with the subjective knowledge or belief that the thing does not yet exist.

Isaac: "3327 Yitschâq; from 6711; *laughter* (i.e. *mockery*)[G12]

kâbash: "3533 kâbash; a prim. root; to *tread* down; hence neg. to *disregard*; pos. to *conquer, subjugate, violate*..."[11]

Glossary

kauchaŏmai: "2744 kauchaŏmai; from some (obsol.) base akin to that of auchĕō (to *boast*) and 2172; to *vaunt* (in a good or bad sense)..."[10.6]

kŏlpŏs: "2859 kŏlpŏs; appar. a prim. word; the *bosom*; by anal. a *bay*: - bosom, creek."[G13]

lalĕō: "2980 lalĕō; a prol. form of an otherwise obsol. verb; to *talk*, i.e. *utter* words; - preach, say, speak (after), talk, tell, utter. Comp. 3004."[45]

lalia: "2981 lalia; from 2980; *talk*: - saying, speech."[44]

Last Adam: The First Adam or the man *formed* by God from *something*; as opposed to the original hosts who were *created* from *nothing*, was the beginning of the redemptive process for *man* undertaken by God: and was completed "It is finished;" by the Last Adam, who was Jesus.

lĕgō: "3004 lĕgō... [... while 4483 is prop. to break silence merely, and 2980 means an extended or random harangue];..."[46]

life or ***living***: reasonably synonymous with "alive" and thus also refers to that *general* state where there is some type of connection

lŏgŏs: "3056 lŏgŏs; from 3004; something *said* (including the *thought*); by impl. a *topic* (subject of discourse), also *reasoning* (the mental faculty) or *motive*; by extens. a *computation*; spec. (with the art. in John) the Divine *Expression* (i.e. *Christ*)"[7]

mancy: "derived from "*manteiā* divination, oracle, from *manteúesthai* to prophesy, from *mántis* prophet; MANTIS..."[44]

mantĕuŏmai: "3132 mantĕuŏmai; from a der. of 3105 (mean. a prophet, as supposed to rave through inspiration); to divine, i.e. utter spells (under pretense of foretelling): - by soothsaying."[40]

237

martureō: "3140 martureō; from 3144; to *be a witness*, i.e. *testify* (lit. or fig.)..."⁹⁹

marturia: "3141 marturia from 3144; *evidence* given (judicially or gen.): - record, report, testimony, witness."⁶

massâ': "4853 massâ' from 5375; a burden; spec. tribute, or (abstr.) porterage; fig. an utterance, chiefly a doom, espec. singing; mental desire: - burden, carry away, prophesy..."²³

meizōn: "3187 meizōn; irreg. compar. of *3173; larger*..."³⁵

metempsychosis: "the term generally recognized to represent that category of reincarnation which maintains the view that reincarnation is kind of a one way street; meaning that there is no possibility of regression. The term "regression" as used here does not mean the "regression" process that involves an individual attempting to find out about past lives, but rather reincarnating to a "lesser state.""

miracle: "something that occurs in the material realm, but is contrary to natural law. In fact in order to be considered a miracle, it *must* contradict natural law or laws; natural law here meaning the law or laws of the material realm."

miqçâm: "4738 miqçâm; from 7080; an *augury*: - divination" (*miqçâm* appears twice in OT)²⁶

Mortal sin: "is called mortal because it is the 'spiritual' death of the soul (separation from God)."¹⁰,¹¹

nâqâh: "5352 nâqâh; a prim. root; to *be* (or *make*) *clean* (lit. or fig.) by impl. (in an adverse sense) to *be bare*, i.e. *extirpated*: - acquit..."³⁹

necromancy: "n. foretelling of the future by communicating with the dead... divination from an exhumed corpse, from Greek

Glossary

nekromanteiā (nekrós dead body + manteiā divination, oracle, from manteúesthai to prophesy..."[44]

nephesh: "5315 nephesh; from 5314; prop. a *breathing* creature, i.e. *animal* or (abstr.) *vitality*. . ."[95]

'ôwv: "178 'ôwv; from the same as 1 (appar. through the idea of prattling a father's name) prop. a mumble, i.e. a water – skin (from its hollow sound); hence a necromancer (ventriloquist, as from a jar): - bottle, familiar spirit;"[45]

palmistry: Palm reading, sometimes called chiromancy; ("chiro" means hand)

papal bull: "a formal proclamation issued by the pope (usually written in antiquated characters and sealed with a leaden bulla)"[111]

penitire: "to regret."[10.13]

Pharisees: "5330 Pharisaiŏs; of Heb. or. [comp. 6567]; a *separatist*, i.e. exclusively *religious*; a *Pharis*(oe)*an*, i.e. Jewish sectary: - Pharisee"[G14] The Pharisees believed in the immortality of the soul, and reincarnation.

philosophunculist: one who speaks or acts in a manner consistent with a proffered level of knowledge or expertise greater than they actually possess.

phrassō: "5420 phrassō; appar. a strength. form of the base of 5424; to *fence* or inclose, i.e. (spec.) to *block* up (fig. to *silence*): - stop."[119]

phrēn: "5424 phrēn; prob. from an obsol. phraō (to *rein* in or *curb*; comp. 5420); the *midrif* (as a *partition* of the body), i.e. (fig. and by impl. of sympathy) the *feelings* (or sensitive nature; by extens. [also in the plur.] the *mind* or cognitive faculties): - understanding."[118]

phrŏnēma: "5427 phrŏnēma; from 5426; (mental) *inclination* or *purpose*..."[117]

phrŏnĕō: "5426 phrŏnĕō; from 5424; to *exercise* the *mind*, i.e. *entertain* or *have* a *sentiment* or *opinion*; by impl. to *be* (mentally) *disposed* (more or less earnestly in a certain direction); intens. to *interest oneself* in (with concern or obedience)..."[116]

physical death: refers to that state where the immaterial part of man (soul) is no longer connected to the material part of man (body).

physical life: is that condition where the immaterial part of man (soul) is connected to the material part (body).

pneuma: "4151 pneuma, from 4154; a *current* of air, i.e. *breath* (*blast*) or a *breeze*; by anal. or fig. a *spirit*, i.e. (human) the rational soul, (by impl.) *vital principle*, mental *disposition*, etc., or (superhuman) an *angel, demon*, or (divine) *God*, Christ's *spirit*, the Holy *Spirit*: - ghost, life, spirit (-ual - ually), mind."[12.7]

pŏiĕō: "4160 pŏiĕō; appar. a prol. form of an obsol. prim; to *make* or *do* (in a very wide application, more or less direct): - abide, +agree, appoint, x avenge..."[134]

profane: (L) "... from the phrase *prō fānō* not admitted into the temple (with the initiates); literally, out in front of the temple (*prō* before, see FOR; and *fānō* ablative case of *fānum* temple;...)"[G15]

prŏphētĕuō "4395 prŏphētĕuō; from 4396; to *foretell* events, *divine speak* under *inspiration, exercise* be prophetic *office*: - prophesy"[50]

Puthōn: "4436 Puthōn; from Puthō (the name of the region where Delphi, the seat of the famous *oracle*, was located); a *python* i.e. (by anal. with the supposed *diviner* there) *inspiration* (*soothsaying*): - divination."[29]

Glossary

qâçam: "7080 qâçam; a prim. root; prop. to *distribute*, i.e. *determine* by lot or magical scroll; by impl. to *divine* : - divine (-r, -ation), prudent, soothsayer, use [divination]." (*qâçam* appears (only) once in OT)²⁷

qâshâh: "7185 qâshâh; a prim. root; prop. to *be dense*, i.e. tough or *severe* (in various applications): - be cruel, be fiercer, make grievous, be ([ask a], be in, have, seem, would) hard (-en, [labour], -ly, thing), be sore, (be, make) stiff (-en, [-necked]).⁷⁸

qeçem: "7081 qeçem; from 7080; a lot; also divination (includ. its fee) oracle; - (reward of) divination, divine sentence, witchcraft." (qeçem appears eight times in the OT) ²¹
"7081 qeçem; from 7080; a *lot*; also *divination* (includ. its *fee*), *oracle*: - (reward of) divination, divine sentence, witchcraft."³¹

reality: the belief or "understanding" of "what a thing is or is not" based upon perception.

realization: The process by which the perception of a "thing or things" produces an awareness, belief or understanding (reality) of said actuality or actualities. *Realization* (process) and *reality* (result) are always less than the actuality, and often incomplete and/or erroneous.

recollection: The process of "remembering." *Recollection* is similar to a reality, but with the subjective knowledge or belief that the thing may no longer exist.

reincarnation: in a very general sense, the reintroduction of that immaterial part of man (soul) into a *new* and *different* physical body (see text)

resurrection: the reintroduction of that immaterial part of man (soul) into the *same* physical body.

241

retrophesy: to obtain knowledge "unnaturally" about the *past*, in the same way and manner that *prophesy* is concerned with the *future*.

rhabdomancy: the use of a wand or rod, such as in searching for underground water; (dowsing using a "divining rod")

rhēma: "rhēma *4487* from *4483*; an *utterance* (individ., collect. or spec); by impl. a *matter* or *topic* (espec. of narration, command or dispute)..."[9]

Sadducees: "4523 Saddŏukaiŏs; prob. from *4524*; a *Sadduc(oe)an* (i.e. *Tsadokian*), or follower of a certain heretical Isr.: - Sadducee."[G16] who did not believe in reincarnation

shâmar: generally translated as "keep" and not "obey." "8104: shâmar; A prim. root; prop. to *hedge* about (as with thorns), i.e. *guard*; gen. to *protect, attend to*, etc.: - beware, be circumspect, take heed (to self), keep (-er, self), mark, look narrowly, observe, preserve, regard, reserve, save (self), sure, (that lay) wait (for), watch (-man)."[G17]

soul: refers to that *immaterial* part of man, often inadequately described as "will, intellect and emotions"

spiritual: can refer to a myriad of immaterial or "breath like" entities.

spiritual death: refers to that state where the immaterial part of man (soul) is disconnected from its original source.

spiritual life: refers to that state where the immaterial part of man (soul) is connected to its original source.

talantŏn: "5007 talantŏn; neut. Of a presumed der. of the orig. form of tiaō (to *bear*; equiv. to *5342*); a *balance* (as *supporting*

Glossary

weights), i.e. (by impl.) a certain *weight* (and thence a *coin* or rather *sum* of money) or *"talent"*: - talent."[24]

têbâh: "8392 têbâh; perh. of for. der.; a *box*: - ark."[123]

tērĕō: "5083 tērĕō; from tĕrŏs (a *watch*; perh. akin to 2334); to *guard* (from *loss* or *injury*, prop. by keeping *the eye* upon..."[SH8]

tetragrammaton: YHWH, the "ineffable" name of God in all of its various spellings, is referred to as the tetragrammaton

Tishbîy: "8664 Tishbîy; patrial from an unused name mean. *recourse*; a *Tishbite* or inhab. of Tishbeh (in Gilead); - Tishbite."[69]

tô'ar: "8389 tô'ar; from 8388; *outline*, i.e. *figure* or *appearance*..."[54]

Transmigration of Souls: "the direction of the soul is generally believed to be related to *karma*, and with this view; one can return as either higher or lower status, including the *type* of life form."

tsâbâ': "6635 tsâbâ' or ts^{e}bâ'âh from 6633; a *mass* of persons (or fig. things), espec. reg. organized for war (an *army*); by impl. a *campaign*, lit. or fig. (spec. *hardship*, *worship*): -appointed time, (+) army, (+) battle, company, host, service, soldiers, waiting upon..."[70]

Ûwrîym: "224 'Ûwrîym; plur. of 217; lights; Urim, the oracular brilliancy of the figures in the Hight Priest's breastplate: - Urim."[49]

wave: is from: "v. 1375 *waven* move back and forth"[G18]

xenoglossia: from *xeno* – foreign, and *glossia* - tongue

xenolalia: from *xeno* – foreign, and *lalia* – some type of speech

yâtsar: "3335 yâtsar; prob. identical with 3334 (through the *squeezing* into shape); ([comp. 3331]); to *mould* into a form; espec. as a *potter*;..."[G19]

yom* or *yôwm (H) "3117 yôwm, from an unused root mean. *To be hot*; a *day* (as the *warm* hours), whether lit. (from sunrise to sunset, or from one sunset to the next), or fig. (a space of time defined by an associated term), [often used adv.]: - age, ... season..." [G20]

BIBLIOGRAPHY

1 Walker, J. Bartholomew, Statists Saving One © 2017 Quadrakoff Publications Group, LLC, Wilmington DE pp. 100
2 *King James Bible* (Genesis 3:17)
3 *King James Bible* (Genesis 2:7)
4 theguardian.com/film/2004/feb/19/science.science
5 *King James Bible* (Revelation 6:9-11)
6 Strong, James, *Strong's Exhaustive Concordance of the Bible* © 1890 James Strong, Madison, NJ p. 46 (Greek)
7 Strong, James, *Strong's Exhaustive Concordance of the Bible* © 1890 James Strong, Madison, NJ p. 45 (Greek)
8 Strong, James, *Strong's Exhaustive Concordance of the Bible* © 1890 James Strong, Madison, NJ p. 78 (Greek)
9 *King James Bible* (Matthew 23:27)
10 *King James Bible* (Genesis 1:28)
11 Strong, James, *Strong's Exhaustive Concordance of the Bible* © 1890 James Strong, Madison, NJ p. 54 (Hebrew)
12 *King James Bible* (Luke 10:18-20)
13 *King James Bible* (Revelation 12:7-9)
14 *King James Bible* (Deuteronomy 18:9-13)
15 *King James Bible* (Deuteronomy 1:1)
16 *King James Bible* (Deuteronomy 34:5-8)

17 *Chambers Dictionary of Etymology*, Copyright © 1988 The H. W. Wilson Company, New York, NY p. 291
18 *Chambers Dictionary of Etymology*. Copyright © 1988 The H. W. Wilson Company, New York, NY p. 291
19 Strong, James, *Strong's Exhaustive Concordance of the Bible* © 1890 James Strong, Madison, NJ p. 68 (Hebrew)
20 Strong, James, *Strong's Exhaustive Concordance of the Bible* © 1890 James Strong, Madison, NJ p. 269
21 Strong, James, *Strong's Exhaustive Concordance of the Bible* © 1890 James Strong, Madison, NJ p. 104 (Hebrew)
22 *King James Bible* (Proverbs 30:1)
23 Strong, James, *Strong's Exhaustive Concordance of the Bible* © 1890 James Strong, Madison, NJ p. 72 (Hebrew)
24 Strong, James, *Strong's Exhaustive Concordance of the Bible* © 1890 James Strong, Madison, NJ p. 703 (Greek)
25 Strong, James. *Strong's Exhaustive Concordance of the Bible* © 1890 James Strong, Madison, NJ p. 24 (Greek)
26 Strong, James. *Strong's Exhaustive Concordance of the Bible* © 1890 James Strong, Madison, NJ p. 71 (Hebrew)
27 Strong, James. *Strong's Exhaustive Concordance of the Bible* © 1890 James Strong, Madison, NJ p. 104 (Hebrew)
28 Strong, James. *Strong's Exhaustive Concordance of the Bible* © 1890 James Strong, Madison, NJ p. 269
29 Strong, James. *Strong's Exhaustive Concordance of the Bible* © 1890 James Strong, Madison, NJ p. 63 (Greek)
30 Strong, James. *Strong's Exhaustive Concordance of the Bible* © 1890 James Strong, Madison, NJ p. 269
31 Strong, James. *Strong's Exhaustive Concordance of the Bible* © 1890 James Strong, Madison, NJ p. 104 (Hebrew)
32 *King James Bible* (Jeremiah 14:14)
33 Strong, James. *Strong's Exhaustive Concordance of the Bible* © 1890 James Strong, Madison, NJ p. 269
34 *King James Bible* (Ezekiel 12:24-25)
35 Strong, James. *Strong's Exhaustive Concordance of the Bible* © 1890 James Strong, Madison, NJ p. 40 (Hebrew)
36 Strong, James. *Strong's Exhaustive Concordance of the Bible* © 1890 James Strong, Madison, NJ p. 269

Bibliography

37 *King James Bible* (Ezekiel 13:6-9)
38 Strong, James. *Strong's Exhaustive Concordance of the Bible* © 1890 James Strong, Madison, NJ p. 269
39 *King James Bible* (Acts 16:16-18)
40 Strong, James. *Strong's Exhaustive Concordance of the Bible* © 1890 James Strong, Madison, NJ p. 46 (Greek)
41 Strong, James. *Strong's Exhaustive Concordance of the Bible* © 1890 James Strong, Madison, NJ p. 22 (Greek)
42 https://www.adventist.org/en/beliefs/ retrieved 5/29/19
43 https://www.adventist.org/en/beliefs/restoration/death-and-resurrection/article/go/-/dead-men-cant-save-you/ retrieved 5/29/19
44 *King James Bible* (1 Samuel 28:1-3)
45 Strong, James. *Strong's Exhaustive Concordance of the Bible* © 1890 James Strong, Madison, NJ p. 9 (Hebrew)
46 *Chambers Dictionary of Etymology*. Copyright © 1988 The H. W. Wilson Company, New York, NY p. 698
47 Strong, James. *Strong's Exhaustive Concordance of the Bible* © 1890 James Strong, Madison, NJ p. 82 (Hebrew)
48 *King James Bible* (1 Samuel 28:4-7)
49 Strong, James. *Strong's Exhaustive Concordance of the Bible* © 1890 James Strong, Madison, NJ p. 10 (Hebrew)
50 *King James Bible* (1 Samuel 28:8-10)
51 *King James Bible* (1 Samuel 28:11-14)
52 Strong, James. *Strong's Exhaustive Concordance of the Bible* © 1890 James Strong, Madison, NJ p. 85 (Comparative Concordance)
53 Strong, James. *Strong's Exhaustive Concordance of the Bible* © 1890 James Strong, Madison, NJ p. 12 (Hebrew)
54 Strong, James. *Strong's Exhaustive Concordance of the Bible* © 1890 James Strong, Madison, NJ p. 122 (Hebrew)
55 *King James Bible* (1 Samuel 28:15-16)
56 *King James Bible* (1 Samuel 28:17-19)
57 *King James Bible* (1 Samuel 15:18)
58 *King James Bible* (1 Samuel 15:14)
59 *King James Bible* (1 Samuel 31:4)
60 *King James Bible* (1 Samuel 25:1)

61 *New American Standard Bible*: 1995 update. 1995 (Acts 1:24-26) The Lockman Foundation: Lahabra, CA
62 *King James Bible* (2 Kings 2:8-9)
63 *King James Bible* (2 Kings 2:10-11)
64 *King James Bible* (2 Kings 2:12-14)
65 *King James Bible* (1 Kings 17:22)
66 *King James Bible* (1 Kings 17:14)
67 *King James Bible* (2 Kings 1:10)
68 *King James Bible* (1 Kings 17:1)
69 Strong, James. *Strong's Exhaustive Concordance of the Bible* © 1890 James Strong, Madison, NJ p. 126 (Hebrew)
70 Strong, James. *Strong's Exhaustive Concordance of the Bible* © 1890 James Strong, Madison, NJ p. 98 (Hebrew)
71 Jewishencyclopedia.com
72 Jewishencyclopedia.com
73 Jewishencyclopedia.com
74 *King James Bible* (1 Samuel 17:45)
75 Strong, James. *Strong's Exhaustive Concordance of the Bible* © 1890 James Strong, Madison, NJ p. 493
76 *King James Bible* (Genesis 1:26-28)
77 Strong, James. *Strong's Exhaustive Concordance of the Bible* © 1890 James Strong, Madison, NJ p. 493
78 Strong, James. *Strong's Exhaustive Concordance of the Bible* © 1890 James Strong, Madison, NJ p. 105 (Hebrew)
79 Walker/Quadrakoff, *MeekRaker Beginnings*...©2011 Quadrakoff Publications Group, LLC Wilmington DE p. 233-236
80 Walker/Quadrakoff, *MeekRaker Beginnings*...©2011 Quadrakoff Publications Group, LLC Wilmington DE p. 236-243
81 Walker/Quadrakoff, *MeekRaker Beginnings*...©2011 Quadrakoff Publications Group, LLC Wilmington DE p. 247-248
82 *King James Bible* (John 1:19-26)
83 *New American Standard Bible*: 1995 update. 1995 (Proverbs 10:19) The Lockman Foundation: Lahabra, CA
84 *New American Standard Bible*: 1995 update. 1995 (Proverbs 18:17) The Lockman Foundation: Lahabra, CA
85 https://www.studylight.org/commentary/matthew/17-13.html)
86 https://www.studylight.org/commentary/matthew/17-13.html)

Bibliography

87 https://www.biblestudytools.com/commentaries/matthew-henry-complete/matthew/17.html)
88 https://www.studylight.org/commentary/matthew/11-14.html)
89 https://www.studylight.org/commentary/matthew/11-14.html)
90 https://www.studylight.org/commentary/matthew/11-14.html)
91 *King James Bible* (Luke 1:17)
92 *The Holy Bible New International Version* ©1984 New International Bible Society, Colorado Springs CO Luke 1:17
93 Strong, James. *Strong's Exhaustive Concordance of the Bible* © 1890 James Strong, Madison, NJ p. 58 (Greek)
94 Strong, James. *Strong's Exhaustive Concordance of the Bible* © 1890 James Strong, Madison, NJ p. 24 (Greek)
95 Strong, James. *Strong's Exhaustive Concordance of the Bible* © 1890 James Strong, Madison, NJ p. 80 (Hebrew)
96 *King James Bible* (Acts 23:6-10)
97 *King James Bible* (Acts 23:11)
98 Strong, James. *Strong's Exhaustive Concordance of the Bible* © 1890 James Strong, Madison, NJ p. 22 (Greek)
99 Strong, James. *Strong's Exhaustive Concordance of the Bible* © 1890 James Strong, Madison, NJ p. 46 (Greek)
100 Strong, James. *Strong's Exhaustive Concordance of the Bible* © 1890 James Strong, Madison, NJ p. 11 (Greek)
101 https://www.biblestudytools.com/commentaries/matthew-henry-complete/matthew/11.html)
102 https://www.studylight.org/commentaries/bnb/hebrews-9.html)
103 *King James Bible* (Genesis 3:19)
104 https://www.studylight.org/commentary/john/1-21.html)
105 *King James Bible* (Matthew 3:3)
106 *King James Bible* (Isaiah 40:3-4)
107 *King James Bible* (Malachi 4:5)
108 *King James Bible* (Malachi 3:2)
109 *King James Bible* (John 1:23)
110 *King James Bible* (Acts 23:11)
111 https://www.thefreedictionary.com/papal+bull)
112 Brin, David, http://www.searchquotes.com/quotation/It_is_said_that_pow

er_corrupts%2C_but_actually_it%27s_more_true_that_power_attracts_the_corruptible._The/234441/
113 Walker, J. Bartholomew, *Statists Saving One* © 2017 Quadrakoff Publications Group, LLC, Wilmington DE p. 136-149
114 *King James Bible* (John 10:27-28)
115 *King James Bible* (Genesis 1:1)
116 Strong, James, *Strong's Exhaustive Concordance of the Bible* © 1890 James Strong, Madison, NJ p. 75 (Greek)
117 Strong, James, *Strong's Exhaustive Concordance of the Bible* © 1890 James Strong, Madison, NJ p. 75 (Greek)
118 Strong, James, *Strong's Exhaustive Concordance of the Bible* © 1890 James Strong, Madison, NJ p. 75 (Greek)
119 Strong, James, *Strong's Exhaustive Concordance of the Bible* © 1890 James Strong, Madison, NJ p. 75 (Greek)
120 *Merriam-Webster.com*
121 *King James Bible* (John 9:1-3)
122 *King James Bible* (Matthew 27:52)
123 Strong, James, *Strong's Exhaustive Concordance of the Bible* © 1890 James Strong, Madison, NJ p. 122 (Hebrew)
124 *King James Bible* (Luke 3:21-22)
125 *King James Bible* (Matthew 3:13-17)
126 *King James Bible* (Mark 1:8-12)
127 *King James Bible* (John 1:29-33)
128 *King James Bible* (John 1:6)
129 *King James Bible* (Matthew 12:31-32)
130 *King James Bible* (Mark 3:28-30)
131 *King James Bible* (Luke 12:10)
132 Walker, J. Bartholomew, *Wisdom Essentials* © 2017 Quadrakoff Publications Group, LLC, Wilmington DE p. 179-180
133 *King James Bible* (John 14:12)
134 Strong, James, *Strong's Exhaustive Concordance of the Bible* © 1890 James Strong, Madison, NJ p. 59 (Greek)
135 Strong, James, *Strong's Exhaustive Concordance of the Bible* © 1890 James Strong, Madison, NJ p. 47 (Greek)

Bibliography

136 Walker, J. Bartholomew, *Wisdom Essentials* © 2017 Quadrakoff Publications Group, LLC, Wilmington DE p. 161-162
137 *King James Bible* (Numbers 14:18)
138 *King James Bible* (Deuteronomy 5:9-10)
139 Strong, James, *Strong's Exhaustive Concordance of the Bible* © 1890 James Strong, Madison, NJ p. 80 (Hebrew)
140 Strong, James, *Strong's Exhaustive Concordance of the Bible* © 1890 James Strong, Madison, NJ p. 17 (Hebrew)
141 Strong, James, *Strong's Exhaustive Concordance of the Bible* © 1890 James Strong, Madison, NJ p. 17 (Hebrew)
142 Strong, James, *Strong's Exhaustive Concordance of the Bible* © 1890 James Strong, Madison, NJ p. 17 (Hebrew)
143 Walker, J. Bartholomew, *Wisdom Essentials* © 2017 Quadrakoff Publications Group, LLC, Wilmington DE p. 89-92
144 Strong, James, *Strong's Exhaustive Concordance of the Bible* © 1890 James Strong, Madison, NJ p. 44 (Greek)
145 Strong, James, *Strong's Exhaustive Concordance of the Bible* © 1890 James Strong, Madison, NJ p. 44 (Greek)
146 Strong, James, *Strong's Exhaustive Concordance of the Bible* © 1890 James Strong, Madison, NJ p. 44 (Greek)
147 *King James Bible* (Acts 19:6)
148 Strong, James, *Strong's Exhaustive Concordance of the Bible* © 1890 James Strong, Madison, NJ p. 963
149 Strong, James, *Strong's Exhaustive Concordance of the Bible* © 1890 James Strong, Madison, NJ p. 20 (Greek)
150 Strong, James, *Strong's Exhaustive Concordance of the Bible* © 1890 James Strong, Madison, NJ p. 62 (Greek)
151 https://www.dictionary.com/browse/glossolalia
152 Shroder, Tom, *Old Souls The Scientific Evidence for Past Lives* © 1999 Tom Shroder, Simon & Schuster, New York, NY

Glossary
Bibliography

G1 https://www.merriam-webster.com/dictionary/amphigory
G2 Strong, James, *Strong's Exhaustive Concordance of the Bible* ©
1890 James Strong, Madison, NJ p. 90 (Greek)
G3 *Chambers Dictionary of Etymology*, Copyright © 1988 The H. W. Wilson Company, New York, NY p. 42
G4 Strong, James, *Strong's Exhaustive Concordance of the Bible* ©
1890 James Strong, Madison, NJ p. 14 (Greek)
G5 *Chambers Dictionary of Etymology*, Copyright © 1988 The H. W. Wilson Company, New York, NY p. 42
G6 Strong, James, *Strong's Exhaustive Concordance of the Bible* ©
1890 James Strong, Madison, NJ p. 28 (Hebrew)
G7 *Chambers Dictionary of Etymology*, Copyright © 1988 The H. W. Wilson Company, New York, NY p. 245
G8 *Chambers Dictionary of Etymology*, Copyright © 1988 The H. W. Wilson Company, New York, NY p. 298
G9 *Chambers Dictionary of Etymology*, Copyright © 1988 The H. W. Wilson Company, New York, NY p. 308
G10 *Chambers Dictionary of Etymology*, Copyright © 1988 The H. W. Wilson Company, New York, NY p. 337
G11 *Chambers Dictionary of Etymology*, Copyright © 1988 The H. W. Wilson Company, New York, NY p. 844
G12 Strong, James, *Strong's Exhaustive Concordance of the Bible* ©
1890 James Strong, Madison, NJ p. 51 (Greek)
G13 Strong, James, *Strong's Exhaustive Concordance of the Bible* ©
1890 James Strong, Madison, NJ p. 43 (Greek)
G14 Strong, James, *Strong's Exhaustive Concordance of the Bible* ©
1890 James Strong, Madison, NJ p. 75 (Greek)
G15 *Chambers Dictionary of Etymology*, Copyright © 1988 The H. W. Wilson Company, New York, NY p. 844
G16 Strong, James, *Strong's Exhaustive Concordance of the Bible* ©
1890 James Strong, Madison, NJ p. 64 (Greek)

Bibliography

G17 Strong, James, *Strong's Exhaustive Concordance of the Bible* © 1890 James Strong, Madison, NJ p. 118 (Hebrew)
G18 *Chambers Dictionary of Etymology*, Copyright © 1988 The H. W. Wilson Company, New York, NY p. 1223
G19 Strong, James, *Strong's Exhaustive Concordance of the Bible* © 1890 James Strong, Madison, NJ p. 51 (Hebrew)
G20 Strong, James, *Strong's Exhaustive Concordance of the Bible* © 1890 James Strong, Madison, NJ p. 48 (Hebrew)

Embedded Bibliography

[In Order of Occurrence]

12.1 *New American Standard Bible*: 1995 update. 1995 (Mal. 3:1) The Lockman Foundation: Lahabra, CA
12.2 *New American Standard Bible*: 1995 update. 1995 (Mal. 4:5) The Lockman Foundation: Lahabra, CA
12.3 *New American Standard Bible*: 1995 update. 1995 (Matt. 17:10-13) The Lockman Foundation: Lahabra, CA
12.4 *New American Standard Bible*: 1995 update. 1995 (Matt. 11:7-14) The Lockman Foundation: Lahabra, CA
12.5 *New American Standard Bible*: 1995 update. 1995 (2Kings 2:11) The Lockman Foundation: Lahabra, CA
12.6 *New American Standard Bible*: 1995 update. 1995 (Luke 1:5-20) The Lockman Foundation: Lahabra, CA

12.7 Strong, James. *Strong's Exhaustive Concordance of the Bible.* ©
1890 James Strong, Madison, NJ p. 58 (Greek)

12.9 *Interlinear Bible Hebrew Greek English, 1 Volume edition.* © 1976, 1977, 1978, 1979, 1980, 1981, 1984. Second Edition, © 1986 Jay P. Green, Sr., Hendrickson Publishers p. 786

12.10 *New American Standard Bible*: 1995 update. 1995 (John 9:1-5) The Lockman Foundation: Lahabra, CA

12.11 Strong, James. *Strong's Exhaustive Concordance of the Bible.* © 1890 James Strong, Madison, NJ p. 10 (Greek)

12.15 *New American Standard Bible*: 1995 update. 1995 (Heb. 9:27-28) The Lockman Foundation: Lahabra, CA

12.16 Strong, James. *Strong's Exhaustive Concordance of the Bible.* © 1890 James Strong, Madison, NJ p.14 (Greek)

12.17 *Interlinear Bible Hebrew Greek English, 1 Volume edition.* © 1976, 1977, 1978, 1979, 1980, 1981, 1984. Second Edition, © 1986 Jay P. Green, Sr., Hendrickson Publishers p. 933 (Heb. 9:27

10.1 *King James Bible* (Ephesians 2:8-9)

10.2 Strong, James. *Strong's Exhaustive Concordance of the Bible.* © 1890 James Strong, Madison, NJ p. 77 (Greek)

10.3 Strong, James. *Strong's Exhaustive Concordance of the Bible.* © 1890 James Strong, Madison, NJ p. 22 (Greek)

10.4 Strong, James. *Strong's Exhaustive Concordance of the Bible.* © 1890 James Strong, Madison, NJ p. 32 (Greek)

10.5 Dean, Dizzy retrieved 5/17
https://www.brainyquote.com/quotes/quotes/d/dizzydean379853.html)

10.6 Strong, James. *Strong's Exhaustive Concordance of the Bible.* © 1890 James Strong, Madison, NJ p. 41 (Greek)

10.7 *King James Bible* (Ephesians 2:4)

10.8 Strong, James. *Strong's Exhaustive Concordance of the Bible.* © 1890 James Strong, Madison, NJ p. 27 (Greek)

10.9 *King James Bible* (Titus 3:5)

10.10 Strong, James. *Strong's Exhaustive Concordance of the Bible.* © 1890 James Strong, Madison, NJ p. 27 (Greek)

Bibliography

10.11 Donovan, Colin B., retrieved 5/17
https://www.ewtn.com/expert/answers/mortal_versus_venial.htm

10.12 Donovan, Colin B., retrieved 5/17
https://www.ewtn.com/expert/answers/mortal_versus_venial.htm

10.13 Etymology Online, retrieved 5/17
http://www.etymonline.com/index.php?term=Repent

10.14 retrieved 5/17
http://www.aboutcatholics.com/beliefs/mortal-sins/

10.15 Donovan, Colin B., retrieved 5/17
https://www.ewtn.com/expert/answers/mortal_versus_venial.htm

10.16 *King James Bible* (1 Corinthians 6:9-10)

10.17 *King James Bible* (1 Corinthians 6:11)

10.18 Fox News retrieved 5/17
http://www.foxnews.com/story/2008/03/11/vatican-adds-seven-new-deadly-sins-including-damaging-environment-and-drug.html

10.19 *King James Bible* (1 Timothy 6::10)

10.20 *King James Bible* (Ecclesiastes 10:19)

10:21 *King James Bible* (Deuteronomy 28:2)

10.22 *King James Bible* (Matthew 25:40)

10.23 *King James Bible* (2 Thessalonians 3:10-12)

SH1. *The Holy Bible, KJV* Exodus 20:6, kingjamesbibleonline.org, retrieved 7 March 2016

SH2. Strong, James. *Strong's Exhaustive Concordance of the Bible.* © 1890 James Strong, Madison, NJ p. 41 (Hebrew)

SH3. Strong, James. *Strong's Exhaustive Concordance of the Bible.* © 1890 James Strong, Madison, NJ p. 41 (Hebrew)

SH4. Strong, James. *Strong's Exhaustive Concordance of the Bible.* © 1890 James Strong, Madison, NJ p. 41 (Hebrew)

SH5. Strong, James. *Strong's Exhaustive Concordance of the Bible.* © 1890 James Strong, Madison, NJ p. 9 (Hebrew)

SH6. Strong, James. *Strong's Exhaustive Concordance of the Bible.* © 1890 James Strong, Madison, NJ p. 118 (Hebrew)

SH7. *The Holy Bible, KJV* John 14:15, *kingjamesbibleonline.org*, retrieved 7 March 2016

SH8. Strong, James. *Strong's Exhaustive Concordance of the Bible.* © 1890 James Strong, Madison, NJ p. 71 (Greek)

AT1 *Chambers Dictionary of Etymology.* Copyright © 1988 The H. W. Wilson Company, New York, NY p.648

AT2 *www.kingjamesbibleonline.org* (KJV) (Matt.5:5) retrieved June 2011

AT3 *www.kingjamesbibleonline.org* (KJV) (Ps. 25:9) retrieved June 2011

AT4 *www.kingjamesbibleonline.org* (KJV) (Ps. 147:6) retrieved June 2011

AT5 *www.kingjamesbibleonline.org* (KJV) (Ps. 76:9) retrieved June 2011

AT6 *www.kingjamesbibleonline.org* (KJV) (Mark 6:52) retrieved June 2011

AT7 *www.kingjamesbibleonline.org* (KJV) (Mark 8:17) retrieved June 2011

AT8 *www.kingjamesbibleonline.org* (KJV) (John 12:40) retrieved June 2011

AT9 *www.kingjamesbibleonline.org* (KJV) (Neh. 9:16) retrieved June 2011

AT10 *www.kingjamesbibleonline.org* (KJV) (Prov. 28:14) retrieved June 2011

AT11 *www.kingjamesbibleonline.org* (KJV) (Prov. 29:1) retrieved June 2011

AT12 Strong, James. *Strong's Exhaustive Concordance of the Bible.* © 1890 James Strong, Madison, NJ p. 63 (Greek)

Other Fine QPG Publications:

MEEKRAKER BEGINNINGS...

From the "inside flap" of *"MeekRaker Beginnings..."*

"The primary purpose of this tome, is the reconciliation of the word of God with science; and to do so in such a manner as to be rendered inarguable by any rational mind. As stated in the Preface: "One must choose between being a "man of science" or a believer," because they are generally considered to be mutually exclusive. If one agrees that words mean things, then an unbiased fair read of God's Word presents no such paradox. But one must read what God actually said, not merely what one thinks He said, what one was told He said, what one wished He said, or would rather He had said."

Statists Saving One:

The Malignant Sophistry of Rights Removal by the Far Left

"...under the umbrella of "liberals" or "liberalism;" (as used today); there are actually two separate and distinct groups:
"True *liberals* believe very much in what they promulgate. They are truly concerned with the welfare of citizens, and they believe in policies that will benefit the same—at least in their view. There are neither nefarious purposes, nor any intellectual dishonesty. Their objective is to improve the quality of life (and longevity), for as many people as possible.
"...Conservatives and liberals can often agree on the *ends*; but vastly disagree on the *means*. Giving a hungry person a fish is kind; but to

conservatives, teaching him how to fish seems to be a better long term solution. It is not that conservatives object to the temporary giving of the fish; but rather they object to *not* teaching him how to fish.

"True liberals believe in the dignity of man; and promulgate policies in furtherance of this belief.

"Statists; the other group usually and often erroneously grouped under the "liberal" umbrella; are another matter. It is because of agreements with liberal *policy* that they are usually grouped under this liberal umbrella; but their *motivations*, *purposes* and *beliefs* are entirely different—arguably antithetical—to true liberalism."

Why should *liberals* read "*Statists Saving One*?"

> To understand that many who may appear to agree with your *means*, have entirely different *ends* in sight; and that these ends are antithetical to liberalism. True liberalism and statism are entirely incompatible. And all along you thought they were your friends.

Why should *conservatives* read "*Statists Saving One*?"

> To understand the difference between liberals and statists; and end the confusion. Many liberals agree with many conservative *ends*, merely proffering a different *means* to achieve them. But statists have entirely different ends in sight—no matter whom they may appear to agree with at any given time.

Why should *statists* read "*Statists Saving One*?"

> To understand the true motivations behind statism; and decide if continued actions are wise. The masquerade is now over. Either change now; or "pack up and go home" while you can, as it will never become any easier in any current statist's lifetime.

Wisdom Essentials—*The Pentalogy*

"That Which is Difficult If Not Impossible to Find Anywhere Else—All In One Volume. Vol. I"

But there are many other effects for which no material cause can be found. In *"Donald Trump Candidacy According to Matthew?,"* his meteoric rise and seeming inability to fail are explained according to Biblical principles. Since this is a non-political work, his success was not actually prophesied, but no other conclusion could possibly have been drawn— *and this was published long before he was even nominated.*

In *"SHÂMAR TO SHARIA,"* the process of radical indoctrination is analyzed, and is shown to be a perversion of that very same thing God instructed man to do with the Commandments, and how this is not in any way limited to terrorists.

"It's Not Just A Theory" examines the relationship between behavior and longevity according to both science and the Scriptures; and *"according to both"* also includes major consistencies.

"Calvary's Hidden Truths" reveals many unknown facts about what actually occurred at that time.

"Inevitable Balance" scientifically and Biblically explains that which is often observed but rarely understood: Why "What Goes Around Comes Around;" AKA *karma*, or the "law of compensation."

OSTIUM AB INFERNO
[The Opening From Hell]

"The Original Monograph - According to the Father, The Christ Son and The Holy Ghost"

What is hell?
Why is there a hell?
What openings from "hell" exist?
What is the truth about "Abraham's Bosom?" And how does this or do these affect man?
What are angels? Are angels named such because of structure or function? Precisely why were some angels sent to hell? Is it true that one third were banished to hell? And when did this all happen?
Much of that which is fanciful has been written about these questions. But the answers should not be sought from that which is the product of men's imaginations—albeit these may provide interesting reading. Rather; the answers should be sought from, and always remain: "according to The Father, The Christ Son, and The Holy Ghost." (Written in English.)

QPG Publications are available wherever you buy fine books.

www.ingramcontent.com/pod-product-compliance
Lightning Source LLC
Chambersburg PA
CBHW030108240426
43661CB00031B/1337/J